T0296822

Ensuring Digital Accessibility through Process and Policy

Ensuring Digital Accessibility through Process and Policy

Jonathan Lazar

Daniel Goldstein

Anne Taylor

AMSTERDAM • BOSTON • HEIDELBERG • LONDON
NEW YORK • OXFORD • PARIS • SAN DIEGO
SAN FRANCISCO • SINGAPORE • SYDNEY • TOKYO
Morgan Kaufmann is an imprint of Elsevier

Acquiring Editor: Todd Green
Editorial Project Manager: Lindsay Lawrence
Project Manager: Punithavathy Govindaradjane
Designer: Greg Harris

Morgan Kaufmann is an imprint of Elsevier
225 Wyman Street, Waltham, MA 02451, USA

ISBN: 978-0-12-800646-7

British Library Cataloguing-in-Publication Data
A catalogue record for this book is available from the British Library

Library of Congress Cataloging-in-Publication Data
A catalog record for this book is available from the Library of Congress

For information on all Morgan Kaufmann publications,
visit our website at www.mkp.com

Working together
to grow libraries in
developing countries

www.elsevier.com • www.bookaid.org

Critical Acclaim for *Ensuring Digital Accessibility through Process and Policy*

"Lazar, Goldstein, and Taylor are a uniquely qualified trio, combining expertise in legal accountability, human-computer interaction, and the perspective of corporations regarding accessibility. Together they offer theoretical and pragmatic insights into why and how the digital world should be accessible, as well as the cultural changes that need to occur to precipitate full inclusion."

–**Michael Stein,** Executive Director, Harvard Law School Project on Disability; Visiting Professor, Harvard Law School; Extraordinary Professor, University of Pretoria Faculty of Law, Centre for Human Rights

"Information technology has enormous potential to make our society more inclusive. Realizing that potential takes a lot of hard work, not just on the technology itself, but also on the legal and policy framework within which it operates. This book lets us learn from those who have been doing that work, a rare opportunity!"

–**Clayton Lewis,** Professor of Computer Science and Fellow of the Institute of Cognitive Science, University of Colorado, Boulder

"*Ensuring Digital Accessibility* is a comprehensive yet easy to follow guide to a fast-moving area of the law. It will be of great use to lawyers, software and web developers, CIOs, and policymakers."

–**Michael Waterstone,** J. Howard Ziemann Fellow and Professor of Law, Loyola University Law School

"This book is a must read for anyone interested in understanding what it means for technology to be fully accessible to individuals with disabilities. The book will be invaluable to a broad audience because it is chock full of technical and legal resources but describes those resources in a way that is understandable to a lay audience. I will rely heavily on this book when I next update my teaching materials in the field of disability discrimination and look forward to its publication."

–**Ruth Colker,** Distinguished University Professor and Heck-Faust Memorial Chair in Constitutional Law, Ohio State University

"*Ensuring Digital Accessibility* is a wonderful explanation of why accessibility to all kinds of technology including computers, smartphones, e-books, and web sites, is so beneficial to society. Certainly the recipients of access benefit, but so do the providers of the information by reaching a wider and more diverse audience. Providing access to users with disabilities is not only the right thing to do, it is the smart thing to do."

–**Richard E. Ladner,** Professor, Department of Computer Science and Engineering, University of Washington

"The authors of this book represent a team that can take a unique perspective on digital accessibility. Dr. Lazar is one of the few academics I know who has taken the time to write multiple books that take academic knowledge about accessibility and organize it into clear and accessible guidelines for the design of digital artifacts. Dan Goldstein is a civil rights lawyer with on the ground experience about what it takes to enforce and create accessibility standards thanks to his leadership in multiple successful lawsuits. Anne Taylor has hands on experience guiding others in the design and use of accessible technologies. Together they are sure to present a practical and grounded perspective on what it takes to *ensure digital accessibility*."

–**Jennifer Mankoff,** Associate Professor, Human Computer Interaction Institute, Carnegie Mellon University

Contents

About the Authors

Dr. Jonathan Lazar is a professor of Computer and Information Sciences and director of the Undergraduate Program in Information Systems at Towson University. Dr. Lazar also founded the Universal Usability Laboratory at Towson University and served as director from 2003 to 2014. Dr. Lazar is involved in teaching and research in the area of human-computer interaction, specifically, web usability, web accessibility for people with disabilities, user-centered design methods, assistive technology, and public policy in the area of human-computer interaction. He has previously published seven books, including "Research Methods in Human-Computer Interaction" (2010, John Wiley and Sons), "Universal Usability: Designing Computer Interfaces for Diverse User Populations" (2007, John Wiley and Sons), and "Web Usability: A User-Centered Design Approach" (2006, Addison-Wesley). Dr. Lazar has published over 140 refereed articles in journals, conference proceedings, and book chapters, and has received research funding from many sources, including the National Science Foundation, the American Library Association, and the Maryland Technology Development Corporation. Dr. Lazar currently serves on the editorial board of ACM Interactions Magazine, the executive board of the Friends of the Maryland Library for the Blind and Physically Handicapped, and on the Executive Committee of ACM SIGCHI (Computer–Human Interaction) as the chair of public policy. Dr. Lazar was named winner of the 2015 AccessComputing Capacity Building Award, the 2011 University System of Maryland Regents Award for Public Service, the 2010 Dr. Jacob Bolotin Award from the National Federation of the Blind, and the 2009 Outstanding Faculty Award in the Fisher College of Science and Mathematics at Towson University. During the 2012–2013 academic year, Dr. Lazar was selected as the Shutzer Fellow at the Radcliffe Institute for Advanced Study at Harvard University.

Daniel F. Goldstein is a founder and Partner of the Baltimore law firm Brown Goldstein Levy. Dan is one of the leading disability rights lawyers in the USA and has served as counsel to the National Federation of the Blind for nearly 30 years. He was the lead lawyer in the National Federation of the Blind lawsuits against Target .com and Scribd, the landmark cases that set precedent regarding the application of access laws to commercial web sites, and has been involved in other cases and agreements involving access to technology, including with AOL, Apple, Amazon, and Cardtronics. His representation of NFB in *Authors Guild v. HathiTrust* established that it is a fair use of copyrighted material to make and distribute print books in digital formats to persons with print disabilities. Dan is a Fellow of the American College of Trial Lawyers, has been listed among Maryland's Top 50 Super Lawyers, and is a 2010 winner of the *Daily Record*'s Leadership in Law Award. In 2011, Dan received the American Bar Association's Paul G. Hearne Award for Disability Rights. This award is presented each year to an individual who has made significant contributions to further the rights, dignity, and access to justice for people with disabilities.

Anne Taylor served as the director of Access Technology at the National Federation of the Blind (NFB) for over ten years. She recently joined Microsoft as senior program manager in the Trusted Experience Team. Anne has worked with companies such as Blackboard, eBay, Microsoft, Apple, Google, Oracle, and Humanware to shape how each of these partners develops and tests their products for use by blind consumers by providing them with feedback and expertise at different stages of the process. In her capacity of Director of Access Technology at the NFB, she also managed the International Braille and Technology Center for the Blind, the most comprehensive consumer evaluation center for nonvisual access technology in the world. During her tenure at the NFB, Anne organized and taught at a number of training events on technology, sharing her expertise and insight on web accessibility, trends, changes, and innovations in the field of Accessible Technology (AT). In addition to this work, she advocates for accessible solutions and disseminates information on the topic by speaking at venues including the California State University at Northridge's Annual International Technology and Persons with Disabilities Conference, EDUCAUSE, Accessing Higher Ground, and Association for Computing Machinery (ACM) conferences. Between the different strands of her work, Anne connects technology professionals, publishers, employers, educators, blind consumers, and many others, aiming for better outcomes for all involved.

Preface

We wrote this book with a mission in mind. We believe that there is a paucity of documentation about digital technology accessibility. There are great international technical standards coming from the Web Accessibility Initiative and that's where the documentation ends. Successful digital accessibility occurs through process and policy, not just a set of technical standards, and therefore, it is necessary to understand the entire context and the entire process. We wrote this book to provide a foundation for understanding the context of digital accessibility. This includes understanding why digital accessibility is important, the history of digital accessibility, how inaccessible content leads to forms of societal discrimination, technical standards, laws, lawsuits, regulations, the methods for evaluating accessibility, compliance monitoring policies and procedures, and best practices. Often, people who are trying to improve digital accessibility are told to just check the technical standards, which are important, but that's not enough to permanently make technology accessible. We know from the human-computer interaction community that technology alone cannot solve a problem. It is equally important to understand the context, to understand the people, to understand the organization developing or hosting the technology. This book documents not only the historical context, the societal context, and the legal and regulatory context, but also includes examples from government, education, and the corporate sectors that demonstrate how accessibility has been successfully integrated into an organizational culture.

We hope that this book will prove useful and usable to computer scientists, educators, technology managers and developers, lawyers, and policymakers. Our own professional histories (as a lawyer, professor, and technology developer, respectively) led us to approach these topics from diverse and, we hope, complementary points of view.

Writing a book is a collaborative process that involves many people. We appreciate the thoughtful reviews of our chapter drafts, provided by Judy Brewer, Harry Hochheiser, Deborah Kaplan, David Lepofsky, Marc Maurer, Michael Stein, Michael Waterstone, and Brian Wentz. We also appreciate the assistance of Michael Levin who greatly contributed to the chapter on International Law and Blake Reid, who helped make the section on the CVAA more accurate and more complete, and especially Clara Van Gerven, Denise Altobelli, and Tyra Wilson. Denise Altobelli, chief paralegal at Brown Goldstein Levy, is always known for her attention to detail, and the book benefited from her wide-ranging skills and Tyra Wilson, assistant to Dan Goldstein, provided logistical support for the book. Clara Van Gerven, access technology content specialist at the National Federation of the Blind, is a true team player, taking on extra work tasks so that Anne Taylor would have more time to concentrate on the book. We would also like to thank the members of the NFB access technology team, Amy Mason and Karl Belanger, for assisting Anne Taylor with accessibility testing products mentioned in the book. Our publisher, Morgan Kaufmann Publishers (part of Elsevier), was always very pleasant to work with, thanks to the support of Lindsay Lawrence, Todd Green, and Meg Dunkerley. We also acknowledge the copyediting support provided by Phyllis Jankowski.

This book would likely not have come to fruition without the generous support of the Radcliffe Institute for Advanced Study at Harvard University. The first author of this book (Jonathan Lazar) was awarded the Shutzer Fellowship for the year 2012–2013, to live and study at Harvard University and to research the connection between human-computer interaction for people with disabilities and disability rights law. Much of the book was written during that fellowship, and the fantastic environment and people of the Radcliffe Institute for Advanced Study made it all possible. The support and encouragement of Judy Vichniac, Rebecca Haley, Sharon Bromberg-Lim, and Mervi Karttunen, all at the Radcliffe Institute, helped make the year-long experience a joyful one. Thanks also go to William Shutzer, who with his family funded the Shutzer Fellowship at the Radcliffe Institute.

Introduction to accessible technology

INTRODUCTION

Digital information, which is stored as a series of zeros and ones, must be transformed to be presented to any of a person's senses, whether or not that person has a disability. Thus, the prevalence of digital information should be good news for people with perceptual or motor disabilities, who have often had limited access to printed and computer-based information. However, developers typically have implemented digital technologies without regard to access by persons with disabilities, and institutional purchasers of those technologies generally have not insisted on accessibility. Even when many cost-effective accessibility solutions exist, they often are not implemented. As a result, gratuitous barriers have been created that stop people with disabilities from accessing digital information and using electronic hardware and software applications. Thus, the barriers to accessing digital information typically are the result of inattention during the technology development process, rather than limitations inherent in the technology. These barriers, these inaccessible technologies, often lead to forms of societal discrimination.

However, a key point often is missing from discussions about accessibility: accessibility is a financial opportunity for businesses. When e-commerce web sites are accessible, the number of potential customers is much higher, and the potential sales are much greater [1]. When e-reader devices are accessible, the devices can be sold to governmental or educational institutions and libraries (which violate the law when they purchase inaccessible e-reader devices). When smartphones are accessible, they can be purchased by a much larger number of people. People with disabilities are consumers, and there is a large base of institutional customers that may purchase only accessible technology. To ignore these potential markets is to ignore great financial opportunities.

Government policies and regulations encourage or require accessibility for information technology (IT) but often are ineffective. International treaties, such as the United Nations Convention on the Rights of Persons with Disabilities (CRPD), specifically mention access to IT (CRPD Article 9 mentions access for persons with disabilities to new information and communications technologies and systems, including the Internet, and Article 21 discusses private entities, mass media, and government providing equal access to information in accessible formats) [2]. However, because of how these policies are implemented, they often are limited in their effectiveness.

This chapter presents the framework for all of the chapters that follow. The authors discuss the meaning of accessible technology and discuss various types of disabilities and technologies. This chapter defines the scope of the topic of accessible technologies, separating accessible technologies from augmentative communication and prosthetics. This chapter also defines the scope of accessible technologies as being very different (and much smaller) than the legal definition of "disability." Finally, this chapter introduces the idea that more effective policies and laws can improve accessibility of IT and benefit people with no disabilities.

DEFINING ACCESSIBLE TECHNOLOGY

Accessible technology is technology that can be utilized effectively by people with disabilities, at the time that they want to utilize the technology, without any modifications or accommodations. People with perceptual or motor disabilities often use alternate input/output programs or devices (such as screen readers, refreshable Braille displays, alternative keyboards, and speech recognition) to secure access to digital information and applications. People who are Deaf or hard of hearing need captioning or American Sign Language (ASL) on video or transcripts of audio. Some mainstream devices (including those of Apple, Inc.) now incorporate these alternate input/output methods with text-to-speech software. If all mainstream content and applications were accessible through these alternative methods of access, the result would be revolutionary for persons with disabilities. First, when a lack of accessibility to mainstream content required the creation of separate channels of information, such as by creating Braille versions of print books, the result had been that only an infinitesimally small fraction of the pool of available information was made accessible to persons with disabilities. Second, when separate devices are created for exclusive use by persons with disabilities, the market is small and the price, high. In addition, separate, clunky devices for people with disabilities exclude them from social interactions and make them feel different [3]. Accessible mainstream devices and content provide the best approach for maximizing access to information.

It is in the best interests of everyone to ensure that mainstream technology is accessible for people with disabilities. If digital information is routinely presented so that it can be accessed through a variety of senses (such as by captioning on video or text-to-speech) and if mainstream electronic devices and applications are usable by all persons with disabilities, the disabilities become irrelevant to the acquisition of information and the use of valued technologies. By contrast, separate and inferior access increases the cost of education while reducing its effectiveness. Moreover, separate and inferior access reduces the effectiveness of persons with disabilities in the workplace and creates the need for additional governmental support of such persons. In addition, when mainstream technology is accessible, the accessibility features also improve usability for the general population without disabilities.

People with disabilities want access to the same digital information, at the same time, and at the same cost as the general population (a concept expanded upon in

Chapter 3). They also want the convenience to engage in the same electronic transactions as the general population through the same user-friendly devices and applications. Thus, the quest for equal access applies to web pages, e-books, operating systems, software applications, smartphones, and any other type of digital information or electronic device. There are real societal limitations that occur when IT is inaccessible. In one instance, because of a technically inaccessible web-based security feature, blind people were not able to sign a petition on the White House web site related to encouraging the rights of blind people [4], thus limiting the rights of blind people to petition their government. Chapter 3 details multiple forms of pricing, employment, and societal discrimination.

Many technologies originally developed to assist persons with disabilities find broader application (see Chapter 2). Scanner technology was born from Ray Kurzweil's decision to build a reading machine for the blind. The first commercially sold e-books were from a company founded by a blind man, George Kerscher, who was frustrated by the lack of accessible information about computer programs. E-books are now popular among the general public. Captioned video is used not only by people who are Deaf or hard of hearing, but also by people who simply want to do keyword searches on the video or watch video in noisy places. Mainstream access to digital information and electronic devices for the minority (those with disabilities) produces a tangible benefit for the majority.

Why hasn't mainstream access been more fully realized? In part, it is a matter of numbers—persons with disabilities are a small part of the population. In part, it is the perception of persons with disabilities as being dependent and in need of care and charity, rather than as persons dealing with personal characteristics requiring adaptation, but who have an equal capacity to lead full and productive lives. However, at a high level, the lack of mainstream accessibility has been the result of governmental and institutional failure to insist on accessibility. As a result, the preponderance of digital information and electronic technology and applications in the marketplace are inaccessible, thereby deepening the segregation and dependence of persons with disabilities and further narrowing their educational, social, and economic opportunities.

There are many examples (expanded upon in Chapter 3) of the societal impacts of inaccessible technology. Students who are blind and don't receive accessible versions of their textbooks early in the semester are excluded from understanding the material and taking part in the discussions; they often must drop out of the class. People who are Deaf who want to take part in a radio show about accessible technology cannot, because the radio show isn't captioned. A Deaf person could easily send in an e-mail question to the radio show panel, if she only knew what was being said during the show. Instead, a Deaf person may receive a transcript posted to the radio station web site two days after the radio show, essentially cutting Deaf people out of the conversation, with no meaningful opportunity to participate in the discussion. When a government agency places a visual CAPTCHA (a security feature) on its web site but doesn't enable an audio option, blind people are unable to e-mail the government agency. If the new US state and federal government health insurance web sites are inaccessible (some of the sites do have accessibility problems), the ability to acquire health insurance can be limited.

There is nothing inherently inaccessible about digital technology, and most aspects of IT accessibility are easy and have been "solved" many years ago. Certain categories (math markup languages, sonified equivalents to large-scale data visualizations) are more technically challenging, but still possible. However, many accessibility solutions (web page markup, e-book accessibility, voting and automated teller machines [ATMs]) are already available and, in some cases, have been in existence for more than a decade. Technical solutions for captioning have existed since the 1970s. These are not difficult solutions. They are simply existing technical solutions that have yet to be implemented because of ineffective policies of governments, companies, organizations, and educational institutions. Work needs to be done in restructuring policies and laws to increase the effectiveness of existing technology solutions.

VARIOUS TYPES OF DISABILITIES

"Disability" is a word that has different meanings. Under the US Americans with Disabilities Act as amended, the starting point is to define an individual with a disability as one who has "a physical or mental impairment that substantially limits one or more major life activities [of that person]" [5]. The UN Convention on the Rights of Persons with Disabilities defines persons with disabilities as "those who have long-term physical, mental, intellectual or sensory impairments which in interaction with various barriers may hinder their full and effective participation in society on an equal basis with others" [2]. Thus, there is a tipping point at which limitations become disabilities; for instance, at some point on the continuum between 20/20 vision and complete blindness, sight limitation becomes defined as a disability. This is true for all issues, whether they be mobility, cognition, or mental status. Moreover, the population of those with disabilities is more fungible than is that of other disfavored groups because a change in one's ethnicity, gender, or sexual orientation generally is not associated with accident or progressive conditions. Many of us are likely to have a disability at some point in our lives.

Within the human-computer interaction world, disabilities often are separated into three different categories: perceptual disabilities (vision and hearing limitations), motor/physical disabilities (limited use of hands, arms, and speech), and cognitive disabilities. These categorizations are based on the functional needs related to computer input and output. This approach of categorizing disability into perceptual, motor, or cognitive disability is a computer-centric view that is based on computer output (primarily affecting people with perceptual disabilities) and computer input (primarily affecting people with motor disabilities). For instance, people who are considered to have perceptual disabilities often need to use different output. Someone who is blind may not be able to effectively use a visual monitor and thus needs a screen reader (synthesized speech output), refreshable Braille display, or other type of tactile output. While it primarily impacts computer output, it also could impact computer input, for instance, if an edit box is associated with a label and both require the use of a mouse or pointing device. Someone who is Deaf needs captioning on video or a transcript of audio files. Typically, people with motor disabilities need to use different types of input; for instance, a person who cannot use a standard pointing device or a mouse potentially could use an ergonomic pointing device or mouse (if the problem is repetitive strain injury, such as carpal tunnel syndrome); keyboard-only with no pointing device; speech recognition (if the problem is limited or no use of hands); or a head-pointing device or mouth joystick (if the problem is no use of hands or speech). Operating systems, software applications, and web sites must be built to be flexible so that they can work properly with various potential input and output devices. Such flexibility is reached by following a set of design guidelines for accessibility (such as the Web Content Accessibility Guidelines 2.0).

From a computing input-output point of view, cognitive impairments are more challenging to understand. The umbrella of cognitive impairments is much broader than those of perceptual or motor impairments, including congenital cognitive impairments (such as Down syndrome), cognitive impairments that occur over time (such as dementia and Alzheimer's disease), and cognitive impairments that occur as the result of an incident (traumatic brain injury, amnesia, and aphasia) [6]. Whereas the research literature on human-computer interaction for people with perceptual or motor disabilities is rich and has at least a 30-year base of knowledge, the research in some areas of cognitive impairment is much more limited, having been done over a shorter amount of time and only for people with specific types of cognitive disabilities (Chapter 2 discusses the history of technology accessibility).

For people with cognitive impairments, information sometimes needs to be transformed, to be presented in a different format. In addition, the research is not always clear about what types of adaptations are needed for people with cognitive disabilities. For instance, in recently published research, people with Down syndrome did not need any type of adaptations for successful interface use. In fact, people with Down syndrome were reported to have higher success rates on visual CAPTCHAs than did people with no disabilities; however, they did have problems with passwords [7]. This is the type of research that is emerging and that in the future likely will affect and influence international interface guidelines. Although international technical interface guidelines (such as WCAG 2.0) are starting to include components related to cognitive impairment, there is no set of clear guidelines available that cover all types of cognitive impairment. Furthermore, some disabilities, such as dyslexia, could be categorized as a cognitive or learning disability (depending on the working definitions), yet what people with dyslexia find helpful is often the same technology that blind people find helpful. For people with dyslexia, hearing the words being read in computer-synthesized speech while visually viewing the words being highlighted can be helpful. People with dyslexia are the largest number of screen reader users [8]. Those with attention deficit hyperactivity disorder (ADHD) often need simultaneous visual and audible input, so they, too, are helped by accessible and flexible interfaces. So the understanding of how to design for cognitive impairment is less comprehensive, and there have been concerns that it is also "less testable."

Disabilities are rarely binary—"you have it or you don't." There are different levels of severity of disabilities, and individuals often have co-occurring disabilities. One of the best-known combinations of disabilities is being deaf-blind; however, few individuals are 100% hearing impaired and 100% visually impaired. Instead, many people who are deaf-blind have some hearing loss and some visual loss and may prefer to use Braille or some combination of hearing aids and magnification.

The word "disability" is often applied, in a legal and human rights context, not only to the perceptual, motor, and cognitive impairments previously described, but also to medical conditions (diabetes, AIDS, cancer, high blood pressure), learning disabilities, mental illness, and other challenges in life (see Chapters 5 and 6 for a discussion of the legal definitions of accessibility). Often such limitations, although fitting under the broad legal umbrella of "disability," are not included in technology-based discussions because there are no obvious impacts on the design of computer interfaces. Someone living with AIDS, cancer, or diabetes doesn't interact with a computer differently from someone with no disabilities. If the diabetes leads to vision loss (a perceptual impairment) or numbness in the fingers (a motor impairment), then that would affect the person's computer usage. Celiac disease might be considered a disability under US law, but intolerance to gluten does not in any way change how a person accesses digital information. Someone with AIDS or cancer might seek web-based information about AIDS or cancer but would do so using the same interaction approach used to search for information about a new car or clothing. The methods for input and output would be no different, and interface accessibility would not be an issue. So, while designing for all disabilities seems to be a challenging goal, many of the legal definitions of disability are not relevant to computer usage. Therefore, the design considerations for IT accessibility are much smaller than for the entire category of disability.

In addition, accessible design is well-defined by international technical standards (to be covered in Chapter 4). When we talk about accessible design in this book, we are referring to accessible design as defined by international technical standards and user performance standards. This means primarily perceptual and motor impairments, as well as the few cognitive and learning impairments that are covered under the international technical standards [6]. For organizations, digital accessibility generally means applying existing solutions, not creating new solutions. A recent lawsuit exemplifies this point about accessibility being "applying existing solutions, not creating new solutions." In the state of Maryland, the Board of Elections had developed a technical solution (in collaboration with the National Federation of the Blind [NFB]) to allow disabled users to mark absentee ballots online, allowing them the ability to privately and independently vote absentee, without asking anyone for help. The Maryland Board of Elections then refused to implement the existing solution, and the NFB sued under the Americans with Disabilities Act and Section 504 of the Rehabilitation Act. The District Court ruled in 2014 that, because an existing technical solution exists, not providing access would deny blind citizens of Maryland equal access to the state's absentee balloting program (U.S. District Court, 2014).

To be fair and honest, the international technical standards do not include every disability group. If one first hears the term "universal usability," one may worry that it means, literally, designing for 100% of the population. Yet doing so is unrealistic. What is realistic is designing to include populations for which there are clear, existing, well-defined, technical standards and technical solutions. These standards help multiple populations, even those not originally envisioned by the standards. For instance, in this book, we often refer to persons with print disabilities and in so doing intend the meaning assigned by George Kerscher, who first coined the phrase "print disabilities" to describe people who cannot effectively read print because of a visual, physical, perceptual, developmental, cognitive, or learning disability. Individuals generally do not claim that they have a "print disability," yet designing for one population of users often helps other populations of users with print-related disabilities.

ACCESSIBILITY HELPS THOSE WITHOUT DISABILITIES

The inclusion of specific accessibility solutions that can address an identified population may provide access to others on the same disability spectrum and other populations with concurrent needs. Solutions that enhance access for a disabled population may enhance access for a nondisabled population or may assist other disability populations for which the technology was not originally intended. For example, many persons with dyslexia use Kurzweil 3000 software, which provides simultaneous audible output and visual display of the text, highlighting the sentence being read in one color and the word being articulated in another [9,10]. This software is also proving to be extremely useful for teaching those learning English as a second language because it provides simultaneous audio-visual information about the spelling and sounds of words. Disability rights laws tend to benefit many parties who do not have disabilities [11], and accessible information technology helps many people without disabilities. Captioning television shows and video clips is helpful for many people who are not Deaf or hard of hearing. Captioning helps people trying to learn a new language; people in noisy settings (such as gyms, bars, restaurants, and airports) who cannot hear the audio portion of clips; and people trying to perform a keyword search through a long video to find the specific segment of interest to them. The keywords, labels, and captions that make a web site or video content accessible also help search engines correctly identify content. Accessibility helps everyone. This also relates to the concept of inclusive and universal design, designing for the broadest population of users possible.

VARIOUS TYPES OF TECHNOLOGIES

In today's society, people use various types of technologies to access digital information: tablet computers, laptop computers, smartphones, e-book readers, and others. This technology diversity is a reality of life. People with disabilities are also users of diverse technologies. This is true in economically developed countries but also in the developing world [12]. Many economically developing countries offer some form of assistive technologies to citizens with disabilities; having such assistive technologies often means the difference between extreme poverty (without access to technology) and economic self-sufficiency [13].

However, given the availability and widespread usage of technologies, contingent barriers in the technologies offered often limit which devices are available for use by people with disabilities. For instance, blind users who want to use a smartphone can't just make the common choice of "iPhone, Android, or Blackberry?" based on the different characteristics of the devices, but must choose based on the relative accessibility of the devices (and, as the next few paragraphs will describe, the decision is even more complex than it first seems). Thus, blind people may tend to favor iPhones and Deaf people Android-based devices because the particular chosen devices are more accessible for the individuals in light of their disabilities (Morris and Mueller, 2014).

MOBILE DEVICES, APPS, AND ACCESSIBILITY

In recent years, there has been an explosion of applications (apps) from a variety of developers, including developers who are not a part of a standard business enterprise. Generally, these apps are designed for mobile smartphones or tablets and tend to be designed for single purposes. The apps are built by a greater diversity of software developers than are more traditional software applications for use on desktop or laptop computers running a more traditional operating system. The device manufacturers have not acted as gatekeepers for the accessibility of apps developed for their devices, so many apps are inaccessible. Apple, Google, and Microsoft have provided guidance to app developers through application programming interfaces (APIs) to allow app accessibility if the developers desire that. Unfortunately, to date, not a single app developer provides any information, prior to purchase, regarding the accessibility of the offered apps.

Another challenge for accessibility in mobile devices is the ability for device manufacturers to customize the operating system (OS). (Please allow us to be technical for a minute!) For instance, in the Android environment, choosing an accessible version of the operating system does not always guarantee that a user will end up with an accessible device. As an example, the Amazon Kindle Fire tablet runs Ice Cream Sandwich, the second most accessible Android OS from Google. However, because Amazon has chosen to turn off the accessibility features in the Android OS, the Kindle Fire does not have all of the accessibility features of Android OS. Similarly, Barnes & Noble's Nook HD runs Ice Cream Sandwich, but Barnes & Noble has made a decision to turn off the accessibility options for all areas of the device except in the Reader application. As a result, the Nook HD is not fully accessible to people with print-related disabilities. To the print disabled, accessibility is not an optional feature. However, as long as the OS providers, such as Apple, Google, and Microsoft, view accessibility as a secondary feature or an optional benefit of the OS and as long as the device manufacturers can choose to turn off the OS accessibility features, inaccessible mobile devices will continue to be a problem.

So, accessibility of devices can be conceptualized at multiple levels: the device and the OS provide the basic accessibility capabilities, the manufacturer configures those in a way that enables (or disables) various possibilities, and the app writers then enact possibilities in their apps. To ensure a good outcome, all parties must coordinate to have full accessibility.

There are bright spots in the area of mobile device accessibility. As of June 2009, blind users have been able to independently access touch screen interfaces on mobile devices. Starting with the iPhone 3GS, Apple Inc. made VoiceOver, the company's screen access program, available by default on every iPhone. Every "iDevice" released by Apple Inc. since then has had built-in accessibility features. However, Apple Inc. did not stop at providing speech access to iDevices; with the release of the iOS4.2, the company also provided Braille support for various refreshable Braille displays by default. With the on-board Braille support, for the first time ever, the print disabled do not have to pay extra for accessibility. Instead, the iPhone is accessible out of the box. Before the release of the Apple iPhone 3GS, the blind user who wanted to have an accessible cell phone had to pay additional money (a significant amount) to purchase screen access software. The additional cost made the option financially out of reach for many people. With the release of recent iPhones, Apple Inc. has set the new standard for accessibility in the mobile phone industry. This has encouraged other industry leaders to include accessibility features out of the box, and as of 2012, all of the major operating systems for cell phones now have some out-of-the-box accessibility features for people with disabilities. The progress with iPhones shows that accessible IT is a technical possibility; it's feasible; and it's a good business decision. For instance, some public school systems are now choosing iPads over Kindles for reading e-books because the iPads offer accessibility. (See Chapter 7 about regulations and e-readers.) It's not technical expertise that's lacking. What is lacking is the *desire*, the *will*, to make IT accessible, and often the policies of public institutions and organizations do not effectively improve the situation.

ACCESSIBILITY IN DESKTOP AND LAPTOP COMPUTERS

The history of accessibility in personal computing is much longer than the history of smartphones. As mentioned, smartphones now often come accessible out of the box, but in many cases, people with disabilities still must purchase extra software or hardware to make their personal computers (PCs) accessible. For people with motor impairments, anything from repetitive strain injuries to paralysis, assistive input devices usually are required. Such devices include modified keyboards: ergonomic keyboards, one-handed keyboards (for people with use of only one hand), keyboards based on the ability to point wrists but not use any fingers, and keyboards designed for use with mouthsticks. Assistive pointing devices include ergonomic mice, mouth joysticks, and foot pedals. For people with no use of their hands or arms, head-tracking or eye-tracking devices might be used. Many of these hardware devices are especially expensive. For people with print-related disabilities, such as blind users, additional accessible software or hardware often must be purchased to make a Windows-based computer accessible. This includes software such as a screen reader (also known as a screen access program or text-to-speech) or screen magnification program (for low-vision users). Additional hardware may include a refreshable Braille display. Every major operating system now includes screen magnification as a built-in feature, and Apple Inc. includes VoiceOver as a built-in screen reader in the MacOS, but Windows does not include a fully functional screen reader. Microsoft has recently set up a partnership with GW Micro to offer a free version of the Window-Eyes screen reader to users who have full licenses for Microsoft Office 2010 or later. Blind people may also choose to purchase a refreshable Braille display, a hardware device often consisting of 40 or 80 Braille cells; however, those devices are expensive, and Braille literacy is low, so this is a less-popular choice.

Users who are Deaf or hard of hearing need captioning (either text captioning or ASL captioning) for multimedia such as videos. When the supplier of the multimedia has not professionally captioned a video, and the Deaf user needs access to the content (say, for employment-related purposes), the Deaf user is left with a few possible choices: do I file a request asking the provider to caption the content?; do I try to use a service, such as Google captioning, that will automatically caption a file for free (often with less-than-ideal results)?; or do I pay to get the file captioned? All of these options are associated with a delay in access to information.

Speech recognition (also known as speech-to-text) is used by a large portion of people, with and without disabilities, in everything from mobile phones and GPS devices (to assist with hands-free calling and map directions) to dictation and controlling software applications. Speech recognition is used not only by people with limited or no use of hands, but also by people with repetitive strain injuries and those whose hands are performing other tasks (such as surgeons in an operating room or people driving a car). Speech recognition is built into both the Windows 8 and MacOS X operating systems. The key goal is to ensure that all of these people, using different forms of input and output, can effectively access web sites, operating systems, software applications, and more. Some of the features that typically make a technology accessible for someone with a perceptual or print disability, such as the ability to access web sites, software applications, and operating systems using only a keyboard and no pointing device, also provide flexibility for people with motor impairment.

HOW DOES ACCESSIBILITY WORK?

How does it work? Screen reader/access software, a popular form of assistive technology, is a good example of how IT is made accessible. The four most popular screen access programs are JAWS for Windows by Freedom Scientific, Window-Eyes by GW Micro, NVDA by NV Access, and VoiceOver by Apple Inc. The primary function of these screen access programs is rendering text content into speech. So how do these screen access programs have the ability to render text into speech?

Screen access software actually receives data directly from the operating system and the browser through an application program interface (API) and, in the context of web pages, the Document Object Model (DOM). This is why the screen access software can pass along information, such as page layout, text attributes, and the location of interactive controls and form fields, to the user. When the web page is designed in compliance with the Web Content Accessibility Guidelines (WCAG 2.0), this works effectively. With a screen access program, users can selectively view content in a word processing application, Portable Document Format (PDF) document, or on a web site and can selectively interact with the various controls of the applications. These accessibility features in a web site, operating system, or application that assist screen reader users also assist other users.

Another common feature of screen access programs is the ability to drive a refreshable Braille display (again, recent MacOS computers have built-in support for a Braille device). Some blind users prefer a Braille device, whereas deaf-blind individuals use refreshable Braille as their primary way to gain access to the computers because speech output is of limited or no use to them. Currently, approximately 30 types of Braille displays are available for purchase in the United States. Refreshable Braille displays can be expensive because of the underlying technology that the manufacturers use to control the refresh rate on the displays. Since the mid-1970s, piezoelectric crystals have been used to push up the pins on the display. No other material has been found that is as responsive for driving the pins. Most Braille displays have a refresh rate of less than 1 second. This rapid refresh rate allows computer users to read or interact with the content very quickly. These displays can be connected to a computer via Bluetooth or USB. These displays then render content in electronic (refreshable) Braille. Another important reason for the high cost of refreshable Braille is the limited manufacturing capacity. Previously, only a few companies in the United States, Japan, and Germany could manufacture these displays. Today, displays are also manufactured in China, and because of the expanded manufacturing capacity, the price of the displays has been decreasing in recent years. By following the operating system, application, and web page accessibility standards, people using all of these different input/output approaches (screen readers, Braille, alternative keyboards, etc.) can have equal access to the operating system, applications, and web pages.

ACCESSIBILITY IN KIOSKS AND VOTING MACHINES

Accessibility isn't limited to personal computers, laptops, and mobile phones. Having access to the various technologies beyond desktop computing and mobile computing is a must. Access to a voting machine to carry out one's civic duty is necessary. Having accessible ATMs to independently conduct personal financial transactions is critical. Both ATMs and voting machines can be made accessible, and there are accessible models in the marketplace. US law (the Help America Vote Act of 2002) mandates that every precinct must have an accessible voting machine for the print disabled to use on Election Day. However, other kiosk-based technologies, such as kiosks at airports, health care facilities, government offices and fast food facilities, often remain inaccessible. Even when ATMs have the potential to be accessible, a bank may have the speech option disabled; thus, an ATM that appears to be accessible to the blind (it may have a Braille keypad or a headphone jack) may still be an inaccessible machine. Requiring a user with a disability to ask another individual for assistance (and possibly provide a banking password to the individual) is an unnecessary risk. When a public kiosk has accessible technology in place, it's important to ensure that it can be physically accessed by someone in a wheelchair; wheelchair access design is not typically a consideration for personal computers or mobile devices but is vital to public kiosks. All of these kiosks, like all IT, have the potential to be accessible. There aren't major, unsolved technical challenges to mainstream access. There ARE existing solutions that have not been implemented. Not using existing solutions and knowledge, and not ensuring accessible information technology, can lead to the various forms of societal discrimination discussed in Chapter 3.

ACCESSIBLE TECHNOLOGY VS. AUGMENTATIVE COMMUNICATION AND PROSTHETICS

We need to be clear when we discuss the differences between accessible technology, augmentative communication, and prosthetics. Accessible technology refers to using different or modified input or output approaches to access the same information, the same web content, the same applications, and the same e-books as those used by people without disabilities. In summary, accessible technology equals access to the same content and the same transactions offered by an application or web site.

Augmentative communication, also known as augmentative and assistive communication (AAC), refers to situations in which an individual has challenges in communicating. For example, augmentative communication is required when someone is unable to speak and has communication needs he or she wants to get across. Understand that we are using the term "speak" to mean spoken language or sign language. If someone cannot use spoken language or sign language, they may be able to use a communications device, which will allow them to select words and have the computer speak those words or allow them to choose items on a screen and to make their wishes be known that way. Although the core technology of computer synthesized speech output may be the same, assistive technology and augmentative communication are used for two different purposes. Assistive technology uses speech output to read to a blind user whatever appears on the screen. The blind user has no trouble communicating his or her wishes through speech. That same computer synthesized speech output can be used by someone who is unable to speak, using a spoken or sign language, to express his or her thoughts and wishes.

Prosthetics were used when an individual lost an arm or a leg, and in the past, these prosthetics were not computerized. However, with technology advances, prosthetics offer more flexibility and variability, which can affect the ways in which someone with a prosthetic interacts with digital technology. It is important to note that in economically developing countries, prosthetics and especially nontechnical devices (wheelchairs, canes) are likely to appear in use before assistive technology or augmentative communication, but these devices may in these contexts be described using the term "assistive technology" [14].

The historical roots of accessible technology, augmentative communication, and prosthetics are different. Accessible technology tends to be developed by the rehabilitation engineering and computer science communities when such technology is related to employment and by the educational community when it is related to learning. Augmentative communication tends to come from the speech pathology community, which is concerned with helping people effectively communicate for life skills, whereas prosthetics tend to come from the medical community.

Sometimes devices may include components of accessible technology, augmentative communication, and prosthetics. However, there is a core difference between accessible technology and the other ones. For prosthetics, an individual needs his or her device and to have it working. For augmentative communication, an individual must have his or her individual communication device, and it must be working. For accessible technology, for someone using an alternative input or output device, it is not enough to simply have his or her input and output device; the individual's alternative input or output device must also interface properly with web sites, operating systems, e-book content, and software applications. If a web site is not designed using the legally required accessibility guidelines, no amount of assistive technology (alternative input or output devices) will help. For public kiosks, such as ATMs, voting machines, and airport check-in centers, accessibility options such as speech output and Braille must be included. A blind user cannot simply walk up to a public kiosk and access the machine using his or her own technology if there is no accessible interface. In using technology with no accessible interface, blind users must surrender their independence, privacy, or on occasion their security (by giving their ATM passwords to another) or the privacy of their electoral choices (in the case of voting machines).

Thus, if a web site does not label its images, edit boxes, and radio buttons in ways that can be detected and reported by screen access technology, a user's assistive technology is rendered irrelevant. An e-book reading device may have accessibility features, but if the e-book content is not marked up properly, the e-book content remains unavailable. When developers render web sites, e-books, operating systems, software applications, and public kiosks in a way that they automatically lock out people with certain types of disabilities, no amount of effort on the part of the individual with a disability will secure access for that person.

An individual with a disability who is locked out of accessing content or applications suffers other types of exclusion (see Chapter 3 for more information on societal discrimination resulting from inaccessible IT). For instance, when a learning management system used in a university class is inaccessible, a student with a disability may not be able to access the assigned readings for the class and may not be able to take part in the ongoing discussions that occur online among classmates. When the individual with a disability asks the professor to make materials available in another format, the professor may see this as an imposition and perceive the student with a disability as less capable. But even if the professor complies, the ongoing discussions and ongoing access to all of the other collaborative and informational features offered by learning management software and the consequences that flow from them also are lost. The disabled student who encounters these barriers inevitably will perform more poorly academically than he or she would have without such barriers. This affects the student's employability upon graduation. Indeed, poor academic performance may reinforce an employer's perception of persons with disabilities being inferior employees, but such performance often was actually caused by inaccessible technology.

VARIOUS TYPES OF POLICIES

Many types of policies can ensure equal access to digital content. Public policies are ones implemented by national, regional, and local governments; multinational governments (such as the European Union); and international organizations involved in human rights, such as the United Nations. These types of public policies often state legal requirements for what types of technologies must be accessible and what organizations are covered by those requirements. As described in Chapter 4, international technical standards often influence these public policies.

Policies take various forms. In terms of government policies, they often start with the creation of laws (which are covered in detail in Chapters 5 and 6). Those laws (also known as statutes), which are broad and general, are implemented through the use of regulations, which provide more technical details needed for implementation (see Chapter 7 for information on regulations). Often, policies of nongovernmental organizations, such as the technical standards provided by the Web Accessibility Initiative of the World Wide Web consortium, influence and are reflected in government policies (see Chapter 4). Other policy mechanisms, such as lawsuits, executive orders, and other legal filings and orders, can help clarify the meaning of statutes and regulations. Even the choice of a government to enforce or not enforce existing rules is a policy mechanism. Budgets obviously play a role as a policy mechanism. If a government publicly states that digital accessibility is important but cuts the budget of the office charged with leading digital accessibility efforts, which action speaks more loudly?

The effectiveness of these public policies can differ, depending on factors such as the level of transparency and reporting required. Typically, public policies that require periodic reporting and the public posting of these reports are more effective. There are also differences in public policies related to enforcement mechanisms and penalties. If technology procured or developed is not accessible, what penalties occur? And what steps are taken to ensure that it doesn't happen again? Public policies also differ in terms of their focus on prioritizing technical guidelines, performance standards, or consultation with disability groups. In addition, development and enforcement of regulations may be decentralized throughout a government. For instance, regulations related to IT accessibility within the US federal government come from multiple agencies: the US Department of Transportation (related to airline web sites and kiosks), the US Access Board (Section 508), the US Department of Justice (the Americans with Disabilities Act), the US Department of Education (Individuals with Disabilities Education Act), and others. There is rarely one agency coordinating all policies related to IT accessibility within a federal government.

Although some policies are governmental public policies, others are the policies of a specific organization, educational institution, company, or professional organization. Such policies are tailored to the specific requirements of that organization, based on the legal requirements for that organization and the priority placed on digital accessibility by the leaders of the organization. Policies often are the framework for taking actions.

As an example of how policies are implemented, consider captioning of videos. Ideally all videos placed online by an organization will already be captioned. But if the video isn't captioned, when someone asks that a video be captioned, if there are good policies and processes in place, a captioning contract (or in-house captioning) exists, and the video captioning is done within 24 hours. If no process is in place, this video is not likely to get captioned in a timely manner. Also, for legacy videos (videos that have been posted in the past), what priority is assigned, and which videos will get captioned first?

The organizational policies specify the point in the development process at which checks are performed to ensure that technologies being developed are accessible. Organizational policies specify how procurement processes are used effectively to acquire accessible technology. The policies and processes provide frameworks for success and also detail methods for easily remedying problems that occur. Accommodation requests that occur one at a time, when someone with a disability requests them, are likely to lead to failure, as well as outright hostility toward those requesting the accommodation. Organizational policies and processes that lead to proactive accessibility, rather than many accommodation requests, should be the goal.

Why are some organizations leaders in accessibility, others followers, and still others outright hostile to the concept? It can depend on the tone of an organization's leaders: do they often discuss digital accessibility? Are they providing funding for it and stressing its importance? Are staff getting credit and kudos for focusing on digital accessibility? It can depend on the history of the organization; some organizations have a long track record of commitment to inclusion and social justice and taking long-term, rather than short-term, views. It can depend on the legal environment in which an organization is operating. Many companies started taking digital accessibility more seriously after the Target (Inc.) settlement, and universities started taking digital accessibility more seriously after the legal settlements with Penn State, the University of Montana, and Louisiana Tech University (see Chapter 5 for more information on these legal settlements). Often, the common link is awareness—leaders being aware of the benefits of digital accessibility and the risks involved with violating laws requiring digital accessibility. See Chapter 10 for case studies of companies, universities, and organizations that have effectively provided digital accessibility.

Merely focusing on the legal risks and penalties misses the major idea. Digital accessibility is good design and good coding, and it is good for everyone. An accessible digital technology can be purchased or used by the broadest segment of the population. Digital accessibility often means that appropriate documentation (within software) was performed. Digital accessibility creates the best technology to empower people. Frank Baitman, CIO of the US Department of Health and Human Services, stated the following:

"Some people say that you should make technology accessible because it's the law, but that's not a good reason. Others say that you should make technology accessible because it's the right thing to do, but that's just charity. You should make technology accessible, because it enables government employees with disabilities to do their job. You should make technology accessible because it enables citizens to effectively interact with their government. Accessibility is about providing good service quality for employees and citizens."

HOW POLICIES AND LAWS CAN LEAD TO IMPROVED ACCESS TO DIGITAL INFORMATION

Many countries have laws relating to information technology accessibility. The United Kingdom, France, Portugal, Australia, Canada, Sweden, and the United States all have laws that relate to information technology accessibility. Some countries require only that government-funded technology, such as government web sites, voting machines, and technology purchased for schools, be accessible. Other countries, including the United Kingdom and the United States, require other types of information technology, even technology not funded by the government, to be accessible. For instance, both the United States (the Americans with Disabilities Act) and the United Kingdom (the Equality Act 2010) require equal access to programs, activities, and services of places of public accommodation and local governments [15]. Thus, a private school, as a place of public accommodation, must still provide equal access to its programs and activities, and to the extent those programs and activities find their expression in or through technology, accessible technology is required.

Many existing disability rights laws focus on the purchasers of technology (government, education, employers). Obviously, requiring *developers* of technology and content to make their devices, applications, and information accessible would directly address the problem. However, rarely do disability rights laws address the development of technologies. Only when IT falls under a specific category (say, communications devices which have their own telecommunications-related laws) can the developers be required to include accessibility. And other existing laws (outside of disability rights laws) generally have not been used as a basis for requiring the development of accessibility.

Those charged with complying with existing laws, such as governmental entities and educational institutions, often ignore the laws. The result is that technology purchasers often make no demand of the IT developers to develop accessible IT. The effect of making market demands is important. When California State University publicly denied procurement contracts to Apple, Blackboard, and other technology companies because of inaccessibility, the companies were encouraged to modify their software to make it accessible [16]. Procurement is starting to be used more effectively as a lever of power for improving accessibility in the European Union (read more about Mandate 376 in Chapters 6 and 7) and the United States (more information is available in Chapters 5 and 7).

There are a number of reasons laws related to IT accessibility have not been effective, and Chapters 7–9 describe in detail the reasons for this lack of success. In multiple countries, there are common reasons for the ineffectiveness of laws. First, it is important to remember that laws are not self-executing. Moreover, regulations and policies must be put into place, as must resources and enforcement mechanisms (see Chapter 7 for more information on regulations). Ongoing compliance monitoring by the government is rare in the government or in the private sector. For instance, between 2003 and 2010, the US Department of Justice did not perform the compliance monitoring for Section 508 regulations within the US government (see Chapter 9 for more information on compliance monitoring). Section 508 requires accessibility when "Federal agencies develop, procure, maintain, or use electronic and information technology." Without reporting, many government agencies stopped complying with Section 508. Similar problems related to IT accessibility have appeared in the United Kingdom [15] and Spain [17]. It is a rare country that has not experienced challenges with IT accessibility [18]. Without any compliance monitoring or enforcement, often the only way to address inequalities is for a disability advocacy group to file a complaint or a lawsuit.

There are many other reasons why laws are often ineffective. Governments often do not give clear guidance, and therefore, there is confusion on what the legal requirements are, what categories of individuals are covered, or what processes must be followed. In some cases, rather than use existing, well-documented international standards for accessibility of interface design (such as WCAG 2.0), national governments modify the interface guidelines. This results in a situation where a country has a specific technical standard, but no documentation or software tools to support their national technical standard, and no base of individuals with expertise in applying that national standard. In some situations, government agencies do an excellent job with their accessibility compliance but are unwilling to share their knowledge, expertise, or techniques with the general public [19]. Other government agencies ignore or violate the law and procure inaccessible technology, such as inaccessible e-books, or build inaccessible web sites. In some instances, national governments indicate that they are not enforcing the law. Because of the way laws related to equal access to information technology have been implemented, such laws have often not been effective. Yet there are entities that are actively working toward accessible IT (see Chapter 10 for case studies of success). Those who experience success often do so through ongoing compliance activities, with results that are public and transparent, which improves accountability. Chapter 10 provides many case studies of success related to IT accessibility.

SUMMARY

The ability and expertise required to make IT accessible for people with many disabilities, in most circumstances already exist. However, because of a lack of knowledge, interest, or motivation, developers often build inaccessible web sites, software applications, e-books, operating systems, and kiosks. Very often the public policies, regulations, and laws that are supposed to encourage improved IT accessibility are ineffective and instead lead to various forms of societal discrimination. But the laws already in place, together with improved regulations and policies, could make a world of difference. This book provides a comprehensive look at laws, policies, regulations, compliance monitoring, and evaluation techniques with the goal of improving the accessibility of information technology.

A NOTE ABOUT THE USAGE OF TERMS

Across different populations of people with disabilities, across different countries, and even within different advocacy groups for the same disability, the terms used to describe people with disabilities are often different. For instance, most people with disabilities prefer "people-first language," in which someone is referred to as a "person with [insert disability]." However, blind people often prefer to be known as "blind people" rather than "people who are blind" or "people who are visually impaired." Deaf people, if they are part of the Deaf culture community, prefer to be known as Deaf people, rather than "people with limited hearing" or something similar. In fact, Deaf people do not view themselves as having a disability; instead, they view themselves as being from a different culture because they communicate using a different language [20]. A term often used is "DHH" meaning "Deaf or hard of hearing," which is designed to be an inclusive term, including both people from the Deaf culture (people who use sign language first), and those who are "oral people," who prefer to speak vocally and lip-read. Those two groups often have very different needs.

There are also different descriptions used in different countries. For instance, in the United Kingdom, "visually impaired" typically refers to people with some residual vision, and "blind" refers to people with no residual vision, but in the United States, "blind" refers more broadly to people with any type of vision loss who use nonvisual techniques, regardless of the level of vision loss. The terms used are not the only things different. The various advocacy groups—from different disabilities, and even within the same disability—often are in disagreement about things such as inclusive education versus separate education, sheltered workshops, and even whether paper currency should have tactile indications of the currency denomination, or whether other issues (e.g., employment and education) deserve more attention. In this book, we have strived to use the most respectful language at all points. We realize that this often will result in a conflict in the type of terminology used. Understand it is never our intent to disrespect anyone with any type of disability.

REFERENCES

[1] Bias R, Mayhew D, editors. Cost-justifying usability: an update for the internet age. Amsterdam: Morgan Kaufmann Publishers; 2005.
[2] United Nations. Convention on the rights of persons with disabilities. Available at: http://www.un.org/disabilities/convention/conventionfull.shtml; 2013.

[3] Shinohara K, Wobbrock J. In the shadow of misperception: assistive technology use and social interactions. Proceedings of the ACM conference on human factors in computing systems 2011;705–14.

[4] Slack D. Blind advocates blast White House. Politico. Available at: http://www.politico.com/politico44/2013/2005/blind-advocates-blast-white-house-164914.html (May 28, 2013).

[5] Bagenstos S. Disability rights law: cases and materials. New York: Thompson Reuters; 2010.

[6] Lazar J, editor. Universal usability: designing computer interfaces for diverse user populations. Chichester, UK: John Wiley & Sons; 2007.

[7] Lazar J, Kumin L, Feng J. Understanding the computer skills of adult expert users with down syndrome: an exploratory study. Proceedings of the ACM conference on assistive technology (ASSETS); 2011. p. 51–8.

[8] Karger J, Lazar J. Ensuring that students with text-related disabilities have access to digital learning materials: a policy discussion. Perspectives on Language and Literacy 2014;40(1):33–8.

[9] Price G. Creative solutions to making the technology work: three case studies of dyslexic writers in higher education. Research in Learning Technologies 2006;14(1):21–38.

[10] Draffen E. Dyslexia and technology. In: Phipps L, Sutherland A, Seale J, editors. Access all areas: disability, technology, and learning. York, UK: TechDis with the Association for Learning Technology; 2002. p. 24–8.

[11] Emens E. Framing disability. University of Illinois Law Review 2012;2012(5):1383–442.

[12] Pal J, Alfaro A, Ammari T, Chatterjee S. A capabilities view of accessibility in policy and practice in Jordan and Peru. The Review of Disability Studies: An International Journal 2013;10(3–4).

[13] Pal J, Lakshmanan M. Assistive technology and the employment of people with vision impairments in India. In: Proceedings of the fifth international conference on information and communication technologies and development; 2012. p. 307–17.

[14] Eide A, Oderud T. Assistive technology in low-income countries. In: MacLachlan M, Swartz L, editors. Disability & international development: towards inclusive global health. New York: Springer; 2009. p. 149–60.

[15] Kuzma J. Accessibility design issues with UK e-government sites. Government Information Quarterly 2010;27(2):141–6.

[16] Keller J. Cal state's strong push for accessible technology gets results. Chronicle of Higher Education. Available at: http://chronicle.com/article/Cal-States-Strong-Push-for/125683/ (December 12, 2010).

[17] Martinez L. Understanding HCI policy in Spain in the context of accessibility. Interactions 2012;19(5):58–61.

[18] Goodwin M, Susar D, Nietzio A, Snaprud M, Jensen C. Global web accessibility analysis of national government portals and ministry web sites. Journal of Information Technology and Politics 2011;8(1):41–67.

[19] Olalere A, Lazar J. Accessibility of U.S. federal government home pages: section 508 compliance and site accessibility statements. Government Information Quarterly 2011;28(3):303–9.

[20] Shapiro J. The deaf celebration of separate culture. No pity: people with disabilities forging a new civil rights movement. New York: Random House; 1994, p. 74–104.

The history of access technology

2

INTRODUCTION

People with disabilities are almost always early adopters of technology. Most people with disabilities believe that assistive technologies can level the playing field, helping those with disabilities to be productive members of society. If being technology-literate is an important asset for people without disabilities, it is even more so for anyone with a disability because knowledge of access technology is seen as key to efficiency in employment and education [1]. For this reason, there is a clear, significant incentive for users with disabilities to take an interest in emerging technologies. However, there are some disincentives to adopting access technology, especially for "newly disabled" users; some of those disincentives are discussed in this chapter.

Access technology historically has not been a one-way street. Many technologies originally designed for people with disabilities have wound up benefitting society at large. The following section provides an overview of some of the ways access technologies have developed and how they have gone on to have illustrious mainstream uses.

The history of access technology is long and storied, and no comprehensive overview is intended here. The aim is to provide some illustrative examples of how such technology comes about, how it is used, how it benefits its users with and without disabilities, and how technology adapts to changing circumstances.

EARLY HISTORY OF ASSISTIVE TECHNOLOGIES (THROUGH THE 1960S)

It may not always be obvious to a general audience, but some of the earliest examples of modern assistive technologies are familiar devices: typewriters, record players and talking books, and TTY for the Deaf and hard of hearing. These are devices that we developed before the well-known disability rights movements.

All of these technologies have dramatically enriched the lives of people with disabilities in ways that no one could have ever imagined. In many cases, these inventions also have been useful to those without a disability.

To appreciate the rich history of access technologies used by populations of people with disabilities, one must have a good understanding of the various benefits of these inventions, so let's have a look at some benefits of well-designed access technologies.

For the blind, the ability to use talking books with accessible digital talking book players, either as students in their pursuit of education, or as professionals, is an extremely important benefit. On many college and university campuses across this country, blind students use their digital talking book players to consume vast amounts of information. With pocket-size digital talking book players, blind students can carry an entire library of books with them. Before the invention of digital talking book players, blind students did not have regular access to a dictionary or encyclopedia because one dictionary takes up as many as 36 hard copy Braille volumes. Textbook transcription was labor intensive and often a manual task. The invention of the digital talking book has eliminated the need for bulky hard copy Braille texts and facilitated access to textbooks that are available in an accessible format. This development allows blind students to have access to dictionaries and other essential books.

For the Deaf and hard of hearing, having access to equipment such as a TTY is extremely valuable. TTY gives them the ability to communicate with family members, friends, and co-workers remotely, via the telephone or the Internet. TTY stands for Teletypewriter. It is also sometimes called a TDD, or Telecommunication Device for the Deaf. TTY is the more widely accepted term, however, as TTYs are used by many people, not just people who are Deaf.

A TTY is a special device that lets people who are Deaf, hard of hearing, or speech-impaired use the telephone to communicate, by allowing them to type messages back and forth to one another instead of talking and listening. A TTY is required at both ends of the conversation in order to communicate. To use a TTY, you set a telephone handset onto special acoustic cups built into the TTY (some TTY models can be plugged directly into a telephone line). Then, type the message you want to send on the TTY's keyboard. As you type, the message is sent over the phone line, just like your voice would be sent over the phone line if you talked. You can read the other person's response on the TTY's text display.

Someone who is not Deaf or hard of hearing can still call a person who is deaf, hard of hearing, or speech-impaired by using the Telecommunications Relay Service (TRS). With TRS, a special operator types whatever you say so that the person you are calling can read your words on his or her TTY display. He or she will type back a response, which the TRS operator will read aloud for you to hear over the phone. Toll-free TRS services are available 24 hours a day, 365 days a year. Of course, many Deaf people today prefer to use text messaging or other current approaches, rather than TTY.

Without TTY and relay call services for communicating long distance, spontaneous contact had in the past been virtually impossible for Deaf and hard of hearing users; however, other options, such as text messaging, have now emerged for some communication situations. Deaf-blind individuals also can use TTY systems with the addition of not necessarily integrated refreshable Braille display. They can type their responses in Braille using the Braille input keyboard on the display. With the addition of the Braille display, a TTY makes getting in touch with friends and family simple for the deaf-blind, a group that is very often overlooked when it comes to technological innovations. The history of the TTY technology is discussed in more detail later in this chapter.

All of the assistive technologies discussed here are widely used by people with disabilities, but these innovations are derived from the ingenuity of inventors who considered the needs of others in their product design long before phrases such as "inclusive design" became popular.

The following sections discuss a brief history of each of these inventions.

THE INVENTION OF THE TYPEWRITER

In 1808, long before the standardized typewriter existed, Italian Pellegrino Turri invented a typing machine and carbon paper for his blind friend Countess Carolina Fantoni da Fivizzano. Turri wanted to create a device that the Countess could use to write to him when he was traveling [2]. His device is the oldest working example of a typewriter. Typewriters may be (mostly) a thing of the past, but the keyboard entry that the typewriter introduced survives in the computer keyboard, which is the main tool used today for text input.

As computing technology continues to evolve and move from desktop to mobile computing, the QWERTY (or AZERTY and other variations) style keyboard is used for sending text messages, surfing the web, and communicating via social media on mobile devices, even when the keyboard is virtual. As a design idea, the QWERTY keyboard has been resilient. The concept that Turri pioneered for the sake of a loved one with a disability is central to most interactions we have with digital information and the Internet.

THE RECORD PLAYER AND THE AUDIOBOOK

When Thomas Edison invented the phonograph in 1877, one of his intended uses of the device was to create audiobooks for the blind. The prolific inventor's listing of this use as a top advantage of phonograph technology should surprise no one; innovation has often been driven by the needs of people with disabilities. With that one declaration, Edison not only promoted the phonograph, but also gave birth to the audiobook [3].

The phonograph and its successors have brought a tremendous amount of enjoyment to the blind and the sighted by giving access to more kinds of music than would ever have been available as live music. The birth of the recording industry has truly made music a universal language and also has made a good number of fortunes along the way, Edison's being not the least among them.

Although in the late 1800s Thomas Edison made known his intention to use phonograph technology to provide the blind with access to recorded books, his desired purpose for the invention did not come to fruition until 1932 in the United States, when the National Library Service for the Blind and the Physically Handicapped (NLS) began exploring the use of phonograph technology to record books for the blind. As expected, the audiobook lending service from the NLS has been extremely popular among the blind and the print-disabled (anyone unable to read print for whatever reason) from the beginning. The following provides a little insight into how the audiobook, now a beloved mainstream format, first entered the public consciousness.

After early efforts to establish libraries for the blind at different institutions across the United States, the NLS became a nationally recognized service in March 1931, when the Pratt-Smoot Act was passed by the US Congress. In this bill, Congress appropriated $100,000 to the Library of Congress to jump-start the lending library service for the blind. The Library of Congress was allowed to make arrangements with the regional libraries nationwide to make Braille books available on loan to the blind. Because the embossed books were difficult and costly to produce, only a few titles were available. In 1933, the NLS began to consider what other types of technologies could assist in getting more books into the hands of the blind. By the early 1930s, Americans were accustomed to enjoying recorded music using Thomas Edison's phonograph technology. It was a natural progression to explore whether a similar type of technology could be used to deliver books to the blind.

In 1933, the important technological breakthrough everyone was hoping for finally occurred. A record format that was suited to recorded books was perfected. Previous formats had accommodated only short recordings; with the new records, human-read books could be recorded at 150 grooves to an inch so that a book of 60,000 words could fit on eight or nine double-faced, 12-inch records. The turntable ran at 33-1/3 revolutions per minute, which made it possible for each record to hold 30 minutes of reading time. The first recordings by the NLS include: the Declaration of Independence; the Constitution of the United States; Washington's farewell address; and Lincoln's Gettysburg address. Several of Shakespeare's plays, including *Hamlet*, also were recorded [4].

At the time, the record players were not provided for the blind free of charge. Frequently, players were purchased on behalf of the blind, either by loved ones or by philanthropic organizations. Eventually, Congress amended the Pratt-Smoot Act to include funding for book players for the blind. The rest is history. Over the years, the NLS has expanded the lending services to support various digital formats, including digital audio and digital Braille [4]. Book players have also advanced significantly, going from heavy desktop record players to pocket-sized players. In recent years, the NLS has made it possible for the blind to download books from the digital library for free. In addition to having access to NLS books on specialized players, the blind can now read digital audio and digital Braille books on an Apple iPhone.

Audio book lending libraries for the blind and print disabled are not unique to the US. In the UK, the Royal National Institute of the Blind (RNIB) has been producing audio books for the blind since 1935. In the early 1930s soldiers who lost their sight in the First World War expressed frustration about the difficulty of reading Braille. The RNIB established an audiobook lending library similar to the NLS in the US to help blind veterans gain access to printed books. The first two titles recorded were *The Murder of Roger Ackroyd*, by Agatha Christie, and *Typhoon*, by Joseph Conrad. Both of these books and others were originally recorded on 12-inch shellac gramophone records at a speed of 24 rpm. A typical novel could take up to 10 records playing at about 25 minutes per side. The recorded version of these books was first mailed out to the patrons on November 7, 1935. The lending service has grown tremendously in the past 80 years. The library now has an impressive collection of digital books in its repository, 22,000 of which are audiobooks [5]. Throughout its history, the lending library has provided books in various formats on various types of reading media ranging from vinyl, to cassette tape, CDs, large print, Braille, and digital download. Since its inception, the RNIB lending library has been working closely with the various publishers to expand the categories of books for the library. However, obtaining publisher's permission to have the books available for production prior to release is not always easy. This can often result in the delayed release of the audio recorded books for the blind. As publishers become more aware of the needs of the print disabled to access audio recorded books, many publishers have been willing to provide content to the RNIB in a timely manner to ensure simultaneous releases of the books. One notable example that set a new standard was the Harry Potter series; with the assistance of the publisher, the RNIB lending library was able to release the specialized format for the blind at the same time as the print version.

Meanwhile, the publishing industry has seen Edison's audiobook grow from a niche use for the blind to a mainstream industry that now tops $1 billion in sales. The book players with which the blind have so long been familiar have transformed into well-used and well-loved audiobook apps on millions of smartphones used by avid sighted readers and blind ones. According to the Audio Publishers Association (APA), in 2011, 38 million more audiobooks were sold than in 2010. This represents a 2.6% increase in total revenues year-over-year [6]. Without Edison's one promotional line, we might not have access to the audio recordings of music or books today. Edison clearly understood that a well-designed piece of technology can be beneficial to everyone, regardless of disability. One can draw a conclusion that due to the popularity of the audio book, gaining access to information via audio has become an acceptable norm. Besides audio books, podcasts are used by millions of people to facilitate learning or to stay informed on various topics of interest.

TTYS FOR THE DEAF AND HARD OF HEARING

Telephones have been used by the hearing population in America since the late 1800s. However, before the invention of Teletypewriter (TTY) technology, the Deaf could not use phones. TTY technology came about in the 1960s thanks to a Deaf scientist, Robert Weitbrecht, and a Deaf orthodontist, James Marsters [7]. With other relevant technology, such as the acoustic coupler used to hold the telephone handset receiver, becoming available, and with more teletype machines available through state programs, Deaf and hard of hearing people could finally have phone conversations with others who had TTY machines. In the next 20 years, the use of TTY technology expanded greatly, keeping pace with the growing TTY device distribution programs in multiple states. More advanced TTY systems were invented and sold in the Deaf consumer market as funding became available to support development [8].

However, for the Deaf and hard of hearing, talking to hearing loved ones or family members was still difficult, if not impossible. To provide greater access, volunteer TTY relay services in the United States were established, initially with limited hours and available only in a few areas, connecting Deaf and hard of hearing TTY users with the hearing population who used standard telephones. The Deaf and the hard of hearing populations had to wait until 1987 to have a reliable relay telecommunication service. California was the first state to establish a statewide telecommunication relay program. Between 1987 and 1990, many states established telecommunication relay services, and the network of the relay services began to grow rapidly nationwide. In 1990, the Americans with Disabilities Act (ADA) title IV, which requires that relay telecommunication services be available for the Deaf and the hard of hearing 24 hours a day in every state and in the US territories, came into effect, and relay services were finally available consistently. Today, anyone who wants to communicate with the Deaf and hard of hearing can simply dial 711 to use relay telecommunication programs.

TTY relay services use a communication assistant (CA). The CA converts voice-to-text and text-to-voice communication. The text is displayed on the user's TTY. Because communication using a TTY is not bidirectional, TTY etiquette was developed to better manage the telephone conversations between the Deaf and hard of hearing populations. People who communicate using a TTY or TTY relay service signal conversation turn-taking by saying or typing "go ahead" (GA) and signal the end of a conversation by saying or typing "stop keying" (SK) [9].

THE 1970S-PRESENT

The 1970s, '80s, and '90s saw the creation of many inventions that were helpful to people with disabilities. This is not accidental in terms of the time period. After the civil rights movement of the 1960s, the disability rights movement took shape beginning in the late 1960s through the early 1970s, culminating in laws being passed that guaranteed people with disabilities the right to education and equal access to government services [10]. As people with disabilities demanded equal rights, there was a demand for equal access to the world of information. Many technologies that are intensely familiar to all today, such as optical character recognition, speech recognition (speech-to-text), screen readers (text-to-speech), and captioning, were developed and introduced during this time period.

During the 1970s-1990s, there was an explosion of interest in access technology. Organizations and corporations, such as the National Federation of the Blind (NFB), technology giant IBM, and the Trace Research and Development Center, all worked as centers of advocacy and technology efforts. The Trace Research and Development Center of the College of Engineering at the University of Wisconsin was established in 1971. The purpose of the Center was to explore new technologies to improve the lives of the people with severe disabilities, especially those who could not communicate verbally [11]. Researchers at the Trace Center coined the term "augmentative communication." The Trace Center was the leader in augmentative communication technology, and the impact of the Center's work was well recognized by the various disability communities [12]. As personal computers (PCs) became more and more popular throughout the 1970s and 1980s, the Trace Center was one of a few leaders in the accessibility field that helped ensure that PCs were accessible to all. In 1984, the Trace Center was the coordinator for the US government and corporate initiatives on computer accessibility. The accessibility guidelines developed by the Trace Center were the foundation for many accepted accessibility standards in use today. Another significant contribution of the Trace Center are the EZ Access techniques, the accessible kiosk design guidelines that came out of this effort. With these accessible design guidelines, ATMs, voting machines, telephones, and other public kiosks can be made accessible to people with disabilities [11].

As mentioned, IBM has made significant contributions to the field of access technology. The IBM Screen Reader was so well known that it gave its name to a whole new species of software: screen access software, most commonly known as screen readers. Details of that work appear later in this chapter. In addition to its screen reader, IBM has made Braille printers, typewriters, and a computer program, the Homepage Reader, which the blind could use to access the web. Much of this outstanding development stemmed from IBM's policy, dating to the 1940s, of hiring people with disabilities. Michael Supa, a blind psychologist, was one of the architects of this policy, and his intervention ultimately resulted in the advances described here. During his 37 years at IBM, Supa created a program for hiring and training employees with disabilities [13]. There is no doubt that when IBM made the decision to integrate staff with disabilities into the company's workforce, it created the environment where accessibility research could thrive. What is more, IBM set a precedent for excellence in hiring a diverse workforce, a legacy that to this day makes the company a leader in successful inclusive practices in business.

A good diversity hiring policy and excellent internal and external work on accessibility in technology are fine starting points, but a large and venerable corporation taking a public stance on accessibility is still a rarity. IBM is one of only a few mainstream companies that has made public statements about its position with regard to various accessibility standards. In 2014, IBM issued a press release stating that it will adopt EPUB3, the latest update to the powerful and flexible EPUB publishing standard, in the company's internal content production to ensure accessibility [14]. Such a clear and open stance from a mainstream company benefits those in the disability community and sets a clear example that building in accessibility from the get-go makes for more efficient business processes than does after-the-fact, add-on accessibility.

OPTICAL CHARACTER RECOGNITION, SYNTHETIC SPEECH, AND THE FLATBED SCANNER

In 1976, Dr. Raymond Kurzweil invented a stand-alone reading machine for the blind. The idea did not come to him out of the blue. When Kurzweil met Dr. Kenneth Jernigan, who was at that time the president of the NFB, he asked Jernigan how he could put his creativity and technological expertise to use for the blind. Jernigan said access to printed text was a major stumbling block for the blind. Working with Jernigan prompted Kurzweil to undertake the task of building a machine to render print into speech [15]. The task required Kurzweil to invent three new technologies that were integrated into one "reading machine."

The first of Kurzweil's foundational breakthroughs was an improved version of omni-font character recognition, which a reading machine requires to accurately recognize printed characters in a variety of fonts and render them into digital text. Next was the speech synthesizer, which was needed to render text into speech. Finally, a flatbed scanner was needed so that the blind could scan hard copy books independently [16]. With Kurzweil's reading machine, the blind community had an opportunity to see the advantages of synthetic speech technology decades before such technology became the everyday feature we now use to receive driving directions in our cars or search results on our smartphones.

Optical character recognition (OCR) technology has become a standard feature in offices and homes worldwide, but one can argue that perhaps the greatest benefit of OCR technology is digital preservation. Millions of books and documents are being scanned, recognized, and preserved every year, and the number of digitized books continues to grow rapidly. The Internet Archive, a nonprofit digital library, has more than five million books in its digital repository. The HathiTrust is even more ambitious; it is a large-scale collaborative repository of digital content from research libraries, subsuming content digitized via the Google Books project and Internet Archive digitization initiatives, as well as content digitized locally by libraries. The Hathi Trust has digitized (as of publication time) 11,023,371 total volumes, 5,754,211 book titles, 286,880 serial titles, 3,858,179,850 pages, and 494 terabytes of data [17], preserving our knowledge and ideas for use by generations to come. One additional benefit of OCR technology, besides book preservation, is that any books that are digitally scanned can simply be made accessible to the print-disabled population.

Imagine your life without wirelessly downloaded e-books to take along when packing light for travel. Imagine life without an automatic check-out terminal at the grocery store or a GPS navigation voice to guide you home. Then compare that reality to critics who claim that researchers working on ways to give equal access to those with disabilities are wasting their time for limited gains.

CAPTIONING

Captioning was first designed to help the Deaf and hard of hearing gain access to television programs. Captioning was first used in television broadcasting by the Caption Center, which was founded in 1972 at the Boston public television station WGBH. The first captioned television program was an episode of Julia Child's renowned cooking show *The French Chef*.

In the beginning, captioning was disruptive to many television viewers. In 1974, a new system called "Closed Captioning" was developed by the Caption Center to provide a better experience for everyone. In the 1970s, only the television sets that were compatible with the Closed Captioning technology could display the captioned content. In the 1990s, the Federal Communications Commission (FCC) made television captioning a requirement for any television set that was 13 inches or larger and available for purchase in the United States. In 2006, the FCC ruled that all broadcast and cable television programs must include captioning [18]. Today, captioning is a popular tool not only for the Deaf and hard of hearing but also people without hearing difficulties who have the ability to see, who use captioning while watching movies, viewing content on the Internet, during class lectures, and at sporting events or loud venues, such as bars, gyms, and airports. Captioning is also an important tool for the deaf-blind to use with a refreshable Braille display to gain access to information. Before captioning, the deaf-blind had access only to content transcribed in Braille. With captioning, many deaf-blind individuals are able to enjoy real-time spoken content, just like the rest of the hearing population. The two popular types of captioning technology are Closed Captions, which typically are used to display prerecorded television content, and Real-Time Captions, which are used to provide access to spoken content during live events.

SPEECH RECOGNITION

Speech recognition technology, also known as "voice recognition technology," is probably one of the most exciting technology developments to become more popular in recent years. In this chapter, the terms "speech recognition" and "voice recognition" are used interchangeably. Speech recognition is ubiquitous and is being used on all computing platforms. Individual consumers do not have to bear any extra cost to be able to take advantage of the voice recognition technology installed on many mainstream devices.

In April 2014, Microsoft released the new speech recognition technology Cortana for the Windows 8.1 Mobile platform [19]. As of April 2014, all Windows mobile phones that have the latest version of Windows Mobile OS installed, regardless of manufacturer, are equipped with speech recognition technology. In recent years, Google has integrated the use of speech recognition technology into practically all of its Nexus phones and tablets and its Google Chrome books. Apple made the Siri speech recognition utility available with the release of the iPhone 4. Now every "iDevice" from Apple has out-of-the-box speech recognition technology available to consumers for free.

Speech recognition has become increasingly popular for drivers using their mobile devices in cars. Because all drivers must be vigilant, keeping their hands on the wheel and eyes on the road, many drivers use speech recognition technology to control telecommunication devices and entertainment systems in their cars. Apple has released CarPlay for the iOS7.1. Cars that are designed to be compatible with the iOS7.1 will have the Apple Siri voice recognition. Many car manufacturers, including Volvo and Mercedes, are planning to integrate Apple's CarPlay into their systems [20]. Product developers are coming up with ways to better utilize this technology. In early April 2014, Amazon released the Amazon Dash, a portable device that one can use to compile a grocery list by voice recognition [21]. Voice recognition is becoming a standard part of any type of networked device.

Voice recognition technology has improved dramatically over the years. Extensive user training is no longer needed for anyone to successfully use speech recognition technology. Many telecommunication companies, banks, and numerous companies in the health care industry are adopting the use of voice recognition technology to help cut costs in daily business operations. Consumers are encountering speech recognition technology through interactive voice response systems that accept speech input. Every time someone says "reservations" to access a hotel booking system, voice recognition is being used. Although the benefits of speech recognition technology have only recently emerged as a commonly used solution for society at large, people with disabilities have been using this technology for more than 30 years.

Speech recognition was first used by people with severe physical disabilities who could communicate well verbally. Speech recognition technology has been used by individuals with physical disabilities to accomplish many daily tasks, including operating a computer, writing, turning a page, and controlling home appliances, such as telephones, radios, fans, curtains, and intercoms. Some use speech recognition to control wheelchairs. The first voice-activated wheelchair with an environmental control unit (ECU) was developed in the late 1970s at Rehabilitation Medicine in New York City [22]. A group of individuals with cerebral palsy has been said to prefer the voice recognition driven wheelchairs to the wheelchairs that were equipped with the breath control systems because it provided the users with quicker access by allowing them to quickly control their wheelchairs with just their voices [23].

Speech Recognition and Learning Disabled Students

The use of speech recognition as a tool for individuals with learning disabilities did not receive much attention until the mid-1980s. The adoption of speech recognition technology for use in classrooms has the capacity to enhance the ability of students with disabilities to write better, according to MacArthur, Graham, and Schwartz. Students with learning disabilities (LDs) are more likely to make spelling, punctuation, and capitalization errors. Continually pausing to correct such errors while writing interrupts the train of thought for such students, who may forget the initial message they wanted to express. In addition, students with LDs may take longer to generate a written narrative than do their peers who do not have LDs. According to De La Paz and Graham (as cited in De La Paz, 1999), students with LDs use a simplified vocabulary when writing to avoid spelling errors, even though they may want to use a more difficult word. These students tend to have a negative attitude about writing in general [24]. The use of voice recognition technology in class may allow such students to focus on the planning and content generation of text, rather than on the mechanics of writing. In addition, speech recognition has the potential to increase the rate of production and positively enhance the overall writing experiences of students with LDs.

SCREEN READER TECHNOLOGY

The late 1980s were a critical juncture in the development of access technology. As the PC rapidly gained ground, work was going on behind the scenes to ensure that PCs were accessible for the blind. Two hubs for this work were IBM and the company that started out as Henter-Joyce.

The introduction by IBM of Screen Reader for DOS in 1988 was a landmark, and the work, spearheaded by Jim Thatcher, developed into a precedent-setting series of programs that gave blind users access to computers by providing speech. The underlying philosophy was one of uncompromising inclusion. "The first and most important principle of the five-point Screen Reader philosophy is that blind users must have access to the same computing environment as their sighted colleagues" [25]. In creating Screen Reader for DOS and its successors for Windows, IBM built on a long-standing tradition of creating in-house solutions for its blind employees and went on to create a commercial product that worked because it was created around the intended user's stated requirements, rather than, as has so often been the case, the untested, hypothetical needs of an undefined user with a disability. Thatcher summarizes the point well when he writes "Screen Reader/DOS and Screen Reader/2 evolved based on the requirements and preferences of IBM employees doing their jobs" [25].

While IBM was developing DOS-compatible screen access software for the company's blind staff, the NFB Research and Development Committee, led by blind inventor Tim Cranmer, was developing a product called the Speaqualizer to help the blind gain access to information on IBM PCs [26]. The Speaqualizer, finalized in 1986, gave speech output to any IBM PC via external hardware. The positive impact of these two types of screen access programs cannot be underestimated.

One engineer, a once-promising motorcycle racer who became blind in a motorcycle accident, ended up making a particularly enduring contribution to the newly developing screen readers. Ted Henter, co-founder of the Henter-Joyce Corporation, created the screen access program Job Access With Speech (JAWS) in 1988, and a new standard was set. JAWS became popular in both DOS and Windows platforms, and it is still the most widely used screen reader [27]. After a series of corporate mergers, the product is now owned by Freedom Scientific.

During the late 1980s and 1990s, JAWS and other screen access programs provided access via speech output only for the blind. However, as technology advanced, and the users' demand increased, most screen access programs in the market added support for the refreshable Braille displays. A refreshable Braille display is a device that has varying numbers of Braille cells on a single line that shows the information on the screen that has focus. A refreshable Braille cell is comprised of two vertical rows of eight pins. Each pin moves individually to form a Braille character. The Braille cells refreshes either when the cursor moves or when screen content changes. The addition of Braille display support to screen readers resulted in the blind and the deaf-blind having choices for how they accessed information on the computer, by using either speech output or Braille output through a refreshable Braille display. Although JAWS is popular for blind Windows PC users, it is no longer the only game in town. Today, blind people have many screen access options, including the Windows-based systems Windows-Eyes from GW Micro, Nonvisual Desktop Access (NVDA) from NV Access in Australia, and SuperNova from Dolphin Computers. With competition, the price of screen access programs has dropped dramatically in some cases. NVDA is free. Apple provides the integrated screen access software VoiceOver with every Mac, without added cost to users. Apple also enables VoiceOver plug-and-play support for most refreshable Braille displays available for purchase worldwide. Microsoft recently announced it is making a free download of Window-Eyes available for every owner of a copy of Windows Office 2010 or later versions, a move that can be expected to further shift a rapidly changing market [28].

ASSISTIVE AND AUGMENTATIVE COMMUNICATION

Professor Gregg Vanderheiden, one of the earliest voices in assistive and augmentative communication (AAC) and founder of the TRACE Center, posits that to understand the development of AAC technology, one should consider the following three aspects, in no particular order of importance: the development of early electromechanical communication and writing systems, research on neurotypical (without disability) child language development, and communication and language boards. All of these products and concepts were explored and developed independently in the 1960s and 1970s. Eventually, the convergence between these three disciplines occurred and resulted in the augmentative and alternative communication technology that is available. AAC technologies are used by individuals who have severe disabilities that cause them to be unable to communicate by themselves. One of the earliest examples of AAC was the electric communication device Patient-Operated Selector Mechanism (POSM), a sip-and-puff typewriter controller invented by Reg Maling in 1960. POSM was used by paralyzed individuals to control a typewriter. Although the POSM was a huge typewriter, when it was released it was considered to be portable. When the POSM was used to communicate, the typist and the reader were facing the same direction. The reader could easily see every word that was typed. This device helped simplify communication between paralyzed individuals and their loved ones. The successors to POSM expanded the options that people could use to drive the typewriter, such as using sip and puff, voice control, or, finally, a directed light beam with the Patient Initiated Lightspot Operated Typewriter (PILOT). The technologies mentioned were not portable, and none allowed face-to-face communication with near eye contact.

Face-to-face communication for those with severe disabilities was not possible until 1973 with the release of the Alan Newell's Talking Brooch. The Talking Brooch and a communication device invented by Toby Churchill called Lightwriter were some of the first portable communication aids. The Talking Brooch was a small display worn on the lapel that could be operated from a hand-held keyboard; the Lightwriter used a longer display and later one display each for the operator and the person with whom he or she communicated. AAC technologies have advanced dramatically in the past 50 years. Currently, thanks to unceasing advocacy efforts from those inside and out of technology companies, we can find many of the AAC accessibility features integrated on various platforms, such as Mac, Windows, UNIX, Linux, and Solaris OS. As tablet and mobile devices have gained popularity, many of these products are able to support AAC technologies [12].

POWER WHEELCHAIRS AND PROSTHETICS

Power wheelchairs evolved with, not only the technology, but also attitudes and advocacy efforts related to people with physical disabilities that limited their mobility. The 1920s saw the introduction of the outdoor motorized "invalid carriage," but it was the combined impacts of antibiotics (and the attendant higher survival rates) and World War II that really moved development forward. In the 1950s, electric indoor/outdoor wheelchairs gradually became more available. Controls and maneuverability improved in the 1950s through the 1970s, and as more diverse and sophisticated means of control became available, mobility continued to become available to more individuals [29].

Electronic prostheses have followed a trajectory not entirely unlike that of motorized wheelchairs. Again, higher survival rates, the cataclysm of World War II, and the Vietnam War did much to move the technology beyond mechanical prostheses and introduce electronically controlled artificial limbs. Technology devised for the benefit of those with disabilities is ahead of the curve. The ability to control an artificial limb by thought alone paves the way for some exciting mainstream uses [30].

CURRENT EVENTS AND TRENDS

Since the mid-1990s, the world has become fully digitized. The introduction of web sites, e-books, e-commerce, and e-government has meant that the world is literally at your fingertips. As an example of how the potential for access to information has changed during the last 20-30 years, consider the potential access to information for blind people. In the past 30 years, Braille production has evolved from an entirely manual process to a mostly automated process. Accessing printed text independently is no longer a dream but a reality through the use of the OCR technology. Accessible personal digital assistants (PDAs) were introduced to the blind long before PDA devices became popular in mainstream society, and the heirs of those devices, the smartphones of today, are increasingly accessible off the shelf. Talking computers no longer exist just in science fiction; they are available for the blind to use at home, in school, and in the office; what's more, these features are being used more and more interchangeably between blind and sighted users. Video conferencing is no longer just a perk for Deaf callers; FaceTime and Skype are available for everyone. Many current touch screen devices allow the blind to interact using gesturing and speech output, without even adding a Braille overlay. These changes have not come about by accident. When devices are designed in a way that is flexible so that they can interact properly with those using assistive technologies, which are essentially alternate input or output devices, the benefits carry over into the general population.

Much of the earlier research (1970s-1990s) focused on technology access for people with perceptual (blind or low vision, Deaf or hard of hearing) or motor (limited or no use of hands, fingers, arms, or voice) impairments. In the early 2000s, the human-computer interaction community began to intensely investigate how to improve access to technology for people with cognitive and intellectual impairments.

Because of the increased incidence of autism, the number of research projects that look at appropriate interfaces or behavioral interventions for computer users with autism has increased. By the definition of the Centers for Disease Control, "Autism spectrum disorder (ASD) is a developmental disability that can cause significant social, communication and behavioral challenges. There is often nothing about how people with ASD look that sets them apart from other people, but people with ASD may communicate, interact, behave, and learn in ways that are different from most other people" [31]. An individual who encounters even one of these difficulties will often have trouble interacting with other people. Many people with autism possess more than one of the characteristics mentioned above. This chapter includes many examples of how inclusive and elegantly designed technology is being used to improve the lives of individuals with disabilities. In that same vein, the autistic population can benefit greatly from well-designed technologies. Rathkey et al.'s 1979 work is one of the earliest studies to show the benefits for those with autism of using computer technology, in this case a micro process-based computer system used to facilitate training for individuals with autism using prompting and data collection. In 1984, data from Panyan demonstrated that computer technology is beneficial to individuals with autism by demonstrating that computer technology can help increase the creativity and learning rate. Properly used computer technology enables individuals with autism to work independently. Finally, the research data from Panyan suggested that computers can assist individuals with maintaining focus as well as helping to improve social behavior–related issues [32].

Individuals with autism encounter sensory overload on a regular basis. Using a computer to present only the relevant information at the relevant time is a great advantage in aiding productivity. In addition, working with a computer cuts down on some of the variables of social interaction that can prove confusing. In both intervention and educational programs, computers have been widely adopted to assist individuals with autism. When there are specific tasks that an individual needs to learn, computers can be programmed to repeat the process until the individual successfully learns what he/she needs to know. To enhance the learning process and to help autistic individuals stay engaged, a computer can also be programmed to respond in such a way as to either affirm the learner's progress or notify him or her that he or she is not yet ready to move on. With this type of response, autistic individuals can make personal adjustments to accommodate their learning style and cognitive ability. As an example, for those who are visual learners, using photos to present information may be best. Others may prefer to have content presented to them in both audio and visual format. Computing offers the tools for that flexibility of format.

While autism research has become more popular, researchers are also looking into computer usage by people with other types of cognitive and intellectual impairments. Researchers at the University of Dundee have focused on computer access for people with memory-related cognitive impairments, such as amnesia, dementia, and Alzheimer's disease [33]. Researchers at Towson University and Loyola University Maryland investigated how people with Down syndrome access technology, with a focus on improving employment outcomes for adults [34].

One of the greatest improvements in providing easy access for everyone is the trend from the mid-2000s for assistive technologies to be included as standard features in technologies purchased out of the box.

The gold star example of this trend toward mainstream inclusion of accessibility features is the work Apple has done on its Macs, particularly its iOS devices. Apple introduced the VoiceOver screen access software for touch screen devices to the blind community in 2009, with the release of the Apple iPhone 3GS and the Apple iPod touch 3rd generation. Note that the Apple iPhone first came out in 2007. With the first generation of the iPhone and the iPod touch, Apple took the US consumer market by storm with its new approach to touch screen devices. Touch screens rapidly became so popular with sighted consumers that any consumer electronic devices that did not adopt a touch screen interface was soon perceived to be obsolete. This was a real problem for the blind community because it meant that accessible devices with physical buttons and keyboards began a rapid decline in popularity and, ultimately, in availability.

The blind were able to maintain their independence at home and in the workplace simply because they were able to use many consumer electronics that had buttons. Even with devices that did not have any speech integrated, a blind user often could, at a minimum, memorize the controls or put tactile marks on them. When more and more consumer electronics and appliance manufacturers decided to design products with only touch controls and no speech output, the blind were left with almost no options. The array of products that were affected negatively by the broad adoption of the touch screen interface ranged from appliances to telecommunication equipment. Businesses, government, and education were deploying the touch screen products at an alarming rate. The problems were real, and the blind community had serious concerns about the implications of this new user interface. Despite efforts to work around the touch screens on phones, such as the solution offered in CodeFactory's MobileSpeak, the basic assumption for many years was that full nonvisual access to touch screens was not possible.

A small group of computer scientists first came up with an elegant solution to the problem of touch screen access. Doctoral student Shaun Kane, with help from fellow student Jeffrey Bigham and guidance from Kane's advisor Dr. Jacob Wobbrock, came up with what they called Slide Rule, a set of accessible gesture controls demonstrated on a touch screen mobile device (a modified iPhone, as it happened), in 2007 [35]. This technical solution made it possible for the blind to use a touch screen with a specific set of swipe gestures. Slide Rule technology was intriguing to the blind community to say the least. In March 2008, Kane and his team released developer tools for the iPhone (S. Kane, personal communication, March 11, 2014). The big question among the users was how to make the Slide Rule technology easier to obtain by average users. In 2009, the Apple iPhone 3GS was released. Integrated in the new device was VoiceOver, screen access software which provided speech feedback and gesture access to the iPhone. VoiceOver has been included in all subsequent releases of the iPhone. VoiceOver, the gestures for which bear some striking resemblances to Kane's work with Slide Rule, offered for the first time fully integrated native screen access software on a smartphone. With the interface, the blind finally had an accessible mobile phone to use without having to pay an additional cost for a speech program.

When the iPhone 3GS was released, all other accessible smartphones in the market required users to install a screen access program to make the phone accessible. These programs added about $300 to the cost of the phone. This kind of cost barrier put accessible cell phones out of reach for many blind individuals, so the impact of the availability of a smartphone that was accessible out of the box is hard to overestimate. Today, the blind no longer have to worry too much about touch screen compatible products being inaccessible. Most of the major companies that drive such devices, including Microsoft, Google, and Amazon, have followed Apple's lead and implemented accessible touch screen interfaces on their products. At the time of this writing, the Apple iPhone and the other iOS devices are the most widely used accessible mobile devices within the blind community [27]. In that first release in 2009, VoiceOver was designed to provide speech output only to the blind. Apple took a giant leap forward by adding support for refreshable Braille displays with the release of the iPhone 4. Over time, Apple has added many other accessibility features, such as hearing aid support and "made for iPhone" hearing aids, magnification and contrast tools, vibration alerts, and Guided Access.

As of the date of this publication, the only major platform that does not provide Braille support is the Microsoft Windows Mobile platform. Given the availability of Braille support in the rest of the mobile market, it seems likely that Microsoft eventually will add Braille support because of market demands. The impact of the accessible touch interface cannot be underestimated. It is another proof that when accessibility is considered to be a part of the design process and not an afterthought, access barriers can be eliminated easily.

HOW ACCESSIBLE TECHNOLOGY HAS CROSSED OVER INTO THE MAINSTREAM

Some of the examples discussed, including the phonograph, typewriter, OCR, and speech recognition, started as assistive technologies designed for specific populations but benefitted society as a whole. This is similar to the often-cited example of how curb cuts on streets assist not only people in wheelchairs, but also people on bikes, those carrying luggage, and parents pushing children in strollers.

These examples highlight technologies that have crossed into the mainstream, but the future is filled with exciting prospects. When engineers and product designers adopt the principle of universal design in their inventions, great things can be expected. Let us consider the benefits of some technologies that are being developed today that can be game changers for us all, regardless of ability. One well-known example is the autonomous vehicle technology that will allow the blind to drive and enable everyone to be more productive on the road, while reducing the number of accidents and saving lives. Three-dimensional (3D) printing is turning out to be the technology of the hour, and some of its most well-published uses are assistive: people are printing inexpensive prosthetics for those who might never have access to them otherwise. Others are using 3D printers to create tactile objects for blind students to use in the classroom, to the envy of their sighted peers. In another area of rapid development, the brain-computing interfaces designed to aid patients in operating prostheses and computers may soon make it possible for all of us to control devices without moving a muscle.

UNDERSTANDING WHY/HOW PEOPLE WITH DISABILITIES ADOPT TECHNOLOGY

It is important to understand how and why people with disabilities choose to use technology. For instance, in the past, people often avoided using hearing aids because of the stigma associated with having such a visible device in their ears. However, today many people have Bluetooth-enabled devices attached to their ears, so there is less stigma attached to using a hearing support device.

Understanding how and why people with disabilities adopt technology leads to an understanding of why people with temporary limitations (such as those on bedrest or with a broken arm) or those who face disability late in life often do not adopt existing accessible approaches to input or output, even if these would be helpful. A senior who ordinarily would not look to computer-synthesized speech output for help, even if functionally blind, often will reconsider that position when confronted with a younger relative using a talking or magnifying tablet. For many reasons, mainstream technology with accessibility features built in can be more appealing than dedicated devices for someone with a disability. Mainstream devices with accessibility features built in have a much lower threshold in cost and availability for newly disabled individuals and a higher adoption rate [36]. The lower cost—usually none for the additional accessibility features—is another important factor in facilitating adoption. The lower cost of integration and maintenance in a workplace is another advantage; when you have the same device as everyone else, it's easier to maintain (similar to how it's easier to find an automotive shop that can fix a Honda or Toyota car, rather than a Lamborghini). These simple facts make the mainstreaming of accessibility such a momentous development.

Although mainstream accessibility offers many advantages, dedicated assistive technology devices do offer incentives for adoption. Access technology companies almost universally provide superior support and training. Because development is focused on one user group, features usually are richer in these specialized devices and software products. Access technology manufacturers are also more responsive to their core consumer base in a way that no large, mainstream technology company serving a much broader audience can match. In addition, government policies in the United States and United Kingdom often specify that government funding (for health care or job rehabilitation) pay for only dedicated devices, not mainstream devices such as iPhones [37].

The most critical factor in access technology adoption is the simplest and incorporates many of the other factors: user buy-in. If the intended user of any device fails to pick it up and use it, the device has failed for that person, but much research and development goes on that ignores this basic tenet. Rule number one of assistive technology design must always be "consult your intended user." Consider the number of research projects and inventions proposed and executed every year that create access technology without involving feedback of people with disabilities. The numbers of such projects and inventions, claiming solutions to problems that in fact do not exist, remain uncounted. Anecdotal evidence from one co-author of this book is that many researchers and inventors who pass through the doors of the NFB are disappointed by the number of user-centered questions regarding the need for assistive technology inventions, because they have neglected getting a user's perspective in their development.

HOW THE CHANGES IN TECHNOLOGY OVER TIME MUST INFLUENCE CHANGES IN SOLUTIONS

It is necessary to understand how access technology developed over time to understand some of the current policy challenges in IT accessibility. For instance, before digital technology, access to information for those who were blind came through Braille-based or recorded material. However, with the advent of digital technology, the same content could be accessed in the same fashion, using identical digital hardware, by blind and sighted alike; only the output differs. When individuals with disabilities had to rely on separate channels for access to information, a specialized office, such as a university office of disability student services, was tasked with providing Braille or accessible digital information. However, when system-wide technology (e.g., learning management systems, intranets, etc.) entered the workplace and education, separate solutions were no longer feasible. A university's disability student services office could not provide an accessible equivalent to inaccessible learning management software or an inaccessible collaborative writing software. The offices that need to have responsibility for IT accessibility are not the "disability" offices but rather the main offices of technology, such as the organizational chief information officer or the director of information technology. More information about this need for a culture change is available in Chapter 11.

SUMMARY

Many people do not realize that the technologies they use on a daily basis originally were designed as access technologies for people with disabilities. Yet access technologies and accessibility features do benefit all users. Not only do most people experience some form of disability in their lives, but even people without disabilities find themselves in situations in which they temporarily cannot look at a display screen (while driving a car), cannot hear a TV (in a noisy airport or bar), or cannot interact with technology using their hands and fingers (while driving or holding a baby). Accessibility features, and the research behind them, help all users have more positive experiences with technologies.

REFERENCES

[1] Yeager P, Kaye SH, Reed M, Doe TM. Assistive technology and employment: experiences of Californians with disabilities. Work J Prevent Assess Rehabil 2006;27(4):333–44.

[2] Taub EA. The blind leading the sighted. *The New York Times*; 1999, October 28, p. G1.

[3] Edison TA. The phonograph and its future. N Am Rev 1878, May;126(262):527–37. Retrieved from http://memory.loc.gov/ammem/ndlpcoop/moahtml/title/lists/nora_V126I262.html.

[4] Library of Congress. NLS: that all may read. Retrieved from Library of Congress: http://www.loc.gov/nls/about_history.html; 2013, June 28.

[5] Royal National Institute of Blind People. Retrieved from http://www.rnib.org.uk/services-we-offer-reading-services/rnib-national-library-service; 2014.

[6] The Audio Publishers Association. Audiobooks are a $1 billion+industry showing steady growth [Press release]. Retrieved from http://www.audiopub.org/press/APASurveyPressReleaseFINAL.pdf; 2013.

[7] Hevesi D. James Marsters, Deaf Inventor, Dies at 85. *The New York Times*; 2009, August 22, p. A26. Retrieved from http://www.nytimes.com/2009/08/23/us/23marsters.html?_r=0.

[8] United States Access Board. (n.d.) 2.0 History of Telecommunications Access for Individuals with Disabilities. Retrieved from http://www.access-board.gov/guidelines-and-standards/communications-and-it/about-the-telecommunications-act-guidelines/background/taac-final-report/2-0-history-of-telecommunications-access-for-individuals-with-disabilities.

[9] National Association of the Deaf. TTY and TTY relay services. Retrieved from National Association of the Deaf: http://nad.org/issues/telephone-and-relay-services/relay-services/tty; 2014.

[10] Shapiro J. No pity: people with disabilities forging a new civil rights movement. New York: Random House; 1994.

[11] The Board of Regents of the University of Wisconsin System. About the Trace Center. Retrieved from http://trace.wisc.edu/about/; 2013.

[12] Vanderheiden GC. A journey through early augmentative communication and computer access. J Rehabil Res Dev 2002;39(5):39–53.

[13] IBM Corporation. The accessible workforce. Retrieved from http://www-03.ibm.com/ibm/history/ibm100/us/en/icons/accessibleworkforce/; 2014.

[14] Schwerdtfeger R. EPUB makes mobile content inclusive & accessible. Retrieved from http://asmarterplanet.com/blog/2014/02/epub-mobile.html; 2014, February 14.

[15] Kurzweil RC. Kenneth Jernigan's Prophetic Vision: Address to National Federation of the Blind Convention Banquet. Retrieved from http://www.kurzweilai.net/kenneth-jernigans-prophetic-vision-address-to-national-federation-of-the-blind-convention-banquet; 2002.

[16] Kurzweil AI Network. Curriculum vitae. Retrieved from http://www.kurzweilai.net/ray-kurzweil-curriculum-vitae; 2010.

[17] Hathi Trust. Statistics and visualizations. Retrieved from http://www.hathitrust.org/statistics_visualizations; 2014.

[18] National Captioning Institute, Incorporated. Retrieved from http://www.ncicap.org/about-us/history-of-closed-captioning/; 2014.

[19] Cortana BJ. (yes!) and many, many other great features coming in Windows Phone 8.1. Retrieved from http://blogs.windows.com/windows_phone/b/windowsphone/archive/2014/04/02/cortana-yes-and-many-many-other-great-features-coming-in-windows-phone-8-1.aspx; 2014, April 2.

[20] Cunningham W. Apple CarPlay lets iOS take over a Mercedes-Benz. CNET. Retrieved from http://www.cnet.com/products/apple-carplay/; 2014.

[21] Robertson A. Amazon announces Dash, a home barcode scanner and microphone. The Verge. Retrieved from http://www.theverge.com/2014/4/4/5582932/amazon-announces-dash-barcode-scanner-microphone-for-amazonfresh; 2014, April 4.

[22] Youdin M, Sell G, Reich T, Clagnaz M, Louie H, Kolwicz R. A voice controlled powered wheelchair and environmental control system for the severely disabled. Med Prog Through Technol 1980;7(2–3):139–43.

[23] Manasse N. Speech Recognition. Retrieved from http://aac.unl.edu/Speech_Recognition.html; 1999.

[24] De La Paz S. Composing via dictation and speech recognition systems: compensatory technology for students with learning disabilities. Learning Disability Q 1999;22(3):173–82.

[25] Thatcher J. Screen reader/2: access to OS/2 and the graphical user interface. In: Proceedings of the first annual ACM conference on assistive technologies (Assets '94), Marina Del Rey. New York, NY: ACM; 1994. p. 39–46.

[26] Cranmer TV. Jacobus ten Broek Library (National Federation of the Blind Institutional Records, File cabinet 9, Drawer 3, Folder AAT/Products/Speaqualizer), Baltimore, MD; 1986 [Letter to Richard Kramer].

[27] WebAIM. Screen Reader User Survey #5 Results. Retrieved from http://webaim.org/projects/screenreadersurvey5/; 2014.

[28] GW Micro. GW Micro Announces Global Window-Eyes Initiative for Users of Microsoft Office [Press release]. Retrieved from http://www.gwmicro.com/News_&_Events/Latest_News/?newsNo=299; 2014, January 14.

[29] Woods B, Watson N. A short history of powered wheelchairs. Assist Technol 2003;15(2):164–80.

[30] Childress DS. Historical aspects of powered limb prostheses. Clin Prosthet Orthot 1985;9(1):2–13. Retrieved from http://www.oandplibrary.org/cpo/1985_01_002.asp.

[31] Centers for Disease Control and Prevention. Autism Spectrum Disorder (ASD). Retrieved from http://www.cdc.gov/ncbddd/autism/facts.html; 2014.

[32] Panyan MV. Computer technology for autistic students. J Autism Dev Disord 1984;14(4):375–82. http://dx.doi.org/10.1007/BF02409828.

[33] Alm N, Astell A, Ellis M, Dye R, Gowan G, Campbell J. A cognitive prosthesis and communication support for people with dementia. Neuropsychol Rehabil 2004;14(1–2):117–34, Special Issue: Technology in Cognitive Rehabilitation.

[34] Ma Y, Feng J, Kumin L, Lazar J. Investigating user behavior for authentication methods: a comparison between individuals with down syndrome and neurotypical users. ACM Trans Accessible Comput 2013;4(4):1–27.

[35] Kane SK, Bigham JP, Wobbrock JO. Slide Rule: making mobile touch screens accessible to blind people using multi-touch interaction techniques. In: Proceedings of ASSETS '08, ACM; 2008. p. 73–80.

[36] Phillips B, Zhao H. Predictors of assistive technology abandonment. Assist Technol 1993;5(1):36–45.

[37] Waller A. Public policy issues in augmentative and alternative communication technologies: a comparison of the U.K. and the U.S. Interactions 2013;20(3):68–75.

The discriminatory impact of digital inaccessibility

3

INTRODUCTION

Before the advent of digital technology, separate formats were often required for effective communication to persons with a variety of disabilities. For example, offering textual content in separate formats for those with print disabilities was not the product of discrimination, but a fact of life. Print was inherently visual, so individuals whose vision or ability to process visually presented material was limited could not access printed text. Pages had to be turned, so those who could not use their hands also required separate content formats.

Textual content in separate (accessible) formats was sparse in quantity, more costly than commercial printed content, and often untimely in availability. Because the market of those with print disabilities appeared to be small and the cost of producing alternate formats, principally Braille, large print, and performed audio, was high, most content produced in alternate formats was created as a matter of charity by nonprofits or governmental entities with limited resources. In addition, until the enactment of laws such as the Chafee Amendment to the Copyright Act in 1996 in the United States (17 U.S.C. § 121), those entities that produced alternate content first sought the publisher's permission. Because granting such permission was not a high priority for most publishers, such requests were often ignored or responded to only after delays of a year or more. Even after the Chafee Amendment eliminated any requirement of permission from the copyright holder to produce accessible versions of printed content, the limited resources to meet a demand for a broad range of content meant that persons with print disabilities could rarely get what they needed when they needed it. In short, what little content became available in alternate formats often came only after long delays.

With digital technology, however, came the possibility that visual and nonvisual presentations of textual content could all be generated from the same source without the necessity of separate production. Historically, the range of content available in separate accessible formats had been severely limited and always after significant delays, due to the need for separate and costly production for a limited market. Digital content makes separate production of text unnecessary, and thus, inaccessible digital textual content represents a discriminatory decision by the content distributor. Content developers only need to develop their digital textual material in universally accessible formats, with proper markup of structural information by following now well-established technical standards. Moreover, digital technology has eased the production of tactile pictorial information.

Organizations of persons with disabilities demand equal access to digital content. As an example, the "Right to Read" Campaign in the United Kingdom specifically addresses e-books with its "same book, same time, same price" campaign. This chapter explores the societal challenges that have arisen for persons with disabilities, not from the disabilities themselves, but from the limited access that digital content and digital technology developers have afforded to date. These include exclusion from participation in our cultural life, limited access to government information, inferior educational opportunities, inability in voting independently and secretly, limited access to bank and other automated machines, and curtailed effectiveness to perform employment functions. These are forms of discrimination, i.e., where people with disabilities are being treated unequally because they are members of a certain group. Some of these forms of discrimination, such as pricing discrimination, also meet the threshold for being a form of illegal discrimination that violates the law. These problems arise when delivery of digital content is not timely or equal in content or cost. Time, content, and price are quantitative measurements. They're easily measured and, with appropriate data, easy concepts to understand. But the societal impacts of inaccessibility go beyond mere quantitative data. When people with disabilities are not able to access digital information, web sites, e-books, and other forms of digital content, it reinforces the stereotype that disability means incapacity far beyond the inherent significance of the disability itself—both to those without disabilities and those who have them.

SEPARATE BUT EQUAL IN THE CONTEXT OF DISABILITY

In 1954, the U.S. Supreme Court, in the landmark "Brown vs. Board of Education" decision, reversed an earlier decision that had allowed for "separate but equal" facilities for Caucasian and African-Americans, by ruling that having public education segregated was inherently unequal. This was not just a ruling on the quantitative measurements of the equality of school facilities (e.g., how many square feet per school, how many students per classroom). Rather, this ruling stated that the core concept of segregation is based on an assumption of inferiority [1]. As has been true for all other excluded groups, the exclusion of persons with disability, whether in the realm of education, employment, housing, or civic affairs, not only promotes a sense of inferiority in those excluded, but presents the actuality of inferior opportunity.

At the core of the disability rights movement has been the demand for an equal opportunity to participate on an equal basis in all aspects of mainstream life. The battle against exclusion has found expression in the insistence on educating children in the most integrated K-12 environment possible, placing adults with intellectual disabilities into community-based settings, rather than institutions in which they are isolated from society (a right established in the US by the Americans with Disabilities Act and elaborated in the *Olmstead* case), eliminating architectural barriers to increase the participation of people in wheelchairs in civic life, and aiming toward competitive employment, rather than sheltered workshops. Insistence from the disability community that mainstream buses and rail public transportation be accessible, rather than having to take a separate "paratransit," shows the emphasis placed on integrated opportunities, not forced exclusion. As technology has become more ubiquitous in mainstream life, equal access to that technology and its benefits has increasingly become a critical issue. The Americans with Disabilities Act in the US, and before it, the Rehabilitation Act, explicitly require mainstream opportunity, allowing separate access only when necessary to achieve integration. "The [ADA] statute's public accommodations title further emphasizes the anti-segregation purpose by prohibiting businesses from providing "different or separate" accommodations to individuals with disabilities except where "necessary" to provide accommodations that are "as effective as [those] provided to others" [2, p. 506].

Laws related to physical access recognize this same goal of integration. For instance, the physical accessibility regulations in the US specify that spaces for wheelchairs in movie theaters must be evenly distributed throughout the theater, not clumped into one section that is only for people with disabilities. The goal is to allow mainstream access whenever possible and whenever the disabled consumer wishes to make that choice.

Because employment is key to integration, and to participation in society, emphasis on employment has always been at the top of the disability rights agenda. To paraphrase the president of the National Federation of the Blind, Dr. Marc Maurer, "It doesn't make a difference if you call me blind, or visually impaired, or low-vision, I want you to call me employed. Because if you can't call me employed, the rest of the names are of little meaning." Much of disability rights litigation centers around the employment of people with disabilities [2] while disability rights organizations insist that sheltered workshops (which separate people with disabilities from others, in non-competitive employment) must pay minimum wage and offer training for mainstream employment.

For people with disabilities to be able to take part in the workforce, the technologies used to communicate among employees, to schedule meetings, to access databases, to do one's work, must be accessible. An employee who cannot access the internal systems with assistive technology cannot do the job as effectively as an employee without a disability. And inaccessible organizational information systems become a barrier to employment, leading to one of two potential, discriminatory outcomes. The first outcome is that employers are less likely to hire someone with a disability, because they know that the person with a disability isn't likely to be able to effectively perform the job using the technology currently existing in an organization. There might also be the misperception that a costly accommodation might be necessary. The other outcome is that, if an individual is already employed but hampered by inaccessible workplace software, other employees may correctly perceive that the disabled co-worker is not fulfilling his or her responsibilities, but attribute it not to the insufficiency of the technology but to the disability. In any event, when a disabled employee misses a meeting because the calendar software was not accessible, it injures the employer, the disabled employee, and his or her colleagues [3]. When an e-mail application doesn't allow blind employees to receive e-mails, to search for them effectively, to flag the important ones, and to create a contacts list, the blind employee is essentially excluded from organizational communication, unable to effectively complete his or her work, through no fault of his or her own [4]. Because inability to access digital technologies leads to exclusion, both socially and in employment, disability advocates have often repeated that mantra: "*same time, same content, same price*." In the next few sections, each one of these topics will be investigated individually.

SAME TIME

It is important that people with disabilities get access to digital information at the same time as people without disabilities. A time delay in access is itself a form of discrimination. When you don't have access to digital content at the same time as others, you are removed from the conversation. For example, a Deaf person who wanted to take part in a radio show about the topic of accessible technology could not do so because the radio show wasn't real-time captioned. If it had been, the Deaf individual could have participated in the call-in discussion by e-mailing questions or comments to the radio show panel. Posting a transcript to the radio station web site 2 days later was too little, too late in that it essentially deprived the Deaf person of the opportunity to contribute to the conversation. Similarly, when an employer only captions workplace videos on request, that employer is ensuring that the Deaf employee will always be the last to know.

A delay in access to accessible e-book content poses the same challenge to people with print-related disabilities. If everyone is reading the new Harry Potter book or the new biography of Winston Churchill and a blind person doesn't have access to that book, then that blind person is cut out of the conversation. That blind person can't take part in book clubs or other discussions about the new and popular book. That becomes societal exclusion.

Sometimes, the logic of technology developers is that they will first place content on the web (or first build a device) and then, at a later time, make it accessible [5]. There is often a time gap in terms of introducing a technology and introducing an accessible version of that technology. Some have estimated that the average time gap is 3 years [6,7]. People with disabilities face exclusion in the time gap between when a technology is introduced and when it is made accessible [5]. The argument that "we don't have any users with disabilities, but we will make a technology accessible upon request" is a faulty one, since the "request" inherently introduces a time delay [5]. If you must make a request for accessible content, by definition, you won't receive the content at the same time as others. Wentz, Jaeger, and Lazar (2011) provide an example of this, from public statements by Cornell University:

> *During the legal controversy over the accessibility of the Amazon Kindle and afterward, representatives from Cornell University have also voiced a similar attitude. When complaints were raised by blind students regarding the inaccessibility of web sites and e-mail at Cornell, although the University agreed to address*

the problems, the statement by the Associate University Counsel implied that Cornell only had a responsibility to provide accessibility upon request, rather than preemptively

A one-at-a-time accommodation of digital content inherently means a time delay and limited access. A delay in making a technology accessible means that, rather than designing with accessibility in mind, which is easy, the developers will need to retrofit, which is not only more technically challenging, but also far more expensive [5]. So the time delay is not only discriminatory, but also greatly increases the cost of the accessibility modifications.

A delay in having access to books and printed materials in education can be especially problematic for any students with a print-related disability (such as inability to read printed text, physically handle printed text, or cognitively process text). For instance, in Australia, university students often face a delay in receiving accessible versions of books and other required reading materials for class [8]. The delay can sometimes be later during the semester, or, very unfortunately, students receive the materials after the semester has ended. The delays are usually longer for class reading materials that are suggested readings, not required readings [8]. Similar delays exist at universities in the United Kingdom [9] and the United States. A recent report from the US Advisory Commission on Accessible Instructional Materials in Postsecondary Education for Students with Disabilities discussed the challenges that students with disabilities face in post-secondary education [10]. Another report from the Association for Research Libraries documents similar problems of university students with print-related disabilities getting access to equal materials in a timely manner [11].

Course-related books, when provided in an accessible format directly from the publisher, can provide nearly instant access for students with print-related impairments. However, when publishers refuse to provide accessible electronic versions of books, universities often must spend the time to turn the print versions of the books into accessible versions, often resulting in a delay to the student in being able to access their course-related books. This delay, when students without disabilities have access to course materials, and students with disabilities do NOT have access to course materials, is a form of unequal treatment, a form of discrimination. The delay in receiving course materials puts students with disabilities at a distinct disadvantage.

Yet, because many publishers are moving to e-books, the opportunity exists for simultaneous mainstream access without regard to disability. Since authors write textbooks, and publishers edit and develop textbooks via computer, books are "born" digital and inherently accessible. It is often the processing of books into e-books that renders them inaccessible. Furthermore, the physical devices from some companies (the dedicated e-book devices) are often built in a way that even if the book content is accessible, the hardware devices are built inaccessibly, even though there is no technical reason that situation needs to exist. As publishers move towards making their books available immediately as e-books, accessible e-books with accessible platforms and hardware could eliminate all three challenges that people with print-related disabilities often face: that there are a limited number of books available in accessible format at higher cost and only after a delay.

Inaccessible e-book devices, when used in post-secondary (higher) education, alone can be a barrier to equal access. For this reason, the civil rights offices of the US Department of Education and US Department of Justice jointly sent out a letter in 2010 to all institutions of higher education in the United States, reminding them that requiring use of inaccessible e-book readers violated both the Americans with Disabilities Act and Section 504 of the Rehabilitation Act [12].

Outside of the realm of education, the issue of accessible e-books also relates to public libraries. A survey of US public libraries (data collected in Oct 2011) found that 76% of libraries are lending e-books and audio books (the content), with 39% lending the e-book devices themselves (hardware) [13]. There has been an advocacy effort by the National Federation of the Blind (in the US) to ensure that libraries that do offer e-book devices will only lend accessible e-books and accessible e-readers, so that blind library patrons can partake of library e-book programs at the same time and in the same way as patrons without disabilities. Public libraries in the US that have recently resolved legal challenges and agreed to offer accessible e-reader devices to their library patrons with print-related disabilities include the Free Library of Philadelphia and the Sacramento Public Library.

Aside from e-books, time delay is often a factor in the accessibility of kiosks. For instance, if ATMs (automated teller machines) are inaccessible to people with disabilities, then people with disabilities have inferior access to their own money, compared to people without disabilities, who can get their cash day or night, including on the weekend. There is nothing about the nature of blindness or a mobility impairment that should require a person who is blind or using a wheelchair to wait for the bank's normal lobby hours to access their cash.

Inaccessible kiosks not only limit access in banking, but frequently, kiosk usage is a requirement for travel, as well. As airlines limit the number of customer service people at an airport, it's unfair to make people with disabilities wait for a very rare human customer service agent, when most passengers can just check in using the automated kiosks (which, like the ATM machines, can be made accessible). Unfortunately, in November 2013, the U.S. Department of Transportation issued regulations that will give airlines up to 3 years to make their web sites accessible (in the year 2016) and 10 years to make 25% of their kiosk fleet accessible (in the year 2023) [14].

There are also many situations in which the value of information drops over time. For instance, individuals with disabilities need access to urgent weather information, to school workplace and government closings due to inclement weather, and emergency information in a timely manner. If there is an evacuation order due to inclement weather, that information is of no value 2 days later. Historically, people with disabilities are often neglected when communicating emergency information [15]. A recent research study documented how many web-based emergency alert sign-up forms in the US are inaccessible, and there are no alternate methods for signing up for these emergency alerts [16]. Federal judges have now ruled unlawful the emergency preparedness plans of New York City and Los Angeles County for, among other things, failure to plan for communicating timely accessible information to those with disabilities [17]. Employment opportunities are, of course, time-sensitive, so delay in access to that information can be the difference between no job and work.

SAME PRICE

Pricing discrimination occurs when a company charges an individual with a disability more for the same product or service than an individual without a disability. When web sites are not accessible, often companies or organizations will say, "under the law, we can make alternate arrangements. Call us, or e-mail us, and we will provide the content, or we will help you make the arrangements." But when it comes to offering separate accommodations in e-commerce, in travel booking, and other forms of inaccessible web content, the separate accommodations often lead to price discrimination. Pricing discrimination occurs most often, due to inaccessible web content, when the lowest prices are available on web sites and aren't available through other methods, and those web sites offering the lowest prices are inaccessible.

Many airlines provide lower prices on their web sites than through other means, such as ticket counters or phone calls. This is true both in the United States and many European countries. If an airline web site isn't accessible, often, the lowest fares (available only on the web site) won't be available to travelers with disabilities. For that reason, the Royal National Institute of Blind People took legal action in January 2012 to force the BMI Baby low-cost airline to make their web site accessible. Before that action was resolved, however, the airline shut down operations [18]. The inaccessibility of airline web sites has been a problem for a number of years [19]. What has changed, however, is that numerous airlines have started providing lower fares on their web site, even charging extra fees for using the call center. Because of this multi-layered penalty for not using the web site, if a web site isn't accessible, persons without disabilities are often charged more than those without. For this reason, the US Department of Transportation issued regulations effective in 2009 requiring that, if an airline web site is inaccessible, an individual with a disability can contact the airline using another method of communication and receive the same low fare offered on the web site and also cannot be charged the "call center fee" [20]. Despite the presence of this regulation (issued in 2008 and in effect in 2009), airlines often do not follow the law. A compliance study done at the end of 2009 established that when individuals called airlines with inaccessible web sites, identified themselves as having a disability, noted the regulation, and asked for fares, they were often not charged the lowest fare, and, often, the airline refused to waive the call center fee. In the data collected in 2009 and published in 2010, US Airways and United Airlines price discriminated against blind individuals in at least a third of the calls [21]. In a follow-up study done 2 years later (data collected in 2011 and published in 2012), some airlines had made improvements in their site accessibility, other airline web sites had become more inaccessible, but the interaction with the call center was still problematic. Of the four airlines evaluated in Fall 2011 (in some cases, different airlines from the previous study), only one airline with an inaccessible web site did not discriminate on price in any situation—United Airlines. However, the other three largest airlines with inaccessible web sites at the time (Alaska, American, and Hawaiian Airlines) all discriminated on price at least one-third of the time [22].

Other forms of public transportation that involve reservations (long trains and buses) also engage in pricing discrimination, denying persons with disabilities the lower fares available only through an inaccessible web site. For instance, the US Department of Justice announced a settlement in May 2011 with the long-distance bus service Megabus, not only requiring that they improve their ability to transport passengers who use wheelchairs, but also requiring that they make their web site accessible, so that the lowest fares available on the web site could become available to all passengers [23]. Recent regulations coming from the U.S. Department of Transportation will require that airlines make their web sites fully accessible by 2016 [14]. These forms of pricing discrimination often do meet the legal threshold for being illegal under various laws.

In addition to transportation, other e-commerce companies offer special "web-only" prices that are not available in their corresponding physical brick-and-mortar stores. When the web site is inaccessible, people with disabilities will not be able to independently take advantage of these web-only prices. In a 2011 study of the 10 largest US companies that offered web-only specials, all 10 companies had web sites with major accessibility barriers [24]. Similar problems arise on aggregator sites—sites that allow an individual to compare products/services and prices across multiple web sites. For instance, a 2012 study of 5 price-comparison web sites in the United Kingdom documented that all five sites had accessibility barriers [25]. Another study of aggregator sites for travel information found that all of them had accessibility barriers [26]. It is clear that inaccessible web sites often lead to forms of pricing discrimination that can violate the law.

SAME CONTENT

Regardless of format, the content presented to someone with a disability should be the *same* content presented to someone without a disability. For example, a restaurant should not offer someone with a disability more limited menu choices than are offered to the general public [2]. Yet when web sites are inaccessible to people with disabilities, when e-books are not provided in an accessible format, people with disabilities have access to less content. This type of exclusion can take many different forms. For instance, there has been a long-running discussion in the Deaf community about edited vs. verbatim captioning. Verbatim captioning is when every single word of spoken dialog appears as captioning, sometimes at a high rate of speed (up to 180 words per minute) [27]. Edited captioning is when words are not included, difficult words are changed into easier words, and old forms of verbiage are modified. Two often-stated goals of edited captioning are to display the captioning at a slower speed (usually less than 140 words per minute) and to modify content so that it is easier to understand for people with lower reading ability [27,28]. The argument for edited captioning is often made when it comes to presenting information for children, although it is questionable as to whether edited captioning really improves comprehension by children and young adults [28]. Yet Deaf advocacy groups often state that to offer anything less than verbatim captioning is censorship and would be limiting their access to information [27]. In a current draft of the W3C guidelines of Media Accessibility User Requirements (as of Dec 2011), the guidelines state:

> *Ideally, captions should be a verbatim representation of the audio; however, captions are sometimes edited for various reasons— for example, for reading speed or for language level. In general, consumers of captions have expressed that the text should represent exactly what is in the audio track. If edited captions are provided, then they should be clearly marked as such, and the full verbatim version should also be available as an option* [29].

Essentially, Deaf groups, in discussing verbatim captioning, are making the same claim that blind groups make for why they don't want alternate web sites—they want access to the same content. Verbatim captioning should also be less expensive to produce, because it requires almost no human editing [27]. (Note: in the UK, the term subtitling is often used to describe the action of captioning, even though there is no language translation involved).

Separate content may often be linked with reduced functionality. For instance, organizations may state that while their main web site isn't accessible, a separate text-only web site or mobile version is accessible. Unfortunately, mobile versions of web sites are often stripped down versions with less functionality. For instance, Facebook encouraged blind subscribers who use screen reader software to use only the mobile version of its website. Facebook's main website, however, had far more functionality than the mobile version, when this was investigated in a research study in 2010 [30]. If someone with a disability wants to use a mobile phone to access web content, that's their choice. But his or her disability shouldn't limit the amount of content that he or she can access. To limit access to social networking conversations and content is to exclude people with disabilities from the 21st century version of the local pub.

Some companies have suggested that people with disabilities should use older versions of software or web sites, rather than the newest versions. For instance, Yahoo! suggested that people utilizing assistive technology use the older "Yahoo Mail Classic," rather than the newest version of Yahoo mail [31]. In another variation of this approach, the *Cumberland News-Times* offer only a limited portion of any article's content on its web site and requires using an inaccessible plug-in (in this specific case, Pressreader) to read the complete article, thereby excluding readers who use assistive technology from access to the entire article [31].

In some cases, companies will admit that their web sites are not accessible, but will say that another, alternate accommodation is available. Under Title III of the US Americans with Disabilities Act (public accommodations), people with disabilities have the right to equally effective communication. In those instances in which a web site is a service of a place of public accommodation, but not the public accommodation itself, the owner or operator of the accommodation may get to choose how access is given to persons with disabilities (2, p. 449). For instance, a blind individual cannot force a restaurant to provide a menu in Braille, as long as the waiters are willing to read the menu out loud. While many people who are Deaf would prefer captioning of video using ASL, the legal requirement is "effective communication," so often, English captioning will be provided, because it is considered "effective communication," although it is not the preferred method for many Deaf people. Thus, some companies have sought to avoid making their web sites accessible by offering alternatives, such as, "call us on the phone, or come into our office, or use a TTY, we will be happy to assist you." Furthermore, web sites that are built to be accessible, to be flexible, not only help people with disabilities, but also users without disabilities who are using alternative devices (such as tablet computers and smartphones). In most instances this "accommodation" will be a poor and unequal substitute. Consider the data collection experiment in the sidebar, which the authors performed in 2011, related to an inaccessible web site, for a major employment aggregator. This example can help explain why providing a separate accommodation is often not equally effective.

WHY YOU NEED ACCESS TO THE SAME CONTENT

An experiment was performed to evaluate the equality of using a job aggregator web site, as compared to calling the job aggregator phone center to ask about jobs. This web site had thousands of jobs available at various different companies. But the web site was inaccessible to screen reader users, and the employment aggregator web site said that blind users should simply call them on the telephone. A total of nine phone calls were made to the employment aggregator, where we identified that we were blind (and the phone calls were primarily made by blind people) and asked the employment aggregator customer service representative about specific job categories in specific states or locations. At the same time, a partner in the research project, using the same search criteria, searched on the web site to see which jobs were immediately available in a given state or location, to determine if the jobs offered over the phone were equivalent to the jobs offered online. In general, when we called the call center, the call center person took one of two approaches, either trying to get us set up with an account with e-mail alerts so that they would not need to read job advertisements to us, or trying to read job advertisements over the phone (but rarely reading ALL of the jobs available), but not both. It is important to note that, by signing up for e-mail alerts, an individual could receive information about jobs when they were newly posted, but not about previously posted jobs (meaning that the content was not the same). The following sections detail what happened in the nine phone calls that were made to the customer service center of the job aggregator web site. In the following descriptions, please note that CC stands for "call center person."

Call 1: The CC stated that there were only two job openings for usability in [eastern state], but a web search on the same keyword came up with 229 job openings.
Call 2: The CC stated the correct number of job openings for usability in [eastern state], but said that we could only apply for these jobs online, and we needed to get a friend to create an account for us.
Call 3: The CC stated that there were no jobs in [major east coast city] for database administrators; however, a web search on the site indicated 458 openings.
Call 4: The CC stated that there were 65 jobs for school psychiatrists in [eastern state], and then, at the CC's request, we narrowed it down to 37 jobs for school psychiatrist located in [major east coast city]. While the figures were generally correct, the CC wouldn't read us the jobs, but offered to create an account and have the jobs sent via e-mail.

Call 5: The CC indicated that there were 168 jobs for customer service located in [major east coast city] (which was the correct figure), but that they could not read them all over the phone to us and only read two jobs over the phone. The CC also noted that most of the jobs require that you apply for the jobs on the aggregator site itself.

Call 6: When we said that we were looking for a job at an IT help desk in [eastern state], the CC asked us to narrow it down since there were too many job postings. When we narrowed it down to help desk manager, there were 5 potential jobs, but rather than reading the job listings, the CC said that they were all older jobs. In reality, those jobs were posted 2, 5, 13, 19, and 20 days ago—not that old, and still open.

Call 7: The CC correctly identified that there were 381 accountant jobs in [eastern state]; however, the CC did not offer to read the job openings over the phone. Instead, she suggested that we sign up for an account on the job aggregator web site, so that we could receive e-mail notices about job postings. The CC also noted that many of the job openings require that we submit an application on the aggregator web site.

Call 8: We called asking about positions as a teacher in [eastern state]. The CC repeatedly asked the search to be narrowed down. When we indicated that we were interested in a math teacher position, the CC said that there were 38 math teacher positions in [eastern state] (which was correct according to the web search that we did). However, later in the call, the CC person insisted that the positions at the elementary and middle school levels were not for math teachers. A web search found that the CC was in error, and those jobs were still available.

Call 9: We called and asked about accounting manager jobs available in [eastern state]. We were told that there were 157 jobs for accounting manager in [eastern state]. The CC would read job openings, but sometimes interjected, "you don't want these job postings—they are over 20 days old, so they are most likely filled" or noted that many of the jobs were with staffing agencies, and remarked, "you really don't want those." While the CC seemed willing to continuously read job postings over the phone, she was attempting to eliminate choices to reduce the number she would have to read.

These calls demonstrate multiple problems that occur for people with disabilities when separate accommodations are offered that do not provide the same content as the web site itself. These problems include:

- the CC attempting to narrow the search using multiple filters so that there were only a few jobs that would need to be read over the phone;
- the CC often said, "oh, we will skip over those jobs, they were posted a long time ago" when they had been posted in the last few weeks and were possibly still open;
- the CC nearly always did a job title search instead of a keyword search, leading to far fewer query results;
- the CC sometimes only read the job title, location, and company, but NOT the actual job advertisement, or skipped over details about certain jobs;
- the CC skipped over job openings at the aggregator company itself that were returned in the web search and that met the job criteria and location. This occurred repeatedly, even when one blind caller specifically asked whether there were any jobs at the aggregator company;
- the CC sometimes reported outright false search results, saying that they needed to change the keywords, because there were no jobs, when in fact there were;
- the CC in one case changed, during the phone call, the number of results reported, saying that there were no more jobs in that category (math), when there were many more; and
- the CC promised to send follow up information about a specific job via e-mail, but did not do so.

In addition, when the CC offered to sign us up for an account:

- the CC often did not ask all of the questions that a typical user would be asked when signing up for an account (details about their experience and qualifications);

- the CC did not read or offer to read the terms of service or privacy policy for the account;
- when job alert e-mails were sent to the blind users, they were simply a list of URLs, linking to web pages on the inaccessible aggregator web site, so the job postings themselves were not e-mailed.

This problem of not having access to the "same content" extends to primary, secondary, and higher education. When e-books are used for educational purposes and the e-books don't work (the content, the platform, or the hardware controlling the content) for students with print disabilities, those students wind up being excluded from the textual information to be mastered. When learning management systems are used in higher education (such as Blackboard, Moodle, DesireToLearn, Sakai), there are two separate concerns related to accessibility: is the learning management system (the software shell) itself accessible, and if so, are teachers and faculty properly marking up their content, rather than placing inaccessible content on the learning management system? Some of the most common accessibility problems related to course content include inaccessible course notes, PowerPoint slides or improperly captioned audio/video material (including clips downloaded from YouTube), and PDF files that are scanned graphics with no markup [32]. Lecture capture, where lectures are recorded and played in the future (often without captioning), is also increasingly problematic, as are social networking software, designed for use within a campus, and e-book hardware required for use in courses, that are inaccessible [33]. For students who simply can't get access to some of the course content at any point in time, this is a clear disadvantage.

Access to content is also problematic with government information. Multiple research articles over a number of years have documented that much of the federal/national and state/municipal government information on the web, both in the US and other countries, is inaccessible. This includes US federal web sites [34,35], US state web sites [36–40], UK government web sites [41], and Chinese government web sites [42]. One of the first multi-national evaluations of government web site accessibility confirmed that it continues to be a problem, regardless of country [43]. Because of the continuing problem of inaccessible government content in the European Union (it has been estimated that only 1/3 of EU government web sites are fully accessible), the EU proposed on Dec 12, 2012, that new regulations be adopted to require accessible government web sites by the end of 2015. These regulations would apply to multiple categories of web sites, including taxes, job searching, education, social security benefits, car registration, birth and marriage certificates, public libraries, and health care [44].

Two recent examples highlight the need for accessibility in the government context. As the result of successful litigation against the Social Security Administration, in 2009, a federal court ruled that agency is required to post and send notices, publications, inquiries, and letters in accessible formats to people who are blind or visually impaired (see http://www.socialsecurity.gov/people/blind/ for more information). In 2014, the United States Department of Education reached a settlement with several blind persons with student loans and the National Federation of the Blind that requires student loan forms, bank statements, notices, and publications to be fully accessible [45]. Heretofore, access to these materials often required the person with a disability to sacrifice his or her privacy to someone who could read the information, and such access was often also untimely, thus leading to a loss of rights. More information about IT accessibility laws in the US is available in Chapter 5; accessibility laws of other countries are discussed in Chapter 6.

The broad array of categories covered under the proposed EU legislation demonstrates that many citizen interactions with government are now occurring online and that accessible government web sites are of the utmost importance to everyday participation as a citizen. Because all citizens should have access to the same government content, not limited or separate content, government web site accessibility needs to improve.

SAME TIME, SAME CONTENT, SAME PRICE, AND NOW . . . SAME HARDWARE AND SOFTWARE

For many years, persons with disabilities preferred separate devices geared to their needs, such as a Kurzweil reader or a Victor Stream Reader. While these devices were more expensive, because of the small market, their specialized nature seemed to promise that the manufacturer would be responsive to consumer concerns. At the same time, with some specialized assistive technology, there could be finger pointing between content developers and specialized technology developers as to where the responsibility lay to make the two work together.

Three new factors have led to a change in the attitudes in the disability community toward accessible hardware and software. The first to occur was the development of closed hardware and content ecosystems, like the first Kindle e-book devices. Although Kindle content can now be somewhat accessible on other devices, Kindle devices were for some time the only road to Kindle content.

The second development was the decision by Apple to build in accessibility out-of-the-box in the iPhone 3 (and subsequent versions), iPod touch, and iPad. Apple executed brilliantly and has given the disability community the option of accessibility in a mainstream product with no additional cost for add-on accessibility software, all at a lower price than for equivalent specialized products. The iPhone, for example, has voice recognition (speech-to-text), screen reader (text-to-speech), and gesturing (including gesturing features for people with limited use of fingers) installed out of the box. Moreover, Apple gives guidance to app developers, through Apple's API, on how to make an app accessible for use on Apple products.

The third, and somewhat ominous development, has come with Google blurring the lines between hardware, software, and content with the development of Chromebooks, Google Drive, and proprietary Google equivalents for common office automation applications (such as MS Word, Excel, and PowerPoint). The low cost of Chromebooks has great appeal to institutional buyers such as primary schools. However, Chromebooks have not historically worked with refreshable Braille displays, and Google's built-in text-to-speech software does not work with non-Google accessible programs, like MS Word and other commonly utilized Microsoft products. Conversely, a student with a disability who has a PC or Apple product has not been able to access anything created with Google proprietary products, like Google Docs, Sheets, or Presentations, and has not been able to see content distributed in Google Drive. For a considerable period of time, Google was non-responsive to the concerns of people with disabilities, pushing software like Google Docs into government and education while it was inaccessible. Thus, a school that bought a Chromebook for its nondisabled students necessarily shut out the disabled student from access to software and content. This conflation of hardware, software, and cloud-based content gives rise to an urgent need to address all. The need is even more apparent when a company like Google spreads its offerings to include everything from educational apps for schools to e-books to movies with a central distribution point like Google Play that may have accessibility barriers and which, in any event, provides the buyer with no information about the accessibility of the various offerings available through that distribution point. Google has now undertaken efforts to address issues involving Android, Chrome, and other proprietary products. As of this writing, there have been significant signs of progress, but nothing approaching equal access. Google is also missing the potential innovation that comes from intentionally building accessibility in from the beginning.

A side benefit to mainstream devices being accessible is that they are typically more elegantly designed. Visual and industrial design generally has not been a driving factor in separate assistive devices, resulting in hardware that is larger and clunkier than what other people without disabilities are using [46]. Separate, expensive, odd, and clunky devices, which identify people as being different, may lead to stigmatization and avoidance of use [47]. While this is not true for some disability populations, for many individuals who are new to having a disability (such as those losing hearing or sight later in life), they are more sensitive about appearing different. So, design makes a big difference. For instance, older adults are often hesitant to wear devices that allow them to identify that they need help in an emergency (such as if they have fallen down). However, when that device is designed so that it looks like jewelry, rather than an assistive device, adoption rates increase [48]. Even if a separate software application is needed (say, for providing public transportation information for individuals who are deaf-blind), installing that app on a standard mobile phone both is more inclusive and reduces the need to carry additional devices around [49].

The best outcome for everyone is if accessibility is integrated into mainstream hardware and platforms, but without destroying the option of specialized devices that may be responsive to a disabled consumer's need, such as a refreshable Braille display or a device that may verbalize prescription information on a chip embedded in the medication container. Expanding the range of accessible mainstream hardware and platforms reduces the cost of disability, enhances the opportunities to stay up to date with the most recent advances in technology, reduces stigmatization, and conveys to those without disabilities the capabilities of disabled users of technology.

SUMMARY

When web sites, e-books, kiosks, hardware devices, operating systems, and other technologies are inaccessible for people with disabilities, it results in discrimination, exclusion, and substantial disadvantage. The history of civil rights shows that segregation of people reinforces a perception that those who are excluded are inferior, both in society at large and in those who are the subject of segregation. For this reason, among others, the disability rights movements have focused strongly on inclusion and integration. Within the context of digital information, the disability rights movements have focused on getting access to the same digital information (not edited or different information), at the same time (without any time delays), and at the same price. Inaccessible technology is an increasingly significant source of exclusion, disadvantage, and discrimination, such as pricing discrimination, employment discrimination, limited access to emergency information, delayed access to necessary readings for university courses, limited access to government content, and exclusion from social events and social networking. Digital technology, when accessible, can be a great opportunity to reduce discrimination and exclusion, to bring people together, instead of increasing existing barriers of discrimination.

REFERENCES

[1] Cottrol R, Diamond R, Ware L. Brown v. Board of Education: caste, culture, and the constitution. Lawrence, KS: University Press of Kansas; 2003.

[2] Bagenstos S. Disability rights law: cases and materials. New York: Thompson Reuters; 2010.

[3] Wentz B, Lazar J. Usable web-based calendaring for blind users. In: Proceedings of the BCS-HCI: the 25th British computing society conference on human–computer interaction; 2011. p. 99–103.

[4] Wentz B, Lazar J. Usability evaluation of e-mail applications by blind users. J Usabil Stud 2011;6(2):75–89.

[5] Wentz B, Jaeger P, Lazar J. Retrofitting accessibility: the inequality of after-the-fact access for persons with disabilities in the United States. First Monday 2011;16(11). Available at: http://firstmonday.org/htbin/cgiwrap/bin/ojs/index.php/fm/article/view/3666/3077.

[6] Kanayama T. Leaving it all up to industry: people with disabilities and the Telecommunications Act of 1996. Inform Soc 2003;19(2):185–94.

[7] Moser I. Disability and the promises of technology: technology, subjectivity and embodiment within an order of the normal. Inform Commun Soc 2006;9(3):373–95.

[8] Harpur P, Loudoun R. The barrier of the written word: analyzing universities' policies to students with print disabilities. J Higher Educ Policy Manage 2011;33(2):153–67.

[9] Whitehouse G, Dearnley J, Murray I. Still "Destined To Be Under-Read?" Access to books for visually impaired students in UK higher education. Publish Res Q 2009;25(3):170–80.

[10] US Department of Education. Report of the advisory commission on accessible instructional materials in postsecondary education for students with disabilities. Available at: http://www.2.ed.gov/about/bdscomm/list/aim/publications.html; 2011.

[11] Association for Research Libraries. Report of the ARL joint task force on services to patrons with print disabilities. Available at: http://www.arl.org/bm~doc/print-disabilities-tfreport02nov12.pdf; 2012.

[12] US Department of Education. Joint "Dear Colleague" letter: electronic book readers. Available at: http://www2.ed.gov/about/offices/list/ocr/letters/colleague-20100629.html; 2010.

[13] Hoffman J, Bertot J, Davis D. Libraries connect communities: public library funding & technology access study 2011–2012. Available at: http://www.ala.org/research/plftas/2011_2012#final%2020report): American Library Association; 2012.

[14] U.S. Department of Transportation. New DOT rules make flying easier for passengers with disabilities. Available at: http://www.dot.gov/briefing-room/new-dot-rules-make-flying-easier-passengers-disabilities; 2013.

[15] Waterstone M, Stein M. Emergency preparedness and disability. Mental Phys Disabil Law Rep 2006;30(3):338–9.

[16] Wentz B, Lazar J, Stein M, Gbenro O, Holandez E, Ramsey A. Danger, danger! Evaluating the accessibility of web-based emergency alert sign-ups in the Northeastern United States. Gov Inform Q 2014;31(3):488–97.

[17] Lewis, R. Ruling on NYC disaster plans for disabled may have far reach. *National Public Radio*. Available at: http://www.npr.org/2013/2011/2009/243998312/ruling-on-nyc-disaster-plans-for-disabled-may-have-far-reach?sc=243998317&f=243991001; 2013.

[18] Royal National Institute for Blind People. RNIB serves legal proceedings on BMIBaby. Retrieved Oct 29, 2012, from http://www.rnib.org.uk/aboutus/mediacentre/mediareleases/mediareleases2012/Pages/pressrelease27Jan2012.aspx; 2012.

[19] Gutierrez C, Loucopoulos C, Reinsch R. Disability-accessibility of airlines' web sites for US reservations online. J Air Transport Manage 2005;11(4):239–47.

[20] U.S. Department of Transportation. Nondiscrimination on the basis of disability in air travel. 14 CFR 382. http://airconsumer.ost.dot.gov/rules/Part%20382-2008.pdf; 2009.

[21] Lazar J, Jaeger P, Adams A, Angelozzi A, Manohar J, Marciniak J, et al. Up in the air: are airlines following the new DOT rules on equal pricing for people with disabilities when websites are inaccessible? Gov Inform Q 2010;27(4):329–36.

[22] Lazar J, Jaeger P, Olalere A, Algarne M, Augustine Z, Brown C, et al. Still up in the air: government regulation of airline websites and continuing price inequality for persons with disabilities online. In: Proceedings of the 13th annual international conference on digital government research. 2012. p. 240–5.

[23] U.S. Department of Justice. Justice Department Announces ADA Settlement with Intercity Bus Company, Megabus. Available at: http://www.justice.gov/opa/pr/2011/May/2011-crt-2625.html); 2011.

[24] Lazar J, Wentz B, Bogdan M, Clowney E, Davis M, Guiffo J, et al. Potential pricing discrimination due to inaccessible web sites. Proc INTERACT 2011;2011:108–14.

[25] AbilityNet. State of the ENation: price comparison sites. Available at: http://www.abilitynet.org.uk/docs/enation/State_of_the_eNation_Report_-_Price_Comparison_Websites_-_April_2012.pdf; 2012.

[26] Lazar J, Biggers D, Delair J, Donnelly M, Eludoyin K, Henin A, et al. Societal inclusion: evaluating the accessibility of job placement and travel web sites. In: Proceedings of the INCLUDE 2011 conference; 2011. Available at, http://triton.towson.edu/~jlazar/papers/aggregator_include2011.doc.

[27] Szarkowska A, Krejtz I, Klyszejko Z, Wieczorek A. Verbatim, standard, or edited? Reading patterns of different captioning styles among deaf, hard of hearing, and hearing viewers. Am Ann Deaf 2011;156(4):363–78.

[28] Ward P, Wang Y, Paul P, Loeterman M. Near-verbatim captioning versus edited captioning for students who are deaf or hard of hearing: a preliminary investigation of effects on comprehension. Am Ann Deaf 2007;152(1):20–8.

[29] Web Accessibility Initiative. Media accessibility user requirements. Available at: http://www.w3.org/WAI/PF/media-a11y-reqs/; 2011.

[30] Wentz B, Lazar J. Are separate interfaces inherently unequal? An evaluation with blind users of the usability of two interfaces for a social networking platform. In: Proceedings of the iSchools 2011 conference (the iConference); 2011. p. 91–7.

[31] Lazar J, Wentz B. Separate but unequal: web interfaces for people with disabilities. User Experience Mag 2011;10(3):12–3.

[32] Fichten C, Ferraro V, Asuncion J, Chwojka C, Barile M, Nguyen M, et al. Disabilities and e-learning problems and solutions: an exploratory study. Educ Technol Soc 2009;12(4):241–56.

[33] Parry M. Colleges lock out blind students online. The Chronicle of Higher Education. Available at: http://chronicle.com/article/Blind-Students-Demand-Access/125695/; December 12, 2010.

[34] Olalere A, Lazar J. Accessibility of U.S. federal government home pages: Section 508 compliance and site accessibility statements. Gov Inform Q 2011;28(3):303–9.

[35] Jaeger P. Assessing Section 508 compliance on federal e-government Web sites: a multimethod, user-centered evaluation of accessibility for persons with disabilities. Gov Inform Q 2006;23(2):169–90.

[36] Fagen J, Fagen B. An accessibility study of state legislative web sites. Gov Inform Q 2004;21:65–85.

[37] Goette T, Collier C, Whilte J. An exploratory study of the accessibility of state government web sites. Univ Access Inform Soc 2006;5(1):41–50.

[38] Lazar J, Beavan P, Brown J, Coffey D, Nolf B, Poole R, et al. Investigating the accessibility of state government web sites in Maryland. In: Langdon P, Clarkson P, Robinson P, editors. Designing inclusive interactions—Proceedings of the 2010 Cambridge workshop on universal access and assistive technology. London: Springer; 2010. p. 69–78.

[39] Rubaii-Barrett N, Wise L. Disability access and e-government: an empirical analysis of state practices. J Disabil Pol Stud 2008;19(1):52–64.

[40] Yu D, Parmanto B. U.S. state government websites demonstrate better in terms of accessibility compared to federal government and commercial websites. Gov Inform Q 2011;28(4):484–90.

[41] Kuzma J. Accessibility design issues with UK e-government sites. Gov Inform Q 2010;27(2):141–6.

[42] Shi Y. The accessibility of Chinese local government Web sites: an exploratory study. Gov Inform Q 2007;24(2):377–403.

[43] Goodwin M, Susar D, Nietzio A, Snaprud M, Jensen C. Global web accessibility analysis of national government portals and ministry web sites. J Inform Technol Polit 2011;8(1):41–67.

[44] European Union. Digital agenda: commission proposes rules to make government websites accessible for all. Available at: http://europa.eu/rapid/press-release_IP-12-1305_en.htm; 2012.

[45] U.S. Department of Education. Settlement agreement between the National Federation of the Blind, et al. & U.S. Department of Education. Available at: https://www.insidehighered.com/sites/default/server_files/files/NFB-DOE%20Settlement_Agreement_FULLY%20EXECUTED.PDF; 2014.

[46] Dawe M. Desperately seeking simplicity: how young adults with cognitive disabilities and their families adopt assistive technologies. In: Proceedings of the 2006 ACM conference on human factors in computing systems (CHI); 2006. p. 1143–52.

[47] Vance A. Insurers fight speech-impairment remedy. *New York Times*; 2009, September 14. Available at: http://www.nytimes.com/2009/2009/2015/technology/2015speech.html?_r=2000&adxnnl=2001&adxnnlx=1354384846-wzP1354384848yRKeRPQN1354384846wA-BaNsueQ.

[48] Hirsch T, Forlizzi J, Hyder E, Goetz J, Stroback J, Kurtz C. The ELDer project: Social, emotional, and environmental factors in the design of eldercare technologies. In: Proceedings of the ACM conference on universal usability; 2000. p. 72–9.

[49] Azenkot S, Prasain S, Borning A, Fortuna E, Ladner R, Wobbrock J. Enhancing independence and safety for blind and deaf-blind public transit riders. In: Paper presented at the proceedings of the SIGCHI conference on human factors in computing systems, Vancouver, BC, Canada; 2011.

Technical standards for accessibility

4

ACCESSIBILITY STANDARDS

Accessibility professionals face many questions from web and product developers; perhaps the most frequently asked one is "where can I learn more about how to make my products and services accessible?" Such a broad question can serve to open a real dialogue on the topic of accessible interfaces and how they relate to usability. Technical standards for accessibility serve as the foundation for international understanding. However, accessibility standards alone do not necessarily yield ideal usability for the consumer. Accessibility, as defined by W3C, is "about ensuring an equivalent user experience for people with disabilities, including people with age-related impairments. For the Web, accessibility means that people with disabilities can perceive, understand, navigate, and interact with websites and tools, and that they can contribute equally without barriers," whereas usability, according to that same source, is "about designing products to be effective, efficient, and satisfying" [1]. The top recommendation for a developer aspiring to create a truly accessible and easy to use product, site, or tool, should always be to involve users with disabilities. Without input from users who rely on access technology as a primary tool, at the design stage, it is difficult to ensure that the products and services that are created are both accessible and user friendly.

Accessible design is a skill that any developer can acquire. Web sites, web applications, or even accessible digital books and accessible documents rely on similar principles, even if there are variations in how they are executed in the different formats. Once the skill is acquired, it is easy to apply it in different environments. With accessibility in mind, and executive level support, creating an accessible product is not an extraordinary or difficult process. A developer with the necessary skills will never have to sacrifice good design for accessibility or vice versa. A good architect who designs an accessible building must follow a strict building code in order to successfully design a safe and accessible building; web standards fulfill that role for website designers and developers.

Accessible design is not an abstract concept, nor does it rely solely on user experiences. The foundation that makes any kind of consensus possible is the range of accessibility standards that are available to help developers to ensure that anyone can benefit from their digital products and services. Individuals with disabilities, similar to the mainstreamed society, consume digital content on many complex platforms; as such, anything short of full accessibility will inevitably cut large swaths of users out. This chapter is a closer look at leading accessibility standards that have gained international acceptance. In addition, we will examine other important accessibility guidelines that are gaining momentum among accessibility experts.

It is important to know that not all accessibility standards are created equal, and that developers must know how to apply the appropriate standard to a given content type during the design process. As an example, if the goal is to have an accessible web site, then the correct accessibility standard to use is the Web Content Accessibility Guidelines (WCAG), version 2.0, priority AA, which is the highest standard achievable across an entire site. However, if the end goal is to design accessible Flash content, then the Adobe accessible Flash design guidelines are needed. In this chapter, we will examine accessibility standards from three major areas of information technology: web accessibility standards, accessible publishing standards, and up and coming accessible guidelines that are likely to become standards in the future.

THE WORLD WIDE WEB CONSORTIUM AND THE WEB ACCESSIBILITY INITIATIVE

In the web accessibility arena, the de facto web accessibility standard comes from the World Wide Web Consortium, usually known simply as W3C (http://www.w3.org/). It is the longevity and credibility of the W3C, and the level of expertise it has attracted to its Web Accessibility Initiative (WAI) (http://www.w3.org/WAI/), that makes the guidelines it issues (which are not, in themselves, legally enforceable) so widely accepted.

Founded in October 1994, a mere 5 years after the invention of the World Wide Web, by the inventor of said web, Tim Berners-Lee, W3C was backed by the organizations who had first spurred on the development of the web and others who were early adopters. These most prominently included the Massachusetts Institute of Technology, the Laboratory for Computer Science, the European Organization for Nuclear Research (best known as CERN), the Defense Advanced Research Projects Agency, and the European Commission [2]. With such heavyweights involved at its genesis, it is unremarkable that W3C was instantly established as an, and likely *the*, authority on matters related to the web.

Work towards creating a web accessibility project started in the fall of 1996, centered around the W3C accessibility page that was maintained by Michael Paciello, which linked to several early web accessibility guidelines including those compiled by Gregg Vanderheiden of the Trace Center. The Web Accessibility Initiative, the body created to hold the new activities, was launched at the Web Conference in Santa Clara in April 1997 [3]. The first version of WCAG (1.0) became final in May of 1999 [4]; WCAG 2.0 came out in 2008. The collaborators listed for the creation of each of these versions is a Who's Who of people and organizations involved in making the web accessible, which is another major factor in the wide adoption of what is a fully voluntary standard. Often those same people and organizations have had a major impact on technology and access technology as a whole, and not just web accessibility. Some of the names mentioned earlier in this book in Chapter 2 on the history of technology accessibility re-surface here—IBM, Microsoft, Gregg Vanderheiden. It is all of these factors that lend the WAI its tremendous influence when setting guidelines.

WEB ACCESSIBILITY STANDARDS

At the heart of the development of standards within WAI are the working groups. The WAI working groups are, among other things, responsible for developing the most commonly used, internationally accepted, web accessibility standard, the WCAG. In order to understand how these web standards come about and continue to develop, it is worth detailing the process by which they become W3C-sanctioned standards. The steps described below apply to all guidelines that stem from the WAI. The following are the stages through which a draft must pass to become a web standard. A more comprehensive description of the process can be found at http://www.w3.org/WAI/intro/w3c-process.php.

- *Working Draft*: Working Drafts are published and announced specifically to ask for review and input from the community. Often there are issues that a Working Group would particularly like input on. Usually multiple Working Drafts of a technical report are published.
- *Last Call Working Draft*: When a Working Group believes it has addressed all comments and technical requirements, it provides the complete document for community review and announces the Last Call.
- *Candidate Recommendation*: The main purpose of Candidate Recommendation is to ensure that the technical report can be implemented. W3C encourages developers to use the technical report in their projects. The technical report is stable at this stage; however, it may change based on implementation experience.
- *Proposed Recommendation*: After there are implementations of each feature of the technical report, W3C announces it as a Proposed Recommendation. At this stage, the report is submitted to the W3C Membership for endorsement.
- *W3C Recommendation (Web Standard)*: Once there is significant support for the technical report from the W3C Members, the W3C Director, and the public, it is published as a Recommendation. W3C encourages widespread deployment of its Recommendations [5].

The WAI group has also developed a plethora of educational resources and technical documents to aid developers and anyone else with interest in web accessibility to find their feet in accessibility implementation.

THE WEB CONTENT ACCESSIBILITY GUIDELINES

The Web Content Accessibility Guidelines (WCAG) are the preferred, and arguably core, accessibility standard for a number of different reasons, and the issuing organization is only one of them. First of all, it is a standard that is the result of a multi-stakeholder effort, and it has received public input at every stage. A second reason for WCAG's success is the simplicity of the underlying principles. In the standard's own phrasing, it requires web content to be perceivable, operable, understandable, and robust (POUR). These four principles are the foundation of the standard, and the model for a number of other guidelines detailed later in this chapter.

"Perceivable" relates to how *available* content is to a given user—i.e., is audio content available to Deaf users through captions; is text highlighting or color coding indicated to screen access software, etc.?

"Operable" refers to the users' ability to interact with content—can they use a keyboard or is a mouse necessary? Can they navigate efficiently? And so forth.

"Understandable" is about how the user processes content, and what the cognitive load is—is navigation consistent? If users make a mistake, can they amend it easily? Etc.

"Robust" pertains to the ability of content to work on as much past, present, and future technology as is feasible [6].

These principles are then put to work in the success criteria, which are the checkpoints by which the WCAG lives and breathes. The success criteria are digitally testable, as well as easily substantiated with usability testing by an access technology user. W3C provides several documents aimed at helping developers assess how to implement WCAG 2.0. These include: "How to Meet WCAG 2.0" (http://www.w3.org/WAI/WCAG20/quickref/); "Techniques for WCAG2.0" (http://www.w3.org/TR/WCAG20-TECHS/); and "Understanding WCAG 2.0" (http://www.w3.org/TR/UNDERSTANDING-WCAG20/). The first document provides a customizable interface for content creators and developers, providing easier access to the other two documents, including HTML code samples and other best practice recommendations that can be used in the web content creation process. Additional implementation references including tutorials are also available (http://www.w3.org/WAI/tutorials/).

The extremely comprehensive approach that the W3Cs WAI working groups adopt when it comes to standards is not only technically based, but incorporates direct feedback from users with disabilities and is keyed to fit their needs. That said, it could never be a working standard if it didn't also have much to offer to those implementing it. In this standard, developers can use simple fixes like image and form labeling to remediate HTML access barriers. Similarly, other developers building and maintaining complex, dynamic websites or web apps will find success criteria for how to handle natural language mark-up and how to manage alerts and focus changes. In the "How to meet WCAG 2.0" document, the success criteria are grouped according to the types of common accessibility barriers present on the web. The following puts some of the guidelines and success criteria into a real-world context. Guideline 1.1 is as good as any place to start. It addresses text alternatives in the following terms: "Provide text alternatives for any non-text content so that it can be changed into other forms people need, such as large print, braille, speech, symbols or simpler language" [7]. One example of a success criterion for this guideline is 1.1.1, "All non-text content that is presented to the user has text alternative that serves the equivalent purpose" [7]. This means that, among other things, images, interactive graphics, links, form fields, etc. must have a label or descriptions as appropriate. The criterion describes, in detail, the scenarios, exceptions, and the recommended techniques for achieving compliance. Other guidelines follow this same template. Guideline 1.2 "Provide[s] alternatives for time-based media" [7], is applicable to the pre-recorded audio content, and pre-recorded video content (level A). This means that synchronized captions must be available for pre-recorded audio content and synchronized audio description must be provided for pre-recorded video content. Again, the specific methods for achieving this goal, with examples, are described.

Guideline 2.1, which requires all elements to be keyboard accessible, can serve as a final example of how one can go from guideline to implementation. This guideline requires that "all functionality for content is operable through a keyboard interface without requiring specific timing for individual keystrokes, except where the underlying function requires input that depends on the path of the user's movement and not just the end point." A simple illustration on how this guideline can be implemented is all controls on the page must be accessible with keyboard. Users must be able to freely move around on the page without having to worry about keyboard traps (i.e., what happens when a user cannot move focus away from an interactive element or control using their keyboard). It is important to note that this guideline does not discourage the use of a mouse or any other pointing devices but only mandates that the same functionality must be available from the keyboard. For example, device-specific event-handlers such as onMouseOver and onClick will have to be replaced with device-independent handlers such as onFocus and onChange. OnMouseOver is an event handler that captures the moment when a pointer (and specifically a pointer) crosses an element boundary; an onClick event happens when a user clicks on an element (with a mouse). By contrast, an onFocus event is triggered when an element receives focus, i.e., when the user navigates to that element. The onChange event is triggered when the value of an element changes, e.g., when the value of a checkbox goes from unchecked to checked.

The robustness of the WCAG is most often in evidence in its capability to adapt to new and changing types of digital content as they are deployed. Everything ranging from mobile web sites to web apps is now the norm, and yet the success criteria of the WCAG are resilient enough to assist the developers in their efforts in designing accessible content for such complex platforms. Each success criterion of the WCAG is formulated as a testable statement that will be either true or false when applied to a specific type of web content. To the extent that is possible, the WCAG standard is truly technology agnostic. When developers design a web site according to the success criteria in the web accessibility standard, the web site will be accessible to people with disability regardless of the combination of browsers, devices, and access technologies that they use to access the site.

Compliance with WCAG is divided into three levels, A, AA, and AAA. Understanding what each of these levels means is central, because they can help prioritize remediation and guide new content. W3C's own materials are a little hesitant, understandably, to ascribe any prescriptive value to the levels. That said, translated into layman terms, the levels translate roughly as follows – A is the groundwork, the indispensable foundation. AA is what you need to have an actually workable site; the house, if you will. AAA is the mark of excellence, but it is explicitly noted that this is not achievable in every instance. For example, A requires that there be audio description or a media alternative and captions for all pre-recorded video content; AA requires captions for live events and audio description for pre-recorded video; AAA requires extended audio description (which adds breaks in the video when natural pauses are insufficient for description) and sign interpreting for pre-recorded video [8].

Developers who decide to adopt the WCAG web accessibility standard will also benefit from the industry-wide support. Web developers can choose from many existing free and paid web accessibility tools that can be programmed to analyze web sites according to the WCAG success criteria in the market (see Chapter 8 for a description of automated accessibility testing tools).

The WCAG success criteria are applicable to more than HTML content. Developers can use the criteria to design accessible Portable Document Format (PDF) files. More detail on the accessible PDF design techniques based on the WCAG criteria can be found at http://www.w3.org/WAI/GL/WCAG20-TECHS/pdf.

In this chapter so far, we have only examined one aspect of the accessible web content. So what does an accessible and inclusive web look like? In order to achieve an accessible web, all of the essential components must work seamlessly together. Web authoring tools must be able to aid developers on how to use accessible coding practice when designing web sites. The most productive method for achieving this is to include both examples and tools for creating accessible, flexible code, and a mechanism to prevent web developers from uploading inaccessible code or inaccessible widgets. Web accessibility validation tools must be able to validate HTML codes and control types to determine whether they are accessible. Furthermore, good validation tools must have a library of techniques on how to implement the WCAG success criteria built in to provide additional guidance to the developers. Once web sites are designed to be accessible, the user agent technologies such as web browsers and screen access software must be able to respect the structure and the integrity of the original code from the author and render content to the users correctly. Finally, the end users must be able to proficiently use access technologies to access information on the web site.

One common example of how all of the essential components must work together to produce an accessible web is an HTML form. In that case, the authoring tool must alert the web designer that the form fields are missing labels before the form is posted. If the designer fails to heed the warning from the authoring tool, then the validation tool needs to be programmed to notify the designers that the HTML form is not properly labeled during the web site quality assurance process. And finally, once the web site is ready for public consumption, the screen access program should not attempt to overcompensate by automatically guessing which label is associated with a particular form field, when the incorrect coding practice is used.

It is hard to overestimate the impact of WCAG. While, as mentioned, WCAG is historically an entirely technical, non-mandatory guideline, it has provided the template for laws worldwide, including in Italy, and as we speak, U.S. Section 508 is being revised in its image. As will be illustrated by other guidelines described in this chapter, WCAG is now the "standard model"—or model standard.

The W3C Web Accessibility Initiative group has always been mindful of the complexity of the various interlocking components of an accessible web. That understanding is what guided the creation of the Authoring Tool Accessibility Guidelines (ATAG) and the User Agent Accessibility Guidelines (UAAG) as standards complementary to the WCAG standards. And these standards are now being utilized for building non-web technologies, as well.

AUTHORING TOOL ACCESSIBILITY GUIDELINES

What are the Authoring Tool Accessibility Guidelines (ATAG)? The main purpose of ATAG is two-fold. Firstly, ATAG provides recommendations on how to make accessible authoring tools so that content creators with disabilities can use the tools independently. Secondly, ATAG can assist authors with accessible content creation by enabling support and promoting the production of content that conforms to WCAG. ATAG is created primarily for designers and developers of the authoring tools. Examples of the types of tool that must utilize ATAG in order to achieve accessibility are the What You See Is What You Get (WYSIWYG) HTML editors; content management systems (CMS), which are tools to centrally create, publish, edit, modify, and review content; and courseware tools. Content creation software such as word processors and desktop publishing tools that have a save as HTML feature can also benefit greatly from the use of ATAG. Multimedia content creation tool developers, blogs and Wiki site owners, photo sharing site owners, and social media tools developers should incorporate ATAG in the designing process of their tools. ATAG is also recommended reading for policy makers, procurement decision makers, and managers. Decision makers such as these can use ATAG to determine whether a given authoring tool is accessible before deployment. Knowing what to look for during, rather than after, the procurement process can pre-empt a host of problems. In those situations where accessibility barriers are uncovered halfway through procurement, ATAG can be used inform the vendor of how to go about removing those barriers. ATAG1.0 [9], approved in 2000, is still the authoritative version. The W3C working group is currently drafting the 2.0 version, and while it is not an approved standard yet, it is the most up-to-date version of the guideline, and this section will focus on ATAG 2.0.

When a tool is designed according to ATAG specifications, this is what you can expect:

- The tool itself is accessible to the web designers with disabilities and web content creators.
- The authoring tool, if used correctly, will produce accessible content by default.

ATAG 2.0

ATAG 2.0 is a candidate recommendation by the ATAG working group and not the W3C official recommended guideline as of March 2015; nevertheless, the developers of authoring tools must strongly anticipate that the ATAG 2.0 will be official soon. It is therefore highly recommended for developers to follow the ATAG 2.0 guideline when developing an authoring tool. Below is an outline of what ATAG 2.0 seeks to achieve:

Part A: Make the authoring tool user interface accessible

- A1 The authoring tool user interface follows applicable accessibility guidelines
  - Ensure that web-based functionality is accessible
  - Ensure that non-web-based functionality is accessible
- A2 Editing-views are perceivable
  - Make alternative content available to authors
  - Ensure that editing-view presentation can be programmatically determined
- A3 Editing-views are operable
  - Provide keyboard access to authoring features
  - Provide authors with enough time
  - Help authors avoid flashing content that could cause seizures
  - Enhance navigation and editing via content structure
  - Provide text search of the content
  - Allow users to manage preference settings
  - Ensure that previews are at least as accessible as user agents
- A4 Editing-views are understandable
  - Help authors avoid and correct mistakes
  - Document the user interface, including all accessibility features

Part B: Support the production of accessible content

- B1 Fully automatic processes produce accessible content
  - Ensure that automatically specified content is accessible
  - Ensure that accessibility information is preserved
- B2 Authors are supported in producing accessible content
  - Ensure that accessible content production is possible
  - Guide authors to produce accessible content
  - Assist authors with managing alternative content for non-text content
  - Assist authors with accessible templates
  - Assist authors with accessible pre-authored content
- B3 Authors are supported in improving the accessibility of existing content
  - Assist authors in checking for accessibility problems
  - Assist authors in repairing accessibility problems
- B4 Authoring tools promote and integrate their accessibility features
  - Ensure the availability of features that support the production of accessible content
  - Ensure that documentation promotes the production of accessible content [10]

For optimal integration, the working group has chosen to model ATAG 2.0's structure closely on WCAG 2.0, and it follows WCAG's breakdown into three conformance levels, A, AA, AAA, with the same basic meaning of minimum/lowest, middle, highest. ATAG 2.0 is split into two parts, part A and part B. Part A deals with making the tool itself accessible; part B tackles the creation of accessible content.

ATAG 2.0 also follows WCAG 2.0 in its use of success criteria for testing standards conformance. The conditions that must be met for a success criterion to be included are as follows:

> *1. For Part A, all success criteria must present* authoring tool user interface-related accessibility issues. *In other words, the user interface issue must cause a proportionately greater problem for authors with disabilities than it causes authors without disabilities and must be specific to authoring tool software, as opposed to software in general.*

> *2. For Part B, all success criteria must present* accessible web content production issues. *In other words, the issue must be specific to the production of accessible web content (WCAG) by authoring tools, as opposed to the production of web content in general.*

> *3. All success criteria must also be* testable. *This is important since otherwise it would not be possible to determine whether an authoring tool met or failed to meet the success criteria. The success criteria can be tested by a combination of machine and human evaluation as long as it is possible to determine whether a success criterion has been satisfied with a high level of confidence.* [11]

Both sets of success criteria must be met for the tool to be considered to be in compliance with the guideline.

The success criteria were assigned to one of the three levels of conformance by the Working Group after taking into consideration a wide range of interacting issues. Some of the common factors evaluated when setting the level in Part A include:

- whether the success criterion is *essential* (in other words, if the success criterion is not met, then even assistive technology cannot make the authoring tool user interface accessible).
- whether it is possible to satisfy the success criterion for *all types of authoring tools* that the success criterion would apply to (e.g., WYSIWYG editors, wikis, content management systems).
- whether the success criterion would impose limits on the "look-and-feel" and/ or function of authoring tools (e.g., limits on the function, design, aesthetic, or freedom of expression of authoring tool developers).
- whether there are workarounds for authors with disabilities if the success criterion is not met [11].

Note that workarounds for authors with disabilities have significant problems associated with them. For example, if scripting is used to make a tool accessible, that script can break any time there are any changes to the tool.

Some of the common factors evaluated when setting the level in Part B include:

- whether the success criterion is *essential* (in other words, if the success criterion is not met, then even authors with a high degree of accessibility expertise would be unlikely to produce accessible content (WCAG) using an authoring tool).
- whether it is possible to satisfy the success criterion for the production of *all web content technologies* that the success criterion would apply to.
- whether the success criterion requires features that would *reasonably be used by authors*.
- whether the success criterion would impose limits on the "look-and-feel" and/ or function of authoring tools (e.g., limits on the function, design, aesthetic or freedom of expression of authoring tool developers) [11].

It will be clear from this summary that the principles set out in version 1.0 of the standard have not been discarded; they have been expanded on and updated, to fit a broad range of possible technologies.

As mentioned previously, the approved version of the ATAG has been in existence since 2000. The current working draft is almost ready for the W3C endorsement. The creation and update of ATAG have not resulted in more than a small handful of web-based or desktop authoring tools that the print-disabled and others with disabilities can use. The most accessible authoring tool is the Microsoft Office desktop client, and that is far from perfect. To give some examples to illustrate that point, Word does not support marking a column a header for the corresponding rows, making it impossible to make complex tables accessible; the same applies to PowerPoint. If the author decides to use a native theme, color and font information is not available to screen access software. Finally, if an author inserts WordArt, that text is not read when navigating through the document with screen access software.

As more people migrate toward cloud- or web-based computing and more content is created on the web using the web-based authoring tools, not having an accessible authoring tool is an increasingly serious problem. The migration to cloud-based productivity has, if anything made the situation worse. The most commonly used tools like the Google Suite are only now beginning to incorporate accessibility considerations into their design process. Others are slower to follow. Individuals with disabilities will most certainly not be able to be as productive in their education or in finding and keeping employment of their choice as their sighted counterparts without access to authoring tools, and there is no question that these are lacking. At the time of this writing, there is not even an accessible HTML editor. It is clear that ATAG is not as widely adopted by the IT industry as it should be. It is imperative that industry players and the user community work together to solve this problem immediately.

USER AGENT ACCESSIBILITY GUIDELINES

In the previous section of this chapter, we mentioned that the essential components of the web must work well together in order to have an accessible web. We have already discussed accessible web content and accessible authoring tools in some detail. The logical next topic is the User Agent Accessibility Guidelines (UAAG).

What is UAAG and who is UAAG designed for? UAAG is a guideline that one can use to evaluate the accessibility of user agent technologies like web browsers, media players, document viewers, and access technology tools that consumers with disabilities use to access information. The core target audience of UAAG are the developers of the tools mentioned above, but policy makers and procurement decision makers can equally use UAAG criteria to determine whether the user agent technologies are accessible, or UAAG can be given to the developers to use to enhance the accessibility features of the tools.

Like ATAG, UAAG has two versions in circulation—the current and referenceable version, 1.0, and the mature draft, 2.0. Because the W3C specifically recommends using version 2.0, even though it is not final, this is the version described below. As with ATAG 2.0, UAAG 2.0 is intended to be consistent with WCAG 2.0 and follows the same structure and the same levels of conformance. As a consequence, the foundational principles will seem very familiar to someone who has used WCAG 2.0, and this helps to shorten the learning curve. More specific information on how UAAG relates to WCAG and ATAG can be found in those sections further on in this chapter.

- PRINCIPLE 1. Perceivable
- PRINCIPLE 2. Operable
- PRINCIPLE 3. Understandable
- PRINCIPLE 4. Programmatic access
- PRINCIPLE 5. Specifications and conventions

The first three principles are consistent with the principles found in the WCAG 2.0. The last two principles are specific to the UAAG 2.0. Principle 4 relates to how the User Agent reveals basic information, supports accessibility, enables write access so the user can modify the state of an element (such as editing a field), and so forth. Principle 5 in essence requires compliance with other accessibility standards, most prominently WCAG 2.0, wherever possible. Each principle has guidelines along with testable success criteria accompanying them, as does WCAG. Much of the value of the UAAG stems from the harmonious integration of the WCAG 2.0 and the ATAG 2.0. Here is what the UAAG working group has to say about the relationship between the three guidelines.

RELATIONSHIP TO THE WEB CONTENT ACCESSIBILITY GUIDELINES (WCAG) 2.0

The W3C recommendation, WCAG, applies to all web content; UAAG provides additional advice on the application user interface.

Some user agents are used to package web content into non-web-based applications, especially on mobile platforms. If the finished application is used to retrieve, render, and facilitate end-user interaction with web content of the end-users choosing, then the application should be considered a stand-alone user agent. If the finished application only renders a constrained set of content specified by the developer, then the application might not be considered a user agent. In both cases, the WCAG 2.0 Guidelines apply to the web content. If the application is not a user agent, application developers are not responsible for UAAG 2.0 requirements that extend beyond WCAG 2.0 requirements. For more detail, see the definition of user agent. [12]

RELATIONSHIP TO THE AUTHORING TOOL ACCESSIBILITY GUIDELINES (ATAG) 2.0

While it is common to think of user agents retrieving and rendering web content for one group of people (end-users) that was previously authored by another group (authors), user agents are also frequently involved with the process of authoring content.

For these cases, it is important for user agent developers to consider the application of another W3C-WAI Recommendation, the Authoring Tool Accessibility Guidelines (ATAG). ATAG (currently 2.0 is in draft) provides guidance to the developers of tools regarding the accessibility of authoring interfaces to authors (ATAG 2.0 Part A) and ways in which all authors can be supported in producing accessible web content (ATAG 2.0 Part B) [12].

When the developers of the user agent technologies ignore the importance of the UAAG criteria, the users suffer. As an example, if screen access software does not report the correct status when the form controls like radio buttons and checkboxes are activated, this is a definite "show-stopper" for users with disabilities. How can a blind person proficiently perform web transactions when they do not know whether the radio buttons or the checkboxes are checked? Much frustration on the web experienced by users with disabilities stems from the fact that developers of access technology and other agent technologies do not adhere to the UAAG success criteria. This is often due to the effort involved in rewriting legacy code to conform with UAAG. Abandoning good code practices in favor of a path-of-least-resistance approach is ultimately counterproductive. Not only are large numbers of consumers excluded by such an approach, but failure to meet UAAG will sabotage efforts by web developers to design inclusive web sites, thereby amplifying the disruptive effect of bad and lazy coding.

ACCESSIBLE RICH INTERNET APPLICATION

The web is constantly changing, and more dynamic content is being pushed out by the developers to the users across the web. Technologically, the semantic information of such content along with the structure, widgets, and behavior must be appropriately conveyed to the user agent technologies, like the browser, and access technologies. The user agent tools need to be able to provide the web users with disabilities with access to the dynamic content as well as advanced user interface web controls, in particular, the web controls that are developed in AJAX, JavaScript, HTML, DHTML, and other related technologies. Before the Accessible Rich Internet Application (ARIA), it was impossible for keyboard users and screen access software users to use complex web controls like the tree controls to navigate the web or to perform complex functions like drag-and-drop in the web browsers. Accessing AJAX-based content change areas that result from user's actions or time-based or event-based updates was also impossible without ARIA. That is why the ARIA guideline was developed. Since the adoption of the ARIA guideline by industry, users of access technologies can quickly navigate through the web sites or web apps using markup like regions and land marks. Accessing content change areas in the Document Object Model without refreshing the entire web page is now possible for the users of access technologies with ARIA alerts and ARIA live regions (live regions are "perceivable regions of a web page that are typically updated as a result of an external event when user focus may be elsewhere" [13]). ARIA 1.0 is the recommended standard developed by the Protocol Format Working Group (PFWG) from W3C on March 2014. Web app developers, web content creators, and user agent technology makers are strongly encouraged to use ARIA element in the development process. Web accessibility validation tool providers also need to ensure that their validation tools can check ARIA content for accessibility. Web developers can use ARIA to ensure that users of access technology can access the "dynamic web." According to the W3C WAI ARIA working group, web authors can use ARIA to define properties or add attributes to the following content types and advance user interface controls:

- Roles to describe the type of widget presented, such as "menu," "tree item," "slider," and "progress meter."
- Roles to describe the structure of the web page, such as headings, regions, and tables (grids).
- Properties to describe the state widgets are in, such as "checked" for a check box, or "has popup" for a menu.
- Properties to define live regions of a page that are likely to get updates (such as stock quotes), as well as an interruption policy for those updates—for example, critical updates may be presented in an alert dialog box, and incidental updates occur within the page.
- Properties for drag-and-drop that describe drag sources and drop targets.
- A way to provide keyboard navigation for the web objects and events, such as those mentioned above [14].

In order to make sense of the ARIA standard, those who are interested at a minimum must be familiar with the following references from the WAI ARIA working group.

The WAI ARIA primer introduces ARIA fundamentals, and types of accessibility barriers that ARIA standard will help solve, as well as the technical approaches to ARIA. It is available at http://www.w3.org/TR/wai-aria-primer.

With the WAI ARIA-authoring practices, a web content creator can learn how to create accessible rich Internet content and accessible rich Internet applications. This document provides detailed examples and advice for not just web authors, but user agent technology developers can also benefit. The WAI ARIA-authoring practice can be found at http://www.w3.org/TR/wai-aria-practices/.

The WAI ARIA User Agent Implementation Guide is a complete recommended guideline for user agent technology developers. This document specifically describes how the developers can expose ARIA features to the accessibility API. Here is the link to the guide: http://www.w3.org/TR/wai-aria-implementation/.

Finally, there are the WAI ARIA 1.0 technical specifications; according to the working group, this is a complete W3C Recommendation web standard, and combines the two previously published WAI-ARIA draft specifications: Roles for Accessible Rich Internet Applications (WAI-ARIA Roles) and the States and Properties Module for Accessible Rich Internet Applications (WAI-ARIA States and Properties). Here is the link to the technical specifications: http://www.w3.org/TR/wai-aria/.

EPUB

Inaccessibility on the web is not the only problem that users with disabilities face when trying to access information. Accessing published content using e-readers, digital book players, tablets, and mobile devices is not straightforward, though unlike its printed counterparts, digital books present no inherent barrier to accessibility. In the past decade the print disabled have been able to read books in, among other formats, a specialized format called the Digital Accessible Information System (DAISY). However, DAISY books had to be produced using a dedicated book production tool, and very often the production process also required human intervention and dedicated book readers. With those limitations, many fewer DAISY books are available for use by the print disabled as compared to the overall numbers of books published on an annual basis. The DAISY standard has served the community of people with disabilities well since its inception in 1994. However, the consensus reached by both the community of people with disabilities and the publishing industry was that there was a clear need to have a more advanced publishing standard that the authors and the publishers can use to produce accessible books and digital documents for all readers.

Enter the International Digital Publishing Forum (IDPF). The IDPF, an international standards and trade association for digital publishing, seeks to promote the standardization of electronic publishing. It was a natural fit, then, for them to work closely with the DAISY Consortium to develop and maintain the EPUB publishing standard. The open, flexible, reflowable (content that adapts how it displays depending on the device it is used on) format was set up as a de facto standard to ensure that publishers can accommodate various reading preferences, platforms, and devices; that basic malleability makes it very suitable for readers with disabilities. EPUB is an incredibly powerful demonstration that in a successful implementation of digital books, the benefits of making sure it works for print-disabled readers, serve to improve the standard across the board, much like optimizing books for mobile devices, will serve to enhance the experience for many users with disabilities.

The current version of the EPUB standard is EPUB 3.0.1, and that version provides the most comprehensive accessibility features. Here is how the IDPF defines EPUB. "EPUB is the distribution and interchange format standard for digital publications and documents based on Web Standards. EPUB defines a means of representing, packaging and encoding structured and semantically enhanced Web content—including XHTML, CSS, SVG, images, and other resources—for distribution in a single-file format" [15]. EPUB allows publishers to produce and send a single digital publication file through distribution and offers consumers interoperability between software/hardware for unencrypted reflowable digital books and other publications. Besides the XML content and the SVG content, EPUB 3.0.1 can also accommodate embedded multimedia content. There are four major components in EPUB-EPUB Publications 3.0, which defines publication-level semantics and overarching conformance requirements for EPUB Publications; EPUB Content Documents 3.0, which defines profiles of XHTML, SVG, and CSS for use in the context of EPUB Publications; EPUB Open Container Format (OCF) 3.0, which defines a file format and processing model for encapsulating a set of related resources into a single-file (ZIP) EPUB Container; and EPUB Media Overlays 3.0, which defines a format and a processing model for synchronization of text and audio [16]. These four components cover every aspect of a digital publication, with an emphasis on creating a final product that is flexible enough to suit a wide variety of users and technologies.

The litmus test for any standard is its rates of adoption. The great benefits of consumers with disabilities being able to read a book and listen to the embedded recordings, or watch videos, all in one book on one device, are moot if the format doesn't catch on. EPUB is significant because, unlike some other standards, and unlike DAISY, it has already gained wide mainstream acceptance, with major content distributors like Apple, Google, and Adobe already supporting EPUB books. When authors and publishers follow the EPUB specifications, it is possible to have accessible books and documents that everyone can consume—right there in the same web store that everyone uses.

APPLYING WCAG 2.0 TO NON-WEB INFORMATION AND COMMUNICATIONS TECHNOLOGIES

WCAG is a powerful standard, and it covers a lot of ground. Not all content and applications are web-based, but these can still benefit from applying some aspects of the WCAG standard. For the developers who want to ensure the accessibility of non-web content and applications, W3C also has issued its "Guidance on Applying WCAG 2.0 to Non-Web Information and Communications Technologies (WCAG2ICT)." The guideline is developed by the WCAG 2.0 ICT task force. This task force works directly with the Web Content Accessibility Guidelines Working Group (WCAGWG).

The guidance document describes how the success criteria of the WCAG 2.0, along with its principles and guidelines, are applicable to non-web Information and Information and Communications Technology (ICT) such as non-web documents and non-web software. On an important side note, WCAG2ICT is not applicable to any software or program that does not have a user interface, like printer drivers. Even though this document is a "working group note" for guidance purposes and not (yet) a recommended standard, it relates to some very critical use cases. Many productivity tools that individuals with disabilities use regularly fall into the non-web ICT category. Examples of such tools include accounting software, inventory database management, antivirus programs, remote PC access utilities, and more; these can make the difference between someone being employed or not, and it is not a marginal use case. More details on the WCAG2ICT can be found on http://www.w3.org/TR/wcag2ict/.

SUMMARY

Well-researched, well-tested, and well-documented standards are a requisite foundation for successful implementations of technology accessibility, and for wider adoption of such standards. The other key to broad adoption is the credibility and the influence of the organization developing the guidelines. It is clear from the preceding review that both the W3C and the IDPF have been leaders in establishing their particular guidelines as the most authoritative. The Web Content Accessibility Guidelines are the most adopted guidelines throughout the world, and they can be adapted for use in non-web technologies where no guidelines currently exist, such as kiosks and embedded devices.

REFERENCES

[1] W3C. Web accessibility and usability working together. Retrieved from http://www.w3.org/WAI/intro/usable; 2010, December 2.
[2] W3C. Facts about W3C. Retrieved from http://www.w3.org/Consortium/facts.html#history; 2012.
[3] Dardailler D. WAI early days. Retrieved from http://www.w3.org/WAI/history; 2009.
[4] W3C. Web Content Accessibility Guidelines 1.0. Retrieved from http://www.w3.org/TR/WAI-WEBCONTENT/; 1999, May 5.
[5] W3C. How WAI develops accessibility guidelines through the W3C process: milestones and opportunities to contribute. Retrieved from http://www.w3.org/WAI/intro/w3c-process.php; 2008.
[6] Summarized from W3C. Web Content Accessibility Guidelines (WCAG) 2.0. Retrieved from http://www.w3.org/TR/WCAG20/; 2008, December 11.
[7] W3C. How to meet WCAG 2.0. Retrieved from http://www.w3.org/WAI/WCAG20/quickref/#text-equiv; 2014, September 16.
[8] W3C. Web Content Accessibility Guidelines (WCAG) 2.0. Retrieved from http://www.w3.org/TR/WCAG20/; 2008, December 11.
[9] W3C. Authoring Tool Accessibility Guidelines 1.0. Retrieved from http://www.w3.org/TR/WAI-AUTOOLS/; 2000, February 3.

[10] W3C. ATAG at a glance. Retrieved from http://www.w3.org/WAI/intro/atag-glance; 2014, March 17.

[11] W3C. Implementing ATAG 2.0: a guide to understanding and implementing Authoring Tool Accessibility Guidelines 2.0. Retrieved from http://www.w3.org/TR/IMPLEMENTING-ATAG20/; 2013.

[12] W3C. User agent accessibility guidelines (UAAG) 2.0. Retrieved from http://www.w3.org/TR/UAAG20/; 2014.

[13] W3C. Accessible Rich Internet Applications (WAI-ARIA) 1.0.4. Important terms. Retrieved from http://www.w3.org/TR/wai-aria/terms; 2014, March 20.

[14] W3C. WAI-ARIA overview. Retrieved from http://www.w3.org/WAI/intro/aria.php; 2014, June 12.

[15] International Digital Publishing Forum. EPUB. Retrieved from http://idpf.org/epub; 2014.

[16] International Digital Publishing Forum. EPUB 3 Overview. Retrieved from http://www.idpf.org/epub/30/spec/epub30-overview.html#sec-intro-overview; 2011.

U.S. laws and lawsuits

5

INTRODUCTION

An animating concept of all civil rights laws is to prevent the denial of equal opportunity for invidious and irrelevant reasons, such as race, gender, religion, and sexual orientation. At the heart of disability civil rights laws is a commitment to provide an equal opportunity to access what society offers: equal access, not equality of result. The latter is a matter of personal achievement.

What distinguishes anti-discrimination laws addressing disability from other civil rights statutes is the nature of the barriers to equal opportunity. In the case of race or gender discrimination, the barriers are generally attitudinal. In the case of disability discrimination, the barriers may also be physical, like stairs with no accompanying ramp or a computer image with no alt tag. Thus, while nondiscrimination in the former case may require refraining from acting in a manner that has a discriminatory impact, equal access for persons with disabilities may also require providing an accommodation or removing a barrier. It is not enough under disability discrimination laws for a restaurant with three steps at the entrance and no ramp, for example, to say to patrons using wheelchairs that they, too, are welcome; rather, to avoid discrimination, it must take the affirmative step, under certain circumstances, to replace or supplement the steps with a ramp. As Justice Ginsburg explained in her concurring opinion in *Tennessee v. Lane*:

> *Including individuals with disabilities among people who count in composing "We the People," Congress understood in shaping the ADA, would sometimes require not blindfolded equality, but responsiveness to difference; not indifference, but accommodation.* [1]

A majoritarian view determines what is considered an "accommodation"; a blind person who turns on his office lights for a sighted visitor or the wheelchair user providing a guest chair to a nondisabled guest are not seen as affording accommodations, but become so when applied to a person whose characteristics are labeled a disability. In both instances, there is a fiscal cost, but in the latter it is seen as a special cost attributable to disability.

Because of the cost of accommodation, disability discrimination laws are unique in setting limits to the obligation not to discriminate and are not a blank check as to the costs that must be borne by an entity subject to these laws when remedial action is required. Thus, concepts like "undue burden" and "fundamental alteration" or, with respect to employment, "reasonable accommodation," as further described in this chapter, often set outer limits on the obligation not to discriminate.

APPLICABILITY OF AMERICAN LAWS TO TECHNOLOGY DEVELOPERS

The various US federal laws barring disability discrimination apply to (a) governmental entities in procurement and in their dealings with the public and their own employees; (b) private and public recipients of federal financial assistance; and (c) places of public accommodations and public transportation [2–8]. Technology developers and vendors have no direct liability for creating inaccessible products and services; rather, they are covered by these laws only to the extent they are employers who must provide an accessible workplace. Amazon, for example, cannot be held liable under federal law for selling inaccessible Kindles to a library, but a library that buys Kindles and lends them to patrons violates the Americans with Disabilities Act (ADA). Thus, the burden of accessibility, from a federal legal standpoint, rests entirely on purchasers or licensees of technology. However, a smattering of state laws may allow for direct action against technology developers. New Jersey's Law Against Discrimination, for example, has a strong aiding and abetting provision, and Massachusetts' Equal Rights Amendment reaches all "programs and activities conducted within the Commonwealth" that discriminate on the basis, among other things, of disability.

THE PACE OF CHANGE IN THE DEVELOPMENT OF TECHNOLOGY AFFECTS THE DESIGN OF LEGAL DEFINITIONS OF ACCESS

The multiplicity of disabilities has implications for legal definitions of accessible technology. The physical design of an ATM, for example, must take into account the heights and depths reachable by a wheelchair user. Accessibility in this circumstance must reflect the variations in the physical characteristics of a human on matters such as reach, but also the variations in the design of wheelchairs. However, while the physical characteristics of wheelchairs and people may change slowly over time, it is possible to write prescriptive standards for accessibility that detail with precision such things as the maximum slope of a ramp or the minimum width for a door. By contrast, the rate of change in digital technology is rapid and can cause poorly designed legal definitions of access to become obsolete.

Thus, in the area of technology, performance or results-oriented standards avoid the risk of straitjacketing change or creating obsolete standards. For example, in response to the adoption of Amazon's Kindle DX at a number of colleges and universities, the Departments of Justice and Education in a letter to all college presidents first explained that:

> *Requiring use of an emerging technology in a classroom environment when the technology is inaccessible to an entire population of individuals with disabilities— individuals with visual disabilities—is discrimination prohibited by the Americans*

with Disabilities Act of 1990 (ADA) and Section 504 of the Rehabilitation Act of 1973 (Section 504) unless those individuals are provided accommodations or modifications that permit them to receive all the educational benefits provided by the technology in an equally effective and equally integrated manner. [9]

The letter then went on to explain that the affirmative obligations of post-secondary institutions under the various federal anti-discrimination statutes are as follows:

Under title III [of the ADA], individuals with disabilities, including students with visual impairments, may not be discriminated against in the full and equal enjoyment of all of the goods and services of private colleges and universities; they must receive an equal opportunity to participate in and benefit from these goods and services; and they must not be provided different or separate goods or services unless doing so is necessary to ensure that access to the goods and services is equally as effective as that provided to others. Under title II, qualified individuals with disabilities may not be excluded from participation in or denied the benefits of the services, programs, or activities of, nor subjected to discrimination by, public universities and colleges. Both title II and Section 504 prohibit colleges and universities from affording individuals with disabilities with an opportunity to participate in or benefit from college and university aids, benefits, and services that is unequal to the opportunity afforded others. [9]

But what is equal access in the eyes of the federal government? Equal access occurs when a student with a visual impairment "can acquire the same information, engage in the same interactions, and enjoy the same services as sighted students with substantially equivalent ease of use" [10]. This is manifestly not a technical standard, but it is one that allows maximum flexibility and avoids the potential for obsolescence as new technology develops.

Acquiring the "same information," does not mean that the technology vendor needs to make blind people see. Rather, this means that when information is communicated by a graphic on a web site, it must be adequately described with an "alt tag" (alternative text description of an image) that screen reader software used by the blind will recognize or by other means that are useful in the context where the graphic appears.

Engaging in the "same interactions" is clear—it would include, among other things, making sure that edit boxes are associated with their labels or that links are labeled, and that error messages are available other than by color-coding.

Finally, because different users have different facility with computers, disabilities aside, the standard "substantially equivalent ease of use" recognizes that exactitude of comparative usability cannot be insisted upon. Rather, what "substantially equivalent ease of use" imports is that a task that the average sighted user can accomplish in 2 minutes should not require that the blind user spend an hour or be forced to guess and try out various unlabeled links to proceed to the next step.

When the federal government has not defined an accessibility standard for a particular technology, as is the case currently, for example, for point of sale machines, the general requirements of equal access still apply [11]. The Department of Justice has proposed, but not promulgated, regulations that would acknowledge that Title III of the ADA (the provision prohibiting discrimination by public accommodations) applies to web sites that act as public accommodations, such as e-commerce entities, and that would make the World Wide Web Consortium's (W3C) Web Content Accessibility Guidelines 2.0 Level AA standard (WCAG 2.0 AA) the measure of accessibility. Those proposed regulations have been mired down in the regulatory process for several years. At the time of writing, there is little indication that promulgation of those regulations is imminent. (This regulation and others are discussed further in Chapter 7.)

Access for persons with disabilities to all the Internet offers in information, commerce and culture should not wait upon the vagaries of regulatory timing. Fortunately, even without a regulation, it is still possible to insist on accessibility by articulating a standard based on the regulatory requirement that public accommodations must engage in communication with persons with disabilities that is as effective as communication to those without disabilities. Put otherwise, equally effective communication would require the public accommodation to provide the same information, same functions, and same transactions to those with disabilities, all with a substantially equivalent ease of use. Thus, a blind user who does not receive an error message that is visible to a sighted one is not getting equally effective communication, whether that is phrased as a WCAG 2.0 AA standard or not.

FEDERAL STATUTES THAT HAVE AN IMPACT ON THE ACCESSIBILITY OF TECHNOLOGY

The federal statutes that are most significant when looking at the landscape of legal obligations applicable to technology access are Sections 504 and 508 of the Rehabilitation Act of 1973, the ADA, the Chafee Amendment to the Copyright Act of 1976 (Chafee Amendment), and the 21st Century Video and Communications Act (CVAA). The CVAA is discussed in Chapter 7 and the remaining statutes are discussed below.

The Individuals with Disabilities Education Act (IDEA) has no measurable impact on the accessibility of technology. While the IDEA can be useful to secure an auxiliary aid, like screen access technology or a refreshable Braille display for an individual school-aged child with a disability, the procedural structure of the act prevents it from being a tool with which to require that educational technology be accessible to all students. Fortunately, a school that must meet the requirements of the IDEA must also satisfy Title II of the ADA, which, by insisting on equal access to a school's programs, may address the need for universally accessible educational technology [12,13].

The Air Carrier Access Act (ACAA) will also not be discussed at length. While it can address such issues as the accessibility of airline kiosks, there is no private right of action; that is, if an airline discriminates against a person with a disability, the injured person has no right to sue. This leaves it to the U.S. Department of Transportation to impose sanctions on any airline that discriminates and to promulgate regulations, but DOT has not focused resources on this issue.

SECTION 504 OF THE REHABILITATION ACT AND TITLE II OF THE ADA

Section 504 of the Rehabilitation Act of 1973 prohibits the executive agencies of the federal government, the United States Postal Service, and recipients of federal financial assistance from denying persons with disabilities participation in and the benefits of, or otherwise discriminating against or excluding such persons from, any "program or activity," solely on the basis of disability [14]. "Program or activity" is broadly defined to include all governmental operations and all the operations of private educational, health care, housing, social service, parks and recreation institutions, and the entirety of a private entity if the federal assistance is extended to the organization as a whole.

Title II of the ADA has a partially overlapping reach, applying only to all nonfederal governmental entities, without regard to federal funding. It provides, succinctly, that:

> *no qualified individual with a disability shall, by reason of such disability, be excluded from participation in or be denied the benefits of the services, programs or activities of a public entity, or be subjected to discrimination by any such entity.* [15]

The obligation to provide all the benefits of a program or activity without regard to disability is limited, however, by the concepts of "fundamental alteration" and "undue financial or administrative burden" [16]. This means that a public entity need not provide access to a program if access would fundamentally alter the nature of that program. Moreover, if access would result in an undue financial or administrative burden, then the public entity is excused from providing equal access. With respect to employment of persons with disabilities by public entities, this statute also requires entities to provide "reasonable accommodations" to qualified persons with disabilities.

The regulations promulgated pursuant to Section 504 clarify further what it means to refrain from discrimination. An entity subject to Section 504 may not:

(i)   Afford a qualified handicapped person an opportunity to participate in or *benefit* from the aid, benefit, or service that is *not equal to that afforded others*;

(ii) Provide a qualified handicapped person with an aid, benefit, or *service* that is *not as effective in affording equal opportunity to obtain the same result*, to gain the same benefit, or to reach the same level of achievement as that provided to others;

(iii) Provide *different or separate aid, benefits, or services* to handicapped persons or to any class of handicapped persons than is provided to others *unless* such action is *necessary to provide* qualified handicapped persons with aid, *benefits*, or services that are *as effective as those provided to others*; (emphasis supplied) [17].

The regulations promulgated pursuant to Title II of the ADA convey the same concepts as Section 504 [18]. For purposes of this book, therefore, the obligations created by Section 504 and Title II can be treated as the same.

Overarching all is the further requirement that "[r]ecipients shall administer programs and activities in the most integrated setting appropriate to the needs of qualified handicapped persons" [19]. The "integration" mandate is critical for it mandates access to mainstream technology and digital content, when that access is feasible using the assistive technology normally used by persons with disabilities. For example, if a governmental agency uses a web site to announce mass transit schedules, that web site should be accessible to the blind. To require a blind person instead to call to get the schedule would not be an integrated setting. Thus, in *Martin v. Metro. Atlanta Rapid Transit Auth.*, the court found that since MARTA made schedule and route information available on its web site, it needed to do so in a fashion that would be accessible to blind users [20]. By contrast, if a college posts a picture of a human cell that identifies each of the various parts, nonvisual access might require a separate solution, such as a tactile graphic with Braille labels, but as a means to an integrated result—blind and sighted students alike having access to a biology class. Thus, a separate provision of services is to be eschewed except when necessary to provide equal access.

Inherent in such regulatory concepts as "equally effective communication" and "all the benefits" of a program or activity is independence and privacy, when those qualities are aspects of programs and activities. Thus, if nondisabled voters are afforded the opportunity to vote privately and independently, then a voting process that requires the disabled person to disclose her vote to another and rely on that third party to cast the ballot does not pass muster under this statute [21]. Discerning the difference between denominations of paper currency only with the assistance of others is unlawful when currency can be designed in different sizes or with tactile markings that enable a blind person to distinguish a $5 dollar bill from a $20. As the D.C. Court of Appeals explained in *American Council of the Blind v. Paulson*:

> *The visually impaired can hardly be "empower[ed] to maximize [their] employment, economic self-sufficiency, independence, and inclusion and integration into society," 29 U.S.C. §701(b)(1), if in everyday transactions they cannot use the paper currency that they possess without the assistance of third persons. Where the basic task of independently evaluating the worth of currency in excess of 99 cents is difficult or impossible, the visually impaired are forever relegated to depend on "the kindness of strangers" to shop for groceries, hire a taxi, or buy a newspaper or cup of coffee.* [22]

How these obligations not to discriminate are met clearly change with changes in technology. For example, at the time that the Rehabilitation Act of 1973 was enacted, government's choices for communicating with the public were limited to in-person meetings, mail, and telephone. For persons with mobility or transportation issues, meetings were difficult. Mail was of little use to persons with visual and certain neurological disabilities, among others. The telephone, unmodified, posed issues for

Deaf people. For each of these communications modalities, it was necessary to provide separate alternatives, such as recorded or Brailled communications for the blind or TTY for the Deaf people. These separate avenues were expensive, required additional ongoing administrative efforts, and usually involved significant delays. From the perspective of the disabled consumer, these accommodations were often hard to secure, of inferior quality, incomplete, and untimely.

Digital information, however, offers the promise of mainstream access: the same information to all, at the same time, through the same modality. Because digital code is not inherently audible, tactile, or visual, but must be converted to be delivered in one or more of those formats, and because hardware and software can be designed to respond to tactile (keyboard and mouse), auditory (voice), and physical (blink of an eye, breath into a straw) commands, it becomes possible for all information to be communicated to all via a single modality [23]. Digital communication of inherently audible information, such as speech, can be communicated through captioning, and inherently visual information, such as pictures, can be communicated through description or an image that can be downloaded and printed as a tactile graphic.

Thus, entities subject to 504 or Title II, when they design or acquire technology or convey digital content, must do so in a fashion that is universally accessible to the same degree to all without regard to disability. Web sites, interactive digital forms, voting machines, among others, are obvious examples of programs and activities that must be designed for universal accessibility. Less obvious but equally applicable examples would be laundry, vending, and cash machines on a university campus.

When an entity does not use digital technology for a particular function, the need for accessibility may require it to do so. For example, some colleges may require students with a manual or visual disability to fill out forms in a paper-print format by hand at a disability student services office in order to request accommodations. To fill out the form with assistance would sacrifice the disabled students' independence and privacy. Thus, the entity must provide an accessible digital form so that the person with a manual or visual disability can have meaningful independent access to the service provided to others. As most paper forms today are "born digital," that is, composed on a computer, this requirement is hardly onerous [24].

The legal limitations on these obligations are "undue hardship" and "fundamental alteration." Courts have rarely found the defense of "fundamental alteration" to apply. If the purpose of a pencil-and-paper test is to test the ability of the student to write legibly, then an electronic test would indeed be a fundamental alteration, but if the test is to determine the student's ability to do mathematics, then an electronic format does not fundamentally alter the nature of the activity.

Undue hardship as a defense refers to a financial or administrative burden. An example of an administrative burden could be an argument by an entity that a student could surreptitiously use the Internet or a calculator for the digital version of a math test or that an accessible format might lend itself to digital piracy of copyrighted information [25].

The regulatory guidance on the existence of an undue burden lists five nonexclusive factors for a court to consider, consisting of (i) the nature and net cost of the accommodation, (ii) the overall financial resources and number of persons employed at the facility involved and the effect on the expenses and resources of the facility, (iii) the overall financial resources and size of the covered entity, (iv) the type of operation or operations of the covered entity, including the composition, structure, and functions of the workforce of such an entity, and (v) the impact of the accommodation on the ability of other employees to perform their duties and the impact on the facility's ability to conduct business [26].

Undue financial burden will therefore usually be a difficult claim for public entities. The massive size of governmental resources and budgets compared to the relatively minor costs of making technology accessible will generally defeat such an argument. Since the legal obligation under these statutes precedes in time the technology acquisition decision, unlike the issue with buildings that may pre-date the ADA, the calculation of cost should focus on what additional cost would have attended the acquisition of accessible technology in the first instance and not the more expensive calculation of retrofitting inaccessible technology. Finally, any consideration of undue economic burden should take into account the cost savings from not administering a separate mode of providing the same program, benefits, and services. Nonetheless, one federal trial court granted a public entity summary judgment on the issue of undue hardship, looking at such issues as the amount the entity had budgeted for accommodations ($15,000) and measuring the cost of remediating the software, rather than the cost of being accessible at the outset. That case is on appeal [27].

PUBLIC COLLEGES: A CASE STUDY IN THE APPLICATION OF TITLE II AND 504 TO CHANGE THE BEHAVIOR OF TECH AND DIGITAL CONTENT VENDORS

Perhaps nowhere has tech become more thoroughly and rapidly embedded than in American education. The reasons for this trend are beyond the scope of this chapter; but, the competition to capture this market and, by implication, the students themselves as they move out of education, is fierce. Educational institutions, pressured by boards of regents, parents, students, and finances, have raced to be the first with the shiniest. Decision making with respect to procuring technology and content is dispersed and decentralized—the French Department decides whether to use Rosetta Stone, while the Finance Department picks the software that will tell students the state of their accounts, and the Chief Information Officer (CIO) selects the learning management software. Meanwhile, the administration, faculty, students, and campus organizations are all posting content to the institution's web site. Before the tech explosion, accessibility to academic content was a matter for the disability services offices, which were expected, for example, to make Braille books or provide readers to blind students. Accordingly, when tech decisions began to be made throughout the academy, it was without thought that these decisions would implicate accessibility in ways that could not be resolved by the disability services office alone. Because schools were not demanding accessibility in procuring educational technology and digital content, the vendors, in the rush to market, had no motivation to take the time to build in accessibility. Certainly, the universities were not paying attention to their own tech development. A 2008 study found that 97% of the home pages of 100 college web sites had significant accessibility barriers [28]. Thus, many students with disabilities, especially those with a sensory disability or manual dexterity issues, face more barriers to an equal opportunity to learn than they faced 15 or 20 years ago.

A sustained campaign by the disability community, involving litigation, education, lobbying, and picketing, coupled with governmental enforcement action is beginning to turn this tide. The effort began, in a sense, when a blind computer science graduate student named George Kerscher, frustrated that he had no accessible texts, created the first commercial e-books in 1988, distributing more than 750 titles over the next 3 years. He patiently waited for the sighted community to appreciate the virtues of these e-books so that there could be an explosion of accessible books.

A print book is inherently visual, so requiring it to be accessible in and of itself would have fundamentally altered its character. Not so a digital book, consisting of zeros and ones and which is not inherently visual, tactile or audible, but must be rendered to be available to one of those senses. However, the direct reach of the ADA and the Rehabilitation Act is to employers, public entities, public accommodations, and entities receiving federal funds. The CVAA had not yet been enacted. Accordingly, the reach of these statutes was more clearly to public institutions. It is against that legal background that the fight for access to information in books began to unfold.

In 2007, Amazon introduced the Kindle, by no means the first e-book reader, but the first to catch fire with the public. George Kerscher and the National Federation of the Blind (NFB) promptly met with the Kindle production team, explained the commercial applications of having the content talk and the marginal additional cost of having the menus talk—a further step that would have made the Kindle accessible to the blind and other persons with disabilities who needed text-to-speech to access the content. In February 2009, the Kindle 2 was introduced with a read-out-loud feature. However, on-screen navigation was not voiced and was therefore inaccessible to the blind. The Association of American Publishers and the Authors Guild sought to have Amazon terminate the read-out-loud feature, believing that it should receive additional payments if digital books were to be voiced as well as visually read. While a digital book that could speak its contents was no more a violation of copyright than a parent reading aloud to a child, the authors and publishers believed that, as a matter of contract, the "rights" to digitally voiced text could be sold separately.

Recognizing that access to digital books would be put beyond the reach of those with print disabilities, the National Federation of the Blind led the formation of the Reading Rights Coalition, composed of 32 nonprofits representing the print-disability community—including, among others, the blind, people with dyslexia and other learning disabilities, those with cerebral palsy, and those with upper spinal cord injuries. The Coalition worked on one hand to protect the inclusion of Text-to-Speech in the Kindle, while simultaneously trying to persuade Amazon to make its menus talk and thus make the device accessible. In addition to meeting with trade publishers and others, the Reading Rights Coalition held a picket of the Authors Guild at which a crowd of people with disabilities made news raising questions as to why the Authors Guild's authors did not want them to read their books.

In May 2009, Amazon announced the launch of its Kindle DX e-book reader, which it had designed for educational use. Because Amazon failed to include accessible navigational controls (talking menus), the device was inaccessible to the blind. Six colleges and universities simultaneously announced they would be deploying the Kindle DX during the 2009–2010 academic year. The NFB and the American Council of the Blind (ACB) filed a complaint in federal court against Arizona State University and filed complaints with the Departments of Justice and Education against the remaining schools (Pace University, Case Western Reserve University, Reed College, Princeton University, and the University of Virginia's Darden School of Business). These complaints alleged that by deploying the inaccessible Kindle, the colleges and universities violated their obligations under Titles II and III of the ADA to provide equal access to their services. While sighted students would benefit from the instant access, note taking, and other services of the Kindle, blind students would be left behind, forced to rely on separate methods of access that are significantly inferior to even the print textbook experience. The NFB, the ACB, and the Department of Justice secured settlements with these schools in which those schools agreed, after the end of that semester, not to deploy inaccessible e-book readers.

While those complaints were pending, other universities stepped forward to publicly pledge they would not adopt e-book technologies on their campus—including the Kindle—unless and until they were accessible. Those universities included Syracuse University, the University of Wisconsin, and the University of Illinois. On March 9, 2010, the Reading Rights Coalition, the Association of American Publishers, and the Authors Guild issued a joint statement, released on the White House blog, supporting mainstream accessibility when books are issued in formats other than print, such as e-books and audio books. Then on June 29, 2010, the Departments of Education and Justice issued the open letter to all college presidents discussed above.

Meanwhile, in September 2008, Apple signed an agreement with the Massachusetts Attorney General and the NFB to make iTunes U accessible to the blind by the end of 2008, a commitment that Apple met and then exceeded: making the iPhone 2 accessible and the iPad accessible from its inception. iBooks, unlike Kindle books, were fully accessible.

While representatives of the disability community began to speak at gatherings of university CIOs and others who might procure educational technology, the NFB in the late summer of 2008 secured congressional approval to establish a Commission on Accessible Instructional Material in Higher Education (AIM Commission), which ultimately issued a report in 2011 recommending that the Access Board establish standards for accessible instructional material and technology.

In 2009, the California State University System refused Blackboard Inc. permission to bid because Blackboard Learn was inaccessible. In so doing, CSU successfully caused Blackboard to focus on making its learning management software accessible. CSU's actions pointed the way to a potentially winning strategy: have the universities create a market demand for accessibility. The strategy, though, had a flaw: because the decision making to deploy accessible content and technology is so dispersed within the academic community, a commitment to accessibility requires the leadership of college presidents, whose agendas are generally formed by the size and imminence of impending crises and emergencies.

Litigation (and the potential for litigation) is one way to overcome that obstacle and get on the agenda of college presidents. In 2011, two blind students, with the assistance of the NFB, sued Florida State University (FSU) to secure their right to accessible math content and software [29]. In March 2012, the case settled, requiring, among other things, FSU's Mathematics Department to procure only accessible digital technology and instructional materials. The settlement required FSU to remove accessibility barriers so that blind students could access the content of the curriculum in an equally effective and integrated manner alongside their sighted peers in courses required for their majors.

In the meantime, Penn State University entered into a voluntary resolution agreement with the NFB that was truly global in scope, requiring, among other things, that Penn State conduct an audit of all of its technology, develop a corrective action plan, require accessibility in procurement of new technology, and remediate all of its web sites [30]. Similarly structured settlements have followed between the Department of Education and (1) the University of Montana, (2) the South Carolina Technical College System, (3) the University of Cincinnati, and (4) Youngstown State University, as well as one between the Department of Justice and Louisiana Tech University that requires accessible digital content as well as accessible instructional technology [31–35]. The Montana and Louisiana Tech settlements are described in greater detail in Chapter 9. The National Federation of the Blind also reached an accessibility agreement with Maricopa Community College [36]. In February 2015, the National Association of the Deaf sued Harvard University and the Massachusetts Institute of Technology for their failure to caption MOOCs (Massive Open Online Courses). The prominence of these defendants may prompt other colleges and universities to address accessibility in a pro-active and systematic way. On April 1, 2015, the Department of Justice reached a settlement with EdX, Inc., the purveyor of hundreds of MOOCs that requires EdX to make its web site and learning platform accessible and to give guidance to content creators on accessible authoring tools and methods [37].

There are indications that these activities are encouraging action by other universities to address accessibility pro-actively. The web pages of Oregon State University, George Mason University, Temple University, North Carolina State University, and Ohio State University have addressed accessibility from the multiple perspectives of procurement, internal training, and best practices. Some of these actions are described in greater detail in Chapter 9. The University of Colorado, Boulder campus, and Penn State University are among those now posting accessibility information about educational software, such as Turnitin [38,39]. In the meantime, professional organizations like the American Library Association and the Association of Research Libraries are urging their members to "buy accessible" and giving guidance to college libraries on how to do so [40].

At the same time, content and educational tech producers are beginning to address accessibility. For example, Pearson and Elsevier, leading academic publishers, have posted accessibility policies [41,42]. Most interesting is sales information that McGraw-Hill has distributed to its sales staff that might best be summarized as, "we are working on accessibility, but our competitors aren't any better" [43]. Certain purveyors of academic digital books, notably Baker & Taylor and CourseSmart, have built a catalog of accessible digital books for use by post-secondary students. The International Digital Publishing Forum has established a set of standards for accessible digital books, ePub3, and a number of textbook publishers are beginning to focus on meeting ePub3 standards for new digital books.

Some of the more expensive Amazon products, like the Kindle Fire, now have menus that the blind can navigate, and Kindle books can be read, after a fashion, by the blind on Apple products, using the iOS app for Kindle books. Unfortunately, even there the navigation is so limited that a disabled student can, in effect, only read the book from beginning to end. Repeating a sentence or a paragraph or jumping to the next paragraph or back a page is not possible for a blind reader of a Kindle book, nor is the ability to change the verbosity to hear a particular word letter-by-letter. Neither endnotes or footnotes are accessible in a Kindle book. And despite the efforts by the Department of Justice Civil Rights Division, the Office of Civil Rights of the Department of Education and disability advocacy organizations, some post-secondary institutions continue to make use of Kindles and Kindle books. The University of Massachusetts, Amherst campus, announced that Amazon will be its exclusive purveyor of books and other campus items, starting in the fall of 2015 [44,45]. If not derailed, this will be sad news for students with disabilities at that institution.

Legislation with bipartisan support that has been introduced in both houses of the U.S. Congress, called the TEACH Act, would authorize the Access Board to set accessibility standards for both digital educational content and educational technology, while the State of Tennessee has passed a similar bill requiring a commission to make recommendations as to standards.

In conclusion, the interim report is that some colleges and universities are hearing that "attention must be paid" and responding, in places, and some digital instructional tech and content vendors are starting to address accessibility. But the current lot of a student who needs screen access or voice command software to access digital content and software or captioning to access videos is still a nightmare of a maze with no exits. The strategy engaged in by disability rights groups has shown promising results, but the outcome of the battle for access is not yet assured.

TITLE III OF THE ADA—PLACES OF PUBLIC ACCOMMODATION

Title III of the ADA addresses disability discrimination by places of public accommodation, a broad term that covers lodging and food establishments, exhibition, entertainment and other places the public gathers, retail establishments, professional offices, transit stations, museums, libraries, zoos, parks, private schools, day care, senior citizen and homeless centers, food banks, adoption agencies, golf courses, health spas, and other places for exercise or recreation [46].

These places of public accommodation shall not discriminate in the "full and equal enjoyment" of the "goods, services, facilities, privileges, advantages, or accommodations" that they offer [47]. This includes the denial of participation in, or an unequal benefit from, that which the public accommodation offers [48]. A separate benefit is permitted only if it is necessary to provide an opportunity equal to, and as effective as, that provided to those without a disability [49]. The public accommodation must afford its offerings in the most integrated setting appropriate to the needs of the individual and must refrain from creating eligibility criteria that screen out persons with disabilities [50,51]. The public accommodation has affirmative obligations to modify policies and procedures and to take such steps as may be necessary to ensure that no one is treated differently because of the absence of auxiliary aids and services, unless such steps would fundamentally alter the nature of the offerings of the public accommodation or result in an undue burden [52].

To what in the digital world does this apply? An ATM is a service offered by a bank, which is, in turn, a place of public accommodation. Thus, ATMs must be accessible to persons with disabilities, a conclusion that mandates not only height and depth requirements to be usable by persons using wheelchairs, but that dynamic information presented visually must be presented audibly to those who cannot see. Movies must be offered by movie theaters so that Deaf patrons can access the dialog [53].

The more critical questions are (1) whether and under what circumstances does Title III apply to web sites; and (2) if some web sites are public accommodations, what is required of the services and goods offered on those web sites?

When Title III was enacted, the Internet, as we know it, did not exist. But Congress made clear "that the types of accommodations and services provided to individuals with disabilities, under all of the titles of this bill, should keep pace with the rapidly changing technology of the times" [54]. Thus, that the Internet was not explicitly mentioned in Title III is not an impediment to that section reaching web sites.

The first official pronouncement on the applicability of Title III to the Internet came in a September 9, 1996, letter from Deval Patrick, then the Assistant Attorney General in charge of the Civil Rights Division at the Department of Justice, to Senator Harkin, responding to a constituent inquiry about the requirement that places of public accommodation make their web pages accessible to persons with visual disabilities. Mr. Patrick responded as follows:

> *Covered entities under the ADA are required to provide effective communication, regardless of whether they generally communicate through print media, audio media, or computerized media such as the Internet. Covered entities that use the Internet for communications regarding their programs, goods, or services must be prepared to offer those communications through accessible means as well.* [55]

The Department of Justice here was expressing an unambiguous view that "off-site" services of a covered entity, such as a web site of a business with a physical establishment, are covered by Title III of the ADA. It did not, however, address whether the web site of a business whose interaction with consumers takes place entirely outside of a physical establishment is a covered entity.

In *Carparts Distribution Ctr. v. Automotive Wholesaler's Ass'n*, the First Circuit Court of Appeals faced the question of whether a health benefit plan that limited lifetime benefits for insureds with AIDS could violate Title III. Although the court did not ultimately answer that question, it held squarely that places of public accommodation under Title III are not "limited to actual physical structures" [56]. The court declined to reach the next issue: whether the ADA merely requires that a public accommodation offer a good or service to all without regard to disability or whether the good or service must be modified to accommodate a person with a disability.

Thereafter, sitting *en banc*, the entire panel of active judges of the Sixth Circuit held that Title III of the ADA applies only to physical places of public accommodation, in a case addressing whether a long-term disability insurance plan offered through an employer could limit benefits for persons with mental illness differently from those with physical disabilities [57].

The Seventh Circuit was the next to be heard, again in the context of an insurance company whose medical insurance capped benefits for insureds with AIDS. It accepted the view that discrimination can be "off-site," and from an establishment that does not have a physical location for interacting with consumers, but held that Title III of the ADA does not require a place of public accommodation to alter its inventory of goods or services to be accessible and therefore did not prohibit insurance policies whose terms discriminated against certain disabilities [58].

That same year, the Second Circuit concluded in a similar insurance context that the ADA was meant to ensure more than physical access, and that a place of business cannot offer a product that discriminates on the basis of disability [59].

In 1999, the NFB sued AOL, Inc. in an effort to secure a judicial determination that a web portal could be a place of public accommodation and that the services of that portal must be altered to be accessible to the blind. However, that case settled in July 2000 without a judicial determination and with AOL agreeing to make its services accessible.

The next year, the Ninth Circuit weighed in, holding that while an insurance agency is a place of public accommodation, an insurance company is not, because there is no disparity between what the physical place of public accommodation offers disabled and nondisabled patrons [60]. Subsequently, in the *Harkins Amusement* case, the Ninth Circuit noted that its earlier holding in *Weyer*, that a place of public accommodation does not need to alter its goods or services, does not apply when the inaccessibility stems from a public accommodation's failure to provide auxiliary aids and services [53].

The Eleventh Circuit Court has weighed in next. In *Rendon v. Valleycrest Productions, Ltd.*, the telephonic auditions for a game show discriminated against Deaf people and those with upper mobility impairments [61]. The Eleventh Circuit noted that the show took place in a studio, a physical place of public accommodation, and held that the auditions, though "off-site," were nonetheless discriminatory and violated Title III. In two unpublished opinions, *Earll v. eBay, Inc., and Cullen v. Netflix*, a panel of the Ninth Circuit concluded that its earlier decision in *Weyer* required it to conclude that e-commerce is not covered by Title III of the ADA [62,63].

These cases make clear that to hold web sites, and goods and services offered on web sites, subject to Title III, disability advocates must address three issues: (1) that Title III applies to virtual places of public accommodations, that is, companies that have no physical retail spaces; (2) that companies with physical retail spaces cannot discriminate in the provision of "off-site" services, and (3) that companies can be required to modify their web sites, and the software they offer, to be accessible. The geographic determination of where a case is brought, then, greatly affects the answers to these questions.

The outcome of three cases addressing the Internet shows the impact of these questions. In *National Federation of the Blind v. Target Corp.*, a trial court in the Ninth Circuit held that Target's web site was covered by Title III as an off-site service of the physical stores, but that those aspects of the web site that do not affect the enjoyment of goods and services in Target stores are not covered by the ADA [64]. Thus, a page showing products sold in Target stores or enabling the ordering from its pharmacy online would be covered, but not a page providing for online payment of a good to be delivered from a warehouse to the consumer. The court rejected Target's claim that making a web site accessible was a fundamental alteration and held that providing the information on a web site by alternative means would require Target to show that the alternative means was equally effective [64]. However, the District Court also found that California's Unruh Act and Disabled Persons Act gave disabled persons the right to access to web sites without regard to whether there was also a physical place of public accommodation [65]. Although Target could have undoubtedly created a separate web site for California residents, the effect of the suit was to make the web site accessible throughout the United States.

More straightforward, a trial court in the First Circuit, following the precedent of *Carparts*, held in *Nat'l Ass'n of the Deaf v. Netflix*, that Netflix's video streaming web site "Watch Instantly," is a place of public accommodation and its services must be modified to provide Closed Captioning for all of its content [66]. On March 19, 2015, the U.S. District Court in Vermont held that Title III of the ADA applied to Scribd, an online library, reasoning that since it offered the services of a public accommodation, the nature of the place from which the services were offered did not affect the scope of the statute [67].

The view of the First, Seventh and Second Circuits that focuses on whether the entity is functioning as a public accommodation is better policy and better law. Without access to the Internet and the services it offers, persons with disabilities will not have equal access to information, to services, cultural opportunities, and social interaction available to the rest of society. That denial relegates those who are excluded to second-class citizenship and ensures that the social integration envisioned by the ADA cannot occur. "[W]hile the Internet is only about 25 years old, 87% of American adults now use the Web. The breadth of this usage—combined with the fact that disabilities are much less apparent online—makes the Internet a unique and prominent venue for removing biases from society; it allows people to interact who might not otherwise communicate offline" [68].

If the law has remained cloudy, it is in part because entities who might argue the degree to which they are subject to Title III have chosen instead to reach settlement agreements to make their web sites and services accessible, rather than having a court decide the issue. This is in part because companies have discovered that compliance costs less than lawsuits and increases market share. According to one report, retrofitting a web site to be accessible could be 10% of web site costs, but phasing in accessibility as the web site is upgraded only adds 1–3% to costs [68]. And, of course, there are public relations costs associated with being an entity that discriminates against those with disabilities.

The recent consent decree between the Department of Justice and the NFB on one hand, and H&R Block on the other, to make both its web site and its online tax filing accessible, sets forth in considerable detail both what and how H&R Block is to become accessible without any required nexus to H&R Block stores [69]. Other cyber entities that have entered into agreements to make their web sites accessible include Peapod (with the Department of Justice), eBay, Monster.com (with the Massachusetts Attorney General and NFB), Amazon, Ticketmaster, Travelocity, Wellpoint, and Charles Schwab [70–75]. Please see Chapter 9 addressing compliance monitoring of such agreements.

Accessibility is not yet the norm on the Internet. Universal accessibility will require not only continued legal advocacy, but the inclusion of accessibility in the curricula for computer scientists and engineers, information technology and HCI graduates, in company policies requiring usability testing and affirmative determinations of accessibility before release, and in employee accountability and visibility.

EMPLOYMENT—TITLE I OF THE ADA AND SECTION 504 OF THE REHABILITATION ACT

Entities with more than 15 employees (ADA Title I) and those receiving federal financial assistance (Section 504 of the Rehabilitation Act) shall not discriminate against their employees on the basis of disabilities. An individual, who with or without reasonable accommodation, can perform the essential functions of the job must be reasonably accommodated and may not be disparately treated because of disability.

Title I covers all aspects of employment from job application procedures through hiring, promotion, compensation, job training, and the like. The statute identifies seven forms of discrimination, several of which are most pertinent to the subject at hand: (1) classifying an employee with a disability in a way that adversely affects his opportunities; (2) using a subcontractor, like an employment agency, that discriminates; (3) using standards, criteria, or methods of administration that discriminate or perpetuate discrimination; (4) failing to make a reasonable accommodation; or (5) using qualification standards, employment tests, or other selection criteria that tend to screen out a class of individuals with disabilities, unless those criteria can be shown to be job-related [76].

Most litigation to date has come up in the context of claims alleging a failure to make a reasonable accommodation. Determining what is a reasonable accommodation is an interactive process between an employer and an employee. An immediate implication of a failure-to-reasonably-accommodate standard is that this standard is ill-suited to create broad-scale change in access to workplace technology. Whether, for example, it is reasonable to have an employee with a manual impairment rely on a fellow employee to enter personal data into HR software or whether the software must be remediated to work with voice command software is not a unitary answer, but will depend on the size and finances of the company, whether the employee had the manual impairment when the software was acquired, and whether there was alternative software that was accessible. If providing an accommodation would cause an undue hardship, the employer is relieved altogether from meeting this requirement.

The "disparate treatment/disparate impact" prong of disability discrimination offers more opportunity for the advocate, since inaccessible online job applications and assessment testing are clearly vulnerable as locking the door to those who are denied access. Yet despite the existence of many inaccessible online job applications posted by major employers, little has been done to challenge inaccessibility in this area [77].

With respect to workplace technology, there are hints, few and far between, that the courts may be receptive. In *Cathcart v. Flagstar Corp.*, the Court upheld a jury verdict that an employer had denied a position to the plaintiff because her disability made her physically unable to use a computer [78]. And in *EEOC v. Echostar Communications Corp.*, the court approved a settlement that required the employer to evaluate the feasibility of making the software used by its customer service representatives accessible with screen access software [79].

The way forward for legal advocates is to attack first inaccessible online job applications and inaccessible assessment testing, while urging the major vendors of HR, accounting, and other cross-industry software to make their software accessible. It may be that with governmental entities that must make their digital offerings accessible to the public, an argument could be framed that "equally effective communication" creates a floor that applies as well to the entity's employees. Nonetheless, although most ADA cases are Title I cases, the structure of its requirements makes it the least suitable for broad-scale changes in accessible technology.

SECTION 508 OF THE REHABILITATION ACT—PROCUREMENT OF ACCESSIBLE TECHNOLOGY BY THE U.S. GOVERNMENT

Enacted in 1998, Section 508 of the Rehabilitation Act, 29 U.S.C. § 794d, ostensibly requires, since the year 2000, that the executive agencies of the federal government, when developing, procuring, maintaining, and using electronic and information technology, to ensure that this technology is accessible to employees and members of the general public who have disabilities [80]. When accessibility would be unduly burdensome, the federal government must offer an alternative means. The legislation directed the Access Board to define the technical and functional performance criteria for accessible electronic and information technology. In turn, the Federal Acquisition Regulatory Council was directed to revise procurement regulations to incorporate the Access Board standards. National security systems are exempt. Beginning in March 1999, and every 2 years thereafter, each agency was to evaluate the accessibility of their technology and, beginning in August 2001, the Attorney General was to issue biennial reports on compliance with Section 508. Finally, someone aggrieved by a violation of Section 508 could file a complaint about technology procured by the federal government 6 months after the issuance of the Access Board standards.

The potential transformative impact of Section 508 was enormous. Because so many tech vendors that sell to the federal government also sell to state and local governments and private enterprises, accessible technology would quickly have spread beyond federal government procurement. Had Section 508 been followed, therefore, accessible workplace technology and accessible public-facing technology would have quickly become the default. Knowledge about how to be accessible and an insistence on accessible product design would have become universal.

Sadly, Section 508 has been staggeringly ineffectual. By 2013, federal agencies, pursuant to GSA's designation of Google Apps as a scheduled item (one, like printers, that can be used without a separate procurement procedure), were implementing inaccessible mail and calendar applications as well Google Docs, the inaccessible collaborative document editing software in the government workplace, thereby shutting out all government employees who must use voice command or screen access technology. In 2014 the Departments of Homeland Security and Labor acquired new telephones with "soft buttons" whose changing functions are reflected only visually on a dynamic screen. These replaced phones that were accessible. Procurement officers write specifications to ensure that only one technology, which is not accessible, is selected. A survey of the home pages of 100 governmental web sites found that 97 had significant barriers [81]. The Department of Justice, which is supposed to issue biennial reports on the government's compliance, issued no reports between 2001 and 2011, but finally issued a report in 2012. The next report should have been issued in 2014, but it was not. The Access Board, recognizing that the original 508 standards are obsolete and, indeed, useless, began the process of issuing new regulations in July 2006. The comment period for the latest draft regulations ended in March 2012, but it was not until February 2015 that the Board announced the issuance of a Notice of Proposed Rulemaking with the text of a proposed rule. The Section 508 regulations are further addressed in Chapter 7 and the use of FOIA requests relating to Section 508 in Chapter 9. Not to be left out, the Federal Circuit, faced with a bid protest by an accessible but unsuccessful contractor to an award to provide Internet job listings for federal employees, held that the federal government can accept a bid from a contractor that says it is "508-compliant with exceptions" even when those exceptions swallow the compliance [82]. Perhaps the attorneys who advise the vendors of Google Apps and the new inaccessible federal phone system on government contracting brought this statute-sized loophole to GSA's attention.

The first challenges by government employees to inaccessible workplace technology are just beginning to make their way through the judicial system. This may, at first blush, seem surprising with a statute more than a decade old. However, given the employment picture for persons with disabilities and the perceived risk that suing your boss will get you fired or make your life a nightmare, it is less surprising that few disabled federal employees file complaints. The response of the Department of Justice to Section 508 complaints has been to raise a host of seemingly frivolous arguments. With respect to government web sites, Justice has asserted on behalf of the Small Business Administration that because the SBA's web site was developed inhouse, it is excluded by the statutory language that "[t]his subsection shall apply only to ... technology that is *procured* by a Federal department or agency not less than 6 months [after the Access Board standards go into effect]" [83]. That language, of course, was only intended to grandfather in technology in use when the standards were promulgated, not to limit the scope of the statute only to procured technology. Equally frivolous, with respect to complaints by a federal employee (even though the statute gives "any individual with a disability" the right to use the courts as permitted by Section 504 of the Rehabilitation Act), the Department of Justice insists that procurement decisions claimed to be in violation of Section 508 can only be pursued under the very limited and deferential review permitted by the Administrative Procedure Act.

The last chapter on Section 508 has not yet been written, but the disability advocacy community needs to support those employees willing to complain, draw Congress's attention to the executive branch's failures, and attract public support for such obvious and common sense items as accessible phones.

THE CHAFEE AMENDMENT TO THE COPYRIGHT ACT

In 1996, Congress amended the Copyright Act to provide that it would not be copyright infringement for a nonprofit organization or a governmental agency that has a primary mission to provide specialized services relating to training, education, or adaptive reading or information access needs of blind or other persons with disabilities to make and distribute previously published nondramatic copyrighted literary works in specialized formats exclusively for the use by the blind and certain other persons with disabilities [84]. This statute, called the Chafee Amendment, after its sponsor, Senator John H. Chafee, presented a compromise agreed upon by the NFB and the Association of American Publishers. The statute explicitly included "digital formats" in the definition of "specialized formats" [85].

For most of its existence, the Chafee Amendment resulted in small-scale but important creation and distribution of limited accessible books for borrowing, principally through the National Library Service of the Library of Congress, Learning Ally (formerly Recording for the Blind and Dyslexic), and Bookshare. The total number of titles available through these sources in 2012 amounted to less than 200,000 books—less than the number published annually in the United States.

In 2004, Google announced that it would partner with the University of Michigan to make a digital copy of its library. Soon thereafter, Google announced partnerships with other universities, amounting today to more than 50, to do the same. A feature of each of these partnerships has been that the university gets a digital copy of its collection to use in accordance with US copyright law.

In 2005, after an initial rebuff from Google, the NFB initiated dialogs with Google's university partners to secure their support in requiring Google to provide the libraries with digital scans that would be accessible to persons with disabilities. This effort was successful, and in 2008, the University of Michigan completed the infrastructure to make the digital scans available to blind students and faculty.

Michigan allowed nondisabled scholars associated with the university to do data mining and searches, activities whose results did not expose expressive material. By contrast, a student or faculty member with a disability making it difficult for that individual to access printed text independently is given a password that allows access to more than 10 million titles.

In 2011, the Authors Guild sued some of the universities partnering with Google in a case called *Authors Guild v. HathiTrust*, alleging that these activities constituted copyright infringement on a massive scale. The NFB and several blind students and faculty intervened as defendants, that is, on the side of the universities, arguing that making the digital library available to blind students and faculty was mandated by the ADA's provisions of equal access and fair use under the Copyright Act and authorized by the Chafee Amendment. The trial judge agreed on all counts, noting that "academic participation by print-disabled students has been revolutionized" by Google's partnership with the libraries [86]. In June 2014, the Second Circuit affirmed that the "fair use" doctrine of copyright law allows the making of accessible digital copies of print books for persons with print disabilities without the permission of the copyright holder [87]. In light of its fair use ruling, the court found no reason to address the scope of the Chafee Amendment. The Second Circuit's opinion opens the way for the storehouse of the collected intellectual capital available in the United States to be open to those with print disabilities and to make print disabilities irrelevant to the conduct of academic research. This would allow those with print disabilities to participate fully in the educational, literary, cultural, and intellectual activities in the United States.

In the summer of 2013, the World Intellectual Property Organization (WIPO) proposed a treaty that would, in essence, make the provisions of the Chafee Amendment law in signatory countries and allow for international sharing of accessible books to persons with disabilities throughout the world the Marrakesh Treaty to Facilitate Access to Published Works for Persons Who Are Blind, Visually Impaired, or Otherwise Print Disabled. The Marrakesh Treaty is addressed in the chapter on international law.

STATE LAWS APPLICABLE TO ACCESSIBLE TECHNOLOGY

Many states have "little ADAs" and some have "little 508s," the latter requiring states to buy accessible technology. In *Hartzell v. Arkansas*, based on a state equivalent to Section 508, a trial court in Little Rock in 2003 preliminarily enjoined the state from continuing to install SAP's inaccessible enterprise resource planning software until it had been made accessible to blind state employees [88]. But many little 508s do not authorize private lawsuits for violations.

By far, the most expansive state law is that of Massachusetts. The Massachusetts Equal Rights Act (MERA), Mass. Gen. Laws ch. 93, § 103, provides as follows: "No otherwise qualified handicapped individual shall, solely by reason of his handicap, be excluded from the participation in, denied the benefits of, or be subject to discrimination under any program or activity within the commonwealth" (MA CONST

Amend. Art. 114). "Any program or activity within the commonwealth," appears to go far further than places of public accommodation, public entities, and entities receiving public funding. Thus, this may be a vehicle by which tech vendors offering programs or activities in Massachusetts can be held to account. The joint effort by the NFB and the Massachusetts Attorney General in 2008, involving Apple, was premised on the idea that iTunes U was a program or activity conducted by Apple in that state, but the reach of the statute was not judicially tested.

California's Unruh Act, Cal. Civ. Code §§ 51(f), 54.1(d) forbids "business establishments of every kind whatsoever" from discriminating against persons with disabilities in the full and equal enjoyment of an establishment's "accommodations, advantages, facilities, privileges, or services." A business establishment need not interact with the public from a place of public accommodation, much less be a public accommodation. Thus, this statute reaches business outside the scope of the ADA. Accordingly, in *NFB v. Target, Inc.* [89] the court held that, unlike the ADA, which applied only to those aspects of target.com that had a nexus to the physical Target stores, the Unruh Act required target.com in its entirety to be accessible [65]. Since that decision, other case law has developed that requires that discrimination reachable by Unruh, but not by the ADA, must be shown to be intentional discrimination.

California also has a Disabled Persons Act, Cal. Civ. Code 51(d), that applies to public accommodations. In *Target*, the court concluded that this act, unlike Title III of the ADA, applied to virtual public accommodations, like a retail web site [65].

The New Jersey Law Against Discrimination (NJLAD), in addition to reaching discrimination against persons with disabilities in a range of activities, prohibits aiding and abetting an act of discrimination [90]. The New Jersey courts have given this provision a broad reading, raising the possibility, for example, that a tech vendor that licensed inaccessible technology to an educational institution in the state might have accessory liability.

SUMMARY

When law and technology are coupled, the results can mark major improvements in the lives of those with disabilities. The tools at hand in the United States for lawsuits and the possibility of lawsuits are valuable tools, but cannot accomplish the task alone. All of the tools available to disability rights advocates, from education to legislation to street demonstrations, must be used if equal access to digital information and technology is to be achieved.

REFERENCES

[1] *Tennessee v. Lane,* 541 U.S. 509, 536; 2004.
[2] Rehabilitation Act of 1973, 29 U.S.C. § 701 *et seq.*
[3] Americans with Disabilities Act, 42 U.S.C. § 12101 *et seq.*
[4] Air Carrier Access Act, 49 U.S.C. § 41705 *et seq.*

[5] Education for All Handicapped Children Act, 20 U.S.C. § 1400 *et seq.*

[6] Fair Housing Act Amendments of 1988, 42 U.S.C. § 3601 *et seq.*

[7] Help America Vote Act, 42 U.S.C. § 15301 *et seq.*

[8] Architectural Barriers Act, 42 U.S.C. § 4151 *et seq.*

[9] US Department of Education. Joint "Dear Colleague" letter: electronic book readers. Available at: http://www2.ed.gov/about/offices/list/ocr/letters/colleague-20100629.pdf; 2010.

[10] US Department of Education. Resolution agreement South Carolina technical college system: accessibility of websites. Available at: http://www2.ed.gov/policy/gen/leg/foia/south-carolina-letter.pdf; 2013.

[11] US Department of Justice. Statement of interest of the USA, *New v. Lucky Brand Dungarees Store, Inc.*: Point of Sale Machines (S.D. Fl. 14-cv-20574). Available at: http://www.ada.gov/briefs/lucky_brand_soi.pdf; 2014, April 10.

[12] *K.M. v. Tustin Unified Sch. Dist.*, 725 F.3d 1088, 1097–98 (9th Cir. 2013).

[13] US Department of Justice. Joint "Dear Colleague" letter: equally effective communication. Available at: http://www2.ed.gov/about/offices/list/ocr/letters/colleague-effective-communication-201411.pdf; 2014, Nov. 12.

[14] 29 U.S.C. § 794.

[15] 42 U.S.C. § 12132.

[16] 28 C.F.R. § 35.164.

[17] 28 C.F.R. § 41.51(b).

[18] 28 C.F.R. § 35.130.

[19] 28 C.F.R. § 41.51(d).

[20] *Martin v. Metro. Atlanta Rapid Transit Auth.*, 225 F. Supp. 2d 1362 (N.D. Ga. 2002).

[21] *Nat'l Fed'n of the Blind v. Lamone*, 2014 WL 4388342 (D. Md. 9/4/14).

[22] *Am. Council of the Blind v. Paulson*, 525 F. 3d 1256, 1269 (D.C. Cir. 2008).

[23] Blanck P. The struggle for web eQuality by persons with cognitive disabilities. Behav Sci Law 2014;32:4–32.

[24] *Brookhart v. Ill. State Bd. of Educ.*, 697 F. 2d 179 (7th Cir. 1983).

[25] *Jones v. Nat'l Conf. of Bar Exam'rs*, 801 F. Supp. 2d 270, 290 (D. Vt. 2011).

[26] 29 C.F.R. § 1630.2(p)(2)(i–v).

[27] *Reyazuddin v. Montgomery Cnty.*, 7 F. Supp. 3d 526 (D. Md. 2014).

[28] Project GOALS Evaluates 100 Pages in Higher Education for Accessibility Against Section 508 Standard, NCDAE Newsletter, April 2008. Available at: http://www.ncdae.org/resources/archives/newsletter/april2008/#goals.

[29] *Toth v. Florida State University*, No. 11-cv-00317 (N.D. Fla., 6/29/2011).

[30] US Department of Education. Settlement agreement with the National Federation of the Blind and Pennsylvania State University (No. 03–11–2020). Available at: http://accessibility.psu.edu/nfbpsusettlement; 2011, September 27.

[31] US Department of Education. Settlement agreement with the University of Montana: Inaccessible Electronic and Information Technology (No. 03–11–2020). Available at: http://www.umt.edu/accessibility/docs/FinalResolutionAgreement.pdf; 2012.

[32] US Department of Education. Settlement agreement with the South Carolina Technical Community College: Accessibility of Website (No. 11–11–6002). Available at: http://www2.ed.gov/about/offices/list/ocr/docs/investigations/11116002-b.pdf; 2013.

[33] US Department of Education. Settlement agreement with the University of Cincinnati: Accessibility of Website (No. 15–13–6001). Available at: http://www2.ed.gov/documents/press-releases/university-cincinnati-agreement.pdf; 2014.

[34] US Department of Education. Settlement agreement with Youngstown State University: Accessibility of Website (No. 15–13–6002). Available at: http://www2.ed.gov/documents/press-releases/youngstown-state-university-agreement.pdf; 2014.

[35] US Department of Justice. Settlement Agreement with Louisiana Tech University: Inaccessible Internet Based Applications (DJ 204-33-116). Available at: http://www.ada.gov/louisiana-tech.htm; 2013.

[36] National Federation of the Blind. Settlement with Maricopa Community College and Mesa Community College for procurement and deployment of accessible electronic and information technology. Available at: https://nfb.org/national-federation-blind-and-maricopa-community-college-district-resolve-litigation; 2014.

[37] US Department of Justice. Settlement Agreement with EdX. Available at: http://www.ada.gov/edx_sa.htm; 2015.

[38] University of Colorado Boulder. Turnitin Accessibility webpage. Available at: http://www.colorado.edu/oit/services/teaching-learning-tools/desire2learn-d2l/help/instructor-support/dropbox/turnitin-accessibility; 2015, April 14.

[39] Penn State University. Accessibility and Usability at Penn State. Available at: http://accessibility.psu.edu/turnitin; 2014.

[40] Association of Research Libraries. Resolution "Purchasing of Accessible Electronic Resources Resolution," adopted July 15, 2009; ARL Accessibility Toolkit. Available at: http://accessibility.arl.org/; 2009.

[41] Elsevier.com. Accessibility policy. Available at: http://www.elsevier.com/about/policies/accessibility-policy; 2015.

[42] Pearson Higher Education. Accessibility statement. Available at: http://www.pearsonhighered.com/educator/accessibility/index.page; 2015.

[43] McGraw-Hill. McGraw-Hill Web Accessibility Compliance Tool Kit. Available at: http://s3.amazonaws.com/StraighterLine/Docs/ADAWebAccessibilityToolKit_M   arch2012.pdf; 2015.

[44] UMassAmherst News & Media Relations. UMass Amherst Collaborates with Amazon.com to Create Virtual Bookstore. Available at: http://www.umass.edu/newsoffice/article/umass-amherst-collaborates-amazoncom; 2015, January 13.

[45] Adams D. Amazon to take over textbook sales at UMass Amherst, The Boston Globe. Available at: http://www.bostonglobe.com/business/2015/01/13/amazon-take-over-textbook-sales-umass-amherst/efshTa9LTGAvsErN5iepOJ/story.html; January 13, 2015.

[46] 42 U.S.C. § 12181.

[47] 42 U.S.C. § 12182(a).

[48] 42 U.S.C. § 12182(b)(1)(A)(i)–(ii).

[49] 42 U.S.C. § 12182(b)(1)(A)(iii).

[50] 42 U.S.C. § 12182(b)(1)(B).

[51] 42 U.S.C. §12182(b)(2)(A)(i).

[52] 42 U.S.C. § 12182(b)(2)(A)(ii)–(iii).

[53] *Goddard v. Harkins Amusement Enter.*, 603 F. 3d 666, 672 (9th Cir. 2010).

[54] H.R. Rep. No. 101–485(11), at 108 (1990), reprinted in 1990 U.S.C.C.A.N. 303, 391.

[55] US Department of Justice. Letter to Senator Tom Harkin from Assistant Attorney General Deval Patrick. Available at: http://www.justice.gov/crt/foia/readingroom/frequent_requests/ada_tal/tal712.txt; 1996.

[56] *Carparts Distrib. Ctr. v. Auto. Wholesale Ass'n*, 37 F. 3d 12, 19 (1st Cir. 1994).

[57] *Parker v. Metro. Life Ins. Co.*, 121 F. 3d 1006, 1014 (6th Cir. 1997).

[58] *Doe v. Mut. of Omaha Ins. Co.*, 179 F. 3d 557 (7th Cir. 1999).

[59] *Palozzi v. Allstate Life Ins. Co.*, 198 F. 3d 28, 32–33 (2nd Cir. 1999).

[60] *Weyer v. 20th Century Fox Film Corp.*, 198 F. 3d 1104 (9th Cir. 2000).

[61] *Rendon v. Valleycrest Prods, Ltd.*, 294 F. 3d 1279 (11th Cir. 2002).

[62] *Earll v. Ebay, Inc.*, 2015 U.S. App. LEXIS 5256 (April 1, 2015).

[63] *Cullen v. Netflix, Inc.*, 2015 U.S. App. LEXIS 5257 (April 1, 2015).

[64] *Nat'l Fed'n of the Blind v. Target Corp.*, 452 F. Supp. 2d 946, 953–54, 955–56 (N.D. Cal. 2006).

[65] *Nat'l Fed'n of the Blind v. Target Corp.*, 582 F. Supp. 2d 1185, 1196–99 (N.D. Cal. 2007).

[66] *Nat'l Ass'n of the Deaf v. Netflix, Inc.*, 869 F. Supp. 2d 196 (D. Mass. 2012).

[67] *Nat'l Fed'n of the Blind v. Scrib'd, Inc.*, 2015 WL 1263336 (D. Vt. 2015).

[68] Areheart B, Stein M. Integrating the Internet, George Washington Law Review, Vol. 83, 2015, n. 14. Available at: http://papers.ssrn.com/sol3/papers.cfm?abstract_id=2420510; 2014, April 4.

[69] US Department of Justice. Settlement agreement with National Federation of the Blind and H&R Block: inaccessible websites and mobile applications. Available at: http://www.ada.gov/hrb-cd.htm; 2014, March 25.

[70] National Federation of the Blind. Agreement with eBay.com to enhance accessibility of eBay's website and mobile application. Available at: https://nfb.org/ebay-and-national-federation-blind-team-optimize-accessibility-site-apps; 2014.

[71] Attorney General of Massachusetts. Agreement between Monster Worldwide, the National Federation of the Blind and MA Attorney General's Office to be fully accessible. Available at: http://www.mass.gov/ago/news-and-updates/press-releases/2013/2013-01-30-monster-agreement.html; 2013.

[72] National Federation of the Blind. Agreement with Amazon.com to promote and improve website accessibility. Available at: https://nfb.org/node/1195; 2007.

[73] National Federation of the Blind. Agreement with Ticketmaster to make website fully accessible to the blind. Available at: https://nfb.org/node/993; 2011.

[74] National Federation of the Blind. Agreement with Travelocity to make website more accessible. Available at: https://nfb.org/node/1006; 2011.

[75] Feingold L. Increase accessibility and usability of website, mobile applications and print materials to blind and visually impaired persons. Available at: http://lflegal.com/category/settlements/web-accessibility-settlements/; 2014, April 12.

[76] 42 U.S.C. § 12112(b).

[77] Lazar J, Olalere A, Wentz B. Investigating the accessibility and usability of job application web sites for blind users. J Usabil Stud 2012;7(2):68–87.

[78] *Cathcart v. Flagstar Corp.*, 155 F. 3d 558 (4th Cir. 1998).

[79] *E.E.O.C. v. Echostar Commc'ns. Corp.*, 2005 WL 2492905 (D. Colo. 2005).

[80] 29 U.S.C. § 794d(a)(1)(A).

[81] Olalere A, Lazar J. Accessibility of U.S. federal government homepages: section 508 compliance and site accessibility statements. Govern Inform Q 2011;28(3).

[82] *Allied Tech. Grp. v. United States*, 649 F. 3d 1320 (Fed. Cir. 2011).

[83] 29 U.S.C. § 794d(f)(1)(B).

[84] 17 U.S.C. § 121.

[85] 17 U.S.C. § 121(d)(4)(A).

[86] *Authors Guild v. HathiTrust*, 902 F. Supp. 2d 445, 449 (S.D.N.Y. 2012).

[87] *Authors Guild, Inc. v. HathiTrust*, 755 F. 3d 87, 101–103 (2nd Cir. 2014).

[88] Order, *Hartzell v. Arkansas* (No. IJ2001–3700) (D. Ct. Pulaski Co. Ark. Aug. 29, 2003).

[89] *Nat'l Federation of the Blind v. Target Corp.*, 452 F. Supp. 2d 946 (N.D. Cal. 2006).

[90] N.J. Stat. Ann. § 10:5–12 (West 2014).

International disability law

6

INTRODUCTION

The past decade reflects much international, supra-national, and national activity directed to the enactment of statutes, regulations, standards, and regulatory bodies that address the accessibility of web sites and software and digital technology. These efforts have yet to translate into significant action anywhere; no nation can claim that its public sector sites, much less those of private concerns, reflect widespread accessibility or even significant sustainable progress. The approaches run the gamut from voluntary performance and process guidelines with the potential for private lawsuits, as is true of the United Kingdom, to mandatory statutory requirements enforceable by a governmental agency, as is true of Norway. Some nations focus on the accessibility of governmental web sites (Sweden), while others (Spain) extend the requirement of accessibility to private organizations providing economically important public services. The last report from the European Union, in 2011, stated that less than 10% of all web sites in the EU were fully accessible (against a WCAG 1.0 AA standard) and only a third of public sector government web sites met that standard [1].

On the international front, the United Nations Convention on the Rights of Persons with Disabilities (CRPD) makes a strong declaration of the rights of persons with disabilities to have equal access to digital information, and the Marrakesh Treaty holds the promise of ending the "book famine" for all of those in the world with print disabilities.

The jury is out on whether any of these promises of equal opportunity, national or international, will be kept, but given the international nature of commercial web sites, there is at least the hope that widespread accessibility of commercial web sites in any one nation could produce international benefits.

The Web Content Accessibility Guidelines (WCAG) are gaining international acceptance by nation states as guidance for web accessibility, whether in policy documents or as enforceable standards. This developing consensus, which the United States may be poised to join, seems a necessary requirement if international digital accessibility is to become reality. This chapter highlights the main features of laws around the world that address digital accessibility.

This chapter surveys international law and the laws of countries outside the United States with respect to access by persons with disabilities to digital content, web sites, and software. These laws are mostly statutory, passed by the legislature of these countries, although the judiciaries of some countries, notably, Canada and Australia, have heard cases on the rights of people with disabilities to have access to accessible technology to fully take advantage of the opportunities that the Internet offers.

The authors of a leading treatise on disability rights distinguish broadly between two models of protection of people with disabilities, the civil rights approach and the human rights approach. On one hand we have the Americans with Disabilities Act in the United States, which focuses on removing barriers to access and allowing equal opportunity for people with disabilities while the other countries look to the inherent dignity and value of people with disabilities using a human rights approach [2]. This latter approach sees states as responsible for removing the social barriers to full participation and integration of persons with disabilities on a basis of equality. Both approaches recognize persons with disabilities as rights holders, and both reject the "medical model" which views people with disabilities as problems to be fixed through medical intervention, if possible, and, if not, to be dealt with charitably. That last view supports welfare for persons with disabilities, but does not attempt to involve people with disabilities in society through employment and full participation and is slowly being recognized as inconsistent with an equal rights narrative for persons with disabilities. However, the "welfare" approach continues in some countries, notably France.

Professor Peter Blanck explains the difference between American and European disability law as follows:

> These divergent approaches flow from a conceptual distinction. Following World War II, disability rights have developed in parallel with and sometimes nurtured by broader concepts of human rights. In contrast, much of United States legislation is rooted in more limited post-Civil War notions of racial injustice, which established tiers of protection. [2]

Despite its shortcomings, which have been discussed earlier in this book, the American model, as seen in the Americans with Disabilities Act and the Rehabilitation Act, has been highly influential abroad. An article written in 2007 noted that "the ADA has played a leading role in developing disability law outside the United States, with more than forty countries adopting formulations of the statute" [3]. That these statutes embody a commitment to equal opportunity in all spheres of modern life does not mean that they share enforcement mechanisms.

In countries that modeled their legal systems on that of England, such as Canada, the United States, and Australia, judicial decisions play a significant role in expounding the scope and content of statutory laws. Moreover, these nations have a tradition of private Attorneys General, that is, that affected citizens who may bring civil rights cases, including disability rights cases, enforcing the provisions of the law. In civil code countries, that is, those modeled on the Napoleonic code, there is less emphasis on judicial interpretations and greater reliance on state enforcement to ensure legal compliance. Like all generalizations, there are exceptions. For example, Spain, a civil code country, has, since 2007, authorized people with disabilities and disability organizations to take ICT accessibility cases to court and seek monetary penalties for breaches of accessibility standards [4].

Canada and Spain were among the first countries to take legislative action prohibiting discrimination against people with disabilities [5]. The Centre for Internet & Society's "Web Accessibility Policy Making: An International Perspective," an encyclopedic work evaluating digital accessibility policies in many countries, classifies the statutes, policies, and guidelines according to their scope ("to what sectors of society does the law apply") and enforceability ("whether or not they have the force of law") (WCAG is translated into many languages) [6]. This report offers the basis for several insights that will be helpful to policy makers as they assemble a digital accessibility policy. First, "[c]ountries whose local languages are alphabet based or that use English as the official medium can leverage the WCAG for their accessibility policy" [6]. Second, countries should create a long-term policy road map that allows them to monitor and achieve compliance with their accessibility regime over time. Third, the report calls for a "systemized forum, committee or board" to "review and monitor implementation and to update policy along with the WCAGs." Finally, the report suggests that a government must have a complaint redress mechanism to ensure timely compliance with guidelines. "This would be a reflection of the commitment to implementation of the legislation and policies and act as a deterrent to non-compliance" [6]. However, the Centre should have added yet two other considerations: the need to educate IT professionals in the requirements of accessibility and the need to give web site operators guidance on how to embed accessibility into their processes.

DISABILITY LAW IN THE UNITED NATIONS: A BRIEF HISTORY

International law refers to the law among states and includes treaties between states as well as customary norms of international law that all states are assumed to follow. Disability issues have a history dating back to the beginning of the United Nations that reflect, first, the medical model of disability, and only later reflect the rights model. The UN General Assembly adopted the Universal Declaration of Human Rights in 1948. That document, together with the International Covenant on Economic, Social and Cultural Rights (ICESCR) and the International Convention on Civil and Political Rights (ICCPR), are considered the International Bill of Rights [5]. However, for more than two decades, the United Nations focused on rehabilitation and cure [7]. In 1971 the UN Declaration on the Rights of Mentally Retarded Persons still viewed disability through a medical lens.

The 1975 Declaration of Rights of Disabled Persons, however, marked the beginning of the UN's adoption of conventions addressing the rights of persons with disabilities.

An important "moment" in international disability law was the decade between 1983 and 1992, which has been termed the Decade of the Disabled. The most tangible outcome was the 1982 World Programme of Action Concerning Disabled Persons (Adopted by the General Assembly on December 3, 1982, by resolution

A/RES/37/52) [8]. In relation to access to technology for people with disabilities, the Programme of Action stated that:

> *Many disabled persons require technical aids. In some countries the technology needed to produce such items is well developed, and highly sophisticated devices are manufactured to assist the mobility, communication and daily living of disabled individuals. The costs of such items are high, however, and only a few countries are able to provide such equipment.* [8]

Note that this was more than thirty years ago, prior to the development of the Internet. On the path to the CRPD, Sweden and Italy proposed disability-specific treaties in 1987 and 1989. Beijing hosted an NGO Summit on Disability in March of 2000. This led to the Beijing Declaration of Rights of People with Disability in the New Century [9].

UNITED NATIONS CONVENTION ON THE RIGHTS OF PERSONS WITH DISABILITIES

The United Nations Convention on the Rights of Persons with Disabilities (CRPD) is modeled after the U.S. Americans with Disabilities Act and promotes the ADA principles of non-discrimination, equality of opportunity, accessibility, and inclusion. The treaty has been ratified by 154 countries but has not yet been ratified by the United States [10]. The United States *signed* the treaty on July 30, 2009, but has yet to *ratify* it under domestic law [11]. Although the treaty has attracted bipartisan support, ratification of the treaty has run into problems with the conservative members of the U.S. Senate who claim that the treaty would undermine American sovereignty [12]. Opponents, led by former Senator Rick Santorum, claim that adopting the treaty will allow international enforcement of American law, will make it easier for people to get abortions, and will undermine their ability to home school their children. Former and current Senators Bob Dole, Bill Frist, and John McCain support the bill and liken it to the Americans with Disabilities Act, signed by President George H.W. Bush. Senators Dole and McCain, both war veterans, and the American Legion, Veterans of Foreign Wars, the Iraq and Afghanistan Veterans of America, and the Wounded Warrior Project all support the treaty [12]. These supporters brush off critics' concerns, arguing that reservations and understandings can be baked into the treaty and should assuage their fellow conservative colleagues' fears.

The CRPD directly addresses the need for equal access to online information for people with disabilities. Countries that sign the treaty pledge to "enable persons with disabilities to live independently and participate fully in all aspects of life." Article 9 of the CRPD specifically calls for States Parties to "take appropriate measures to ensure to persons with disabilities access, on an equal basis with others, to … information and communications, including information and communications technologies and systems [10]. Article 21 not only requires countries to "[provide] information intended for the general public to persons with disabilities in accessible formats and technologies appropriate to different kinds of disabilities," but to take all steps necessary for persons with disabilities to participate fully in public discourse. Moreover, the CRPD requires States Parties to submit reports on the Convention's implementation to a monitoring body [13].

MARRAKESH TREATY

The Marrakesh Treaty to Facilitate Access to Published Works for Persons who are Blind, Visually Impaired, or otherwise Print Disabled, often known as the "Marrakesh Treaty," is the other significant international disability rights document with a major impact on digital content [14]. The key problem addressed by the Marrakesh Treaty is the "book famine"[15]. Book famine describes the reality that only 1-5% of all published books ever make it into any accessible format that people with print disabilities can read [22]. A 2013 study published by the World Health Organization counts the number of blind people in the world at 285 million, 90% of whom are living in the developing world [16]. The Marrakesh Treaty is one attempt to address the needs of this group, but all of those with a print disability, whether because of sight, lack of manual dexterity, or processing issues, will benefit from this treaty.

The Marrakesh Treaty sought to ease copyright restrictions that prevented the reproduction and distribution of books in a format accessible to print-disabled readers. Under the Marrakesh Treaty, contracting parties agree to create an exception to their national copyright laws to allow for the reproduction and distribution of published works for print-disabled people that would otherwise run afoul of the author's intellectual property rights. The treaty allows for the cross-border sharing of works that are reproduced and distributed in a form that is accessible to visually impaired people.

The key language of the treaty reads as follows:

Article 4—National Law Limitations and Exceptions Regarding Accessible Format Copies

1. (a) Contracting Parties shall provide in their national copyright laws for a limitation or exception to the right of reproduction, the right of distribution, and the right of making available to the public as provided by the WIPO Copyright Treaty (WCT), to facilitate the availability of works in accessible format copies for beneficiary persons. The limitation or exception provided in national law should permit changes needed to make the work accessible in the alternative format.
(b) Contracting Parties may also provide a limitation or exception to the right of public performance to facilitate access to works for beneficiary persons.

Ratifications

Fifty-one member states of the World Intellectual Property Organization (WIPO) signed the Marrakesh Treaty on June 27, 2013. By mid-2014, 82 countries had signed. However, signatures are not enough; the treaty will not be in effect until 20 nations have ratified, that is, have officially approved the treaty. At that point, the treaty creates obligations under the domestic law of the signatory nations. (In international law, ratification is "[t]he final establishment of consent by the parties to a treaty to be bound by it, usu. including the exchange or deposit of instruments of ratification" [17].) India was the first country to ratify the Treaty on June 24, 2014 [18]. Since then, Argentina, El Salvador, Mali, Singapore, the United Arab Emirates, Uruguay, and Paraguay have also ratified.

THE EUROPEAN UNION

The European Union (EU) Charter of Fundamental Rights states that it protects people with disabilities. The EU has passed three "action plans" that are intended to bring an accessible Internet to more Europeans. The plans do not carry the force of law, but are meant to encourage member states to voluntarily make their web sites accessible. Although the plan comports with WCAG guidelines, an EU report, dated 2011, found that only a small fraction of EU-wide public web sites conform to WCAG 1.0 (1). In the four years since that report, the European Union has published no further reports on the progress of member nations in developing accessible web sites.

The European Union's Mandate M 376 resulted in the European Standard Organization publishing European Standard EN 301 549 in 2014 [19]. The standard defines "functional accessibility requirements for information and communication technology products and services" [20]. These standards are in accordance with WCAG 2.0 [21]. (Note: detailed information about EU Mandate M 376 is provided in Chapter 7—Regulations.)

In 2015, the European Commission published "The Digital Agenda for Europe," intended to stimulate the economies of the member states and maximize their citizens using digital technology [22]. Some countries, such as Sweden, have listed accessibility and usability as priority strategic goals [23]. The impact of the EU's actions, which have proceeded in fits and starts, cannot yet be determined.

STATUTORY AND CASE LAW ON DIGITAL ACCESSIBILITY

The sections that follow outline the major efforts of selected countries to promote digital accessibility through law, agency guidance, and sometimes, the courts.

SPAIN

Spain got an early start on accessibility of ICT, establishing voluntary standards for hardware, software, and web sites in 1998 [4]. In 2002, Spain required that by December 2005, all governmental web sites be accessible [4]. However, a Royal Decree in 2007 imposed the same requirement on the same web sites to be met by

2008 [4]. Also, in 2007 legislation was passed providing for fines for inaccessible web sites, extending the requirement of accessibility to private companies performing significant public services, such as banks, utilities, transportation, and the like and authorizing people with disabilities and organizations of persons with disabilities to bring private actions. Spain is also seeking to require "buy accessible" for government procurement [4]. Nonetheless, as one author observed, "the real impact of these policies has been quite limited" [4].

UNITED KINGDOM

The United Kingdom's Equality Act of 2010 superseded separate acts targeted toward distinct groups, such as the Sex Discrimination Act of 1975, the Race Relations Act of 1976, and the Disability Discrimination Act of 1995. It addresses discrimination against persons with disabilities in services and public functions, work, education, associations, and transport services. Section 20 of the Equality Act 2010 has three requirements relating to persons with disabilities. First, if a criterion or practice puts a person with disabilities "at a substantial disadvantage in relation to a relevant matter in comparison with persons who are not disabled," the entity using such criterion or engaging in that practice must "take such steps as it is reasonable to have to take to avoid the disadvantage." Second, "where a physical feature puts a disabled person at a substantial disadvantage in relation to a relevant matter in comparison with persons who are not disabled," the responsible party must "take such steps as it is reasonable to have to take to avoid the disadvantage." Third, it requires that where a person with disabilities would, "but for the provision of an auxiliary aid, be put at a substantial disadvantage in relation to a relevant matter in comparison with persons who are not disabled, [the responsible party] take such steps as it is reasonable to have to take to provide the auxiliary aid." Most relevant here, the Act states: "where the first or third requirement relates to the provision of information, the steps which it is reasonable for [the responsible actor] to have to take include steps for ensuring that in the circumstances concerned the information is provided in an accessible format" [24].

Under the Disability Discrimination Act, the predecessor statute to the Equality Act, regulatory guidance required service providers to make their web sites accessible [13]. This guidance did not carry over under the Equality Act, and compliance with performance standards, such as WCAG, is voluntary [13].

The British Standards Institute has promulgated a Web Accessibility Code of Practice, known as BS 8878, that addresses an oft-overlooked issue: the process by which accessibility is incorporated into business processes. This code helps an organization:

1. understand why digital inclusion and accessibility make good business sense;
2. embed inclusion responsibility strategically across key job roles and into key policies;
3. follow a user-centered production process which identifies the key decisions which affect inclusion and which are taken in a web product's lifecycle;

4. adopt an informed way of making these decisions;

5. adopt a way of documenting these decisions to provide a log for assessing accessibility risk and proving conformance with BS 8878; and

6. synchronize these activities with similar processes for the inclusive design of non-digital products [25].

These standards are an important complement to WCAG.

AUSTRALIA

The Disability Discrimination Act (DDA) was passed in 1992. The Australian Human Rights Commission is authorized under section 67(1)(k) of the DDA to issue guidelines for the purpose of avoiding discrimination [26]. The act outlaws both direct and indirect discrimination against persons on account of their disabilities, and requires "reasonable adjustments" in the provision of services [27,28]. A case brought by a blind individual under this statute, *Maguire v. Sydney Organizing Committee for the Olympic Games*, is an early digital access case that led to judicial decisions in 1999 and 2000 [29].

Bruce Lindsay Maguire filed a complaint with the Human Rights and Equal Opportunity Commission alleging that the Sydney Organizing Committee for the Olympic Games (SOCOG) discriminated against him on the basis of his disability by failing to make the contents of its web site available to him in Braille. Specifically, the web site contained the ticket book, which allowed people to apply for tickets to the Olympic Games events. Maguire was unable to apply for tickets for himself and his two children and was told by a manager via telephone that a Braille copy could not be made available because it was a matter of "costs and percentages." Maguire, blind since birth, alleged a violation under the Disability Discrimination Act of 1992 because SOCOG did not intend to provide him with a Braille copy of the ticket book.

The court concluded that the ticket book on the web site was a relevant service comprehended by the definition of "service" in the Disability Discrimination Act. The court reasoned that:

> [g]iven the nature and extent of the entertainment services to be provided at the Olympic Games in Sydney in 2000, the provision of tickets to members of the public required of the respondent that it develop an efficient ticketing process and, at the same time, advertise it extensively, so as to ensure that all persons were properly informed on all matters necessary for and relating to their proposed participation in the entertainment provided by means of the Games program ... In the provision of the ticket book, [SOCOG] provided services within the meaning of the definition and of section 24 of the Act. It is also clearly arguable that the same conclusion is available if one had regard to the reference to 'recreation' in subparagraph (b) of the definition and to paragraph (f) thereof.

The next year, the court addressed the issue of whether an inaccessible web site violated the DDA:

The respondent in constructing its web site (and its Ticket Book) was intending to offer a service to the public. In the case of the web site that service consisted in the provision of a large body of information. By the form and content of its web site the respondent sought to make the information available. Because of the manner in which that information was made available, it could be accessed by a sighted person. Because of the manner which that information was made available it could not be accessed by a blind person because of his or her disability. This meant that, in respect of the same information, the respondent, in the manner in which it used its computer technology to service the needs of the public to have access to that information, made it available to sighted persons, but it made it unavailable or only partly available to a blind person because of the latter's disability. It follows that, because of his or her disability, the blind person was treated less favorably by the respondent than the sighted person. That in my view constitutes direct discrimination within the meaning of section 5 of the DDA.

The interplay between cases and regulatory action is reflected by the promulgation of Australia's "World Wide Web Access: Disability Discrimination Act Advisory Notes" as an outgrowth of *Maguire v. SOCOG* (2000). The Advisory Notes, "intended to assist individuals and organizations involved in the ownership or development of web resources, by clarifying the requirements of the DDA in this area, and explaining how compliance with them can be best achieved," are described in the sidebar.

The Advisory Notes do not have direct legal force, but the Australian Human Rights Commission and other anti-discrimination agencies may consider them in responding to complaints under the Disability Discrimination Act. Actions in accordance with the notes, the notes' authors suggest, should make it far less likely that an individual or organization would be subject to complaints about the accessibility of their web site or other web resource.

The Advisory Notes explain that just like in the context of physical buildings, web sites should be designed with accessibility in mind.

Accessibility of buildings and other aspects of the physical environment is best achieved through careful planning and attention to detail, rather than by adding accessibility features at the end of the design process. Similarly, creating accessible web content should be an integral part of the web design cycle, and accessibility features should be incorporated into all aspects of the design process. (Advisory Notes, 1.2) [26]

The Advisory Notes also give technical guidance on what constitutes a failure to operate an accessible web site by including a list of Ten Common Web Accessibility Failures:

Web developers should ensure that they design their web sites so as to avoid [common web accessibility failures], and should take steps to rectify them if they are already present.

1. Failure to include appropriate text descriptions (such as "alt-text" labels) for images;
2. Failure to provide accessible alternatives when using a visual CAPTCHA;
3. Failure to use technologies (such as Flash and JavaScript) in ways that are accessible;
4. Failure to use HTML features appropriately to indicate content structure such as the hierarchy of headings;
5. Failure to explicitly associate form input controls with their labels;

6. Failure to ensure sufficient difference between foreground (text) colour and background colour;
7. Failure to identify data tables with Summary or Caption, and failure to mark up data tables correctly;
8. Failure to provide a way for users to disable content such as advertisements from flashing rapidly (rapidly flashing content may cause seizures in susceptible individuals), and failure to provide a way for users to stop a page from auto-refreshing;
9. Failure to ensure that web pages can be used from the keyboard (that is, without the mouse);
10. Failure to alert the user to changes on a web page that are triggered automatically when selecting items from a dropdown menu.

It is beyond the scope of these Advisory Notes to provide technical advice about how to rectify these failures. In most cases, however, they represent non-compliance with various WCAG 2.0 Success Criteria (see section 4.3.1 below for a brief explanation of WCAG 2.0 Success Criteria), and the W3C provides a comprehensive range of technical documentation about how to comply with WCAG 2.0. Web developers who need further advice or clarification should seek the assistance of a web accessibility consultant [26].

The Advisory notes anticipate a web site provider's defense of undue hardship, which is a defense under the DDA, but explain that:

[w]eb designers and content providers should note that unjustifiable hardship has to be demonstrated and cannot simply be assumed. In particular, stylistic preferences rather than functional requirements are highly unlikely to be accepted as constituting a basis for a defense of unjustifiable hardship (other than in cases where the artistic form of a site is a significant function). This does not imply any attempt to prohibit innovative design. It does mean that design must address access requirements, directly or by provision of alternative means of access.

The extensive guidance in the Advisory Notes along with the Disability Discrimination Act itself gives Australia the status of a leader when it comes to digital accessibility.

CANADA

In *Jodhan v. Attorney General of Canada*, the Supreme Court of Canada was faced with the question of whether government web sites were required to be accessible to blind people. The Court concluded that a person with a disability had demonstrated two systemic failures that underlie the government's failure to provide online services in a manner that is accessible to the visually impaired [30]. In reaching that decision, the Court was guided by Canada's charter, which explicitly recognizes people with disabilities. Charter s. 15(1) explains that:

Every individual is equal before and under the law and has the right to the equal protection and equal benefit of the law without discrimination and, in particular, without discrimination based on race, national or ethnic origin, colour, religion, sex, age or mental or physical disability. [Charter s. 15(1)]

Quoting the language of Justice La Forest in *Eldridge v. British Columbia (Attorney General)*, at para. 56, the court stated: "[i]t is an unfortunate truth that the history of disabled persons in Canada is largely one of exclusion and marginalization. ... As a result, disabled persons have not generally been afforded the 'equal concern, respect, and consideration' that § 15(1) of the Charter demands. ... One consequence of these attitudes is the persistent social and economic disadvantage faced by the disabled" [31].

Standards and Guidelines in Canada

The *Jodhan* Court determined that the government had failed to implement Canada's Common Look and Feel (CLF) 1.0 standard guidelines that the Canadian government had directed its departments and agencies to implement nine years earlier. The CLF 1.0 standard consisted of four standards and two guidelines to ensure that government web sites conformed to a common look and feel and were "designed to ensure that online services be provided in an efficient and professional manner" [30].

Federal institutions had an implementation deadline of December 31, 2008, for the CLF 2.0 standard issued on January 1, 2007 [30]. The "Policy Statement" of the Communications Policy stated:

Government must:

Employ a variety of ways and means to communicate, and provide information in multiple formats to accommodate diverse needs. Government information must be broadly accessible throughout society. The needs of all Canadians, whose perceptual or physical abilities and language skills are diverse, must be recognized and accommodated. Information must be accessible so citizens, as responsible members of a democratic community, may be aware of, understand, respond to and influence the development and implementation of policies, programs, services and initiatives. Information must be available in multiple formats to ensure equal access. All means of communication - from traditional methods to new technologies - must be used to reach and communicate with Canadians wherever they may reside. Modern government requires the capacity to respond effectively over multiple channels in a 24-hour, global communications environment.

The Court reviewed their decisions on substantive equality and Charter s. 15(1).

Substantive equality, as contrasted with formal equality, is grounded in the idea that: 'The promotion of equality entails the promotion of a society in which all are secure in the knowledge that they are recognized at law as human beings equally deserving of concern, respect and consideration': Andrews, at p. 171, per McIntyre J., for the majority on the s. 15 issue.

Pointing out that the concept of equality does not necessarily mean identical treatment and that the formal "like treatment" model of discrimination may in fact produce inequality, McIntyre J. stated (at p. 165):

To approach the ideal of full equality before and under the law — and in human affairs an approach is all that can be expected — the main consideration must be the impact of the law on the individual or the group concerned. Recognizing that there will always be an infinite variety of personal characteristics, capacities, entitlements and merits among those subject to a law, there must be accorded, as nearly as may be possible, an equality of benefit and protection and no more of the restrictions, penalties or burdens imposed upon one than another. In other words, the admittedly unattainable ideal should be that a law expressed to bind all should not because of irrelevant personal differences have a more burdensome or less beneficial impact on one than another.

The *Jodhan* court then stated: "[t]he law should not have a less beneficial impact on the blind than on sighted persons" [30]. They described this case as one of "adverse effects discrimination," which "is not a question of whether ... discrimination is motivated by an intentional desire to obstruct someone's potential" but as the disproportionate impact on one group as the result of practices or systems applied in a uniform way [30].

The Court ultimately held that the failure to accommodate blind people "perpetuates a disadvantage which undermines the dignity of the visually impaired" [30]. The *Jodhan* court analogized the case of an accommodation to the physical design of a building for a person in a wheelchair to the "visually impaired [who] similarly seek independent access to online services and dignity without physical limitation" [30].

Accessibility for Ontarians with Disabilities Act

In 2005, the Government of the Province of Ontario, Canada, passed the Accessibility for Ontarians with Disabilities Act (AODA). Ontario is one of only two Canadian provinces that have a disability rights law. The overall goal of the AODA is to make Ontario a fully accessible province by the year 2025. The AODA addresses accessibility in five areas of life: Customer Service, Information and Communications, Employment, Transportation, and the Built Environment [32]. The purpose of the act is to "benefit all Ontarians by, (a) developing, implementing and enforcing accessibility standards in order to achieve accessibility for Ontarians with disabilities with respect to goods, services, facilities, accommodation, employment, buildings, structures and premises on or before January 1, 2025, and (b) providing for the involvement of persons with disabilities, of the Government of Ontario and of representatives of industries and of various sectors of the economy in the development of the accessibility standards." Under AODA, web sites must be compatible with the WCAG 2.0 standards, which means they must be perceivable, operable, understandable, and robust.

The detailed web site provisions are found in Part II, "Information and Communication Standards," Section 14: "Accessible web sites and web content":

(1) The Government of Ontario and the Legislative Assembly shall make their internet and intranet web sites and web content conform with the World Wide Web Consortium Web Content Accessibility Guidelines (WCAG) 2.0, at Level AA, and shall do so in accordance with the schedule set out in this section.

(2) Designated public sector organizations and large organizations shall make their internet web sites and web content conform with the World Wide Web Consortium Web Content Accessibility Guidelines (WCAG) 2.0, initially at Level A and increasing to Level AA, and shall do so in accordance with the schedule set out in this section.

In 2015, Ontario's Economic Development Minister Brad Duguid reported that 60% of private sector organizations subject to the AODA failed to file mandatory accessibility self-reports by the end of 2014. Nonetheless, the Ontario Government planned to reduce the number of organizations that it would audit for web site accessibility [33]. As we have seen repeatedly, the gap between legal promises of accessibility and states' willingness to act on those promises, in Ontario as elsewhere, is large. Note that more information about compliance with the AODA is available in Chapter 9.

IRELAND

For Ireland, accessibility is mentioned in the Equal Status Act, the Employment Equality Act, and the Disability Act. The Equal Status Act (2000, 2004) includes a reasonable accommodation provision and as the Centre for Internet and Society suggests, "prima facie, the Act would appear to cover discrimination in the provision of online and web based services" because it says that a "failure by the provider of a service to do all that is reasonable to accommodate the needs of a person with a disability by providing special treatment or facilities, if without such special treatment or facilities it would be impossible or unduly difficult for the person to avail himself or herself of the service" [14]. Ireland's National Disability Authority follows the WCAG 1.0 standards in the policy document, "New Connections—A Strategy to realize the potential of the Information Society," which suggests Web Accessibility Initiative's (WAI) Web Content Accessibility Guidelines [14]. One issue here is that the guidelines only apply to public sector web sites and are not mandatory [14]. The National Disability Authority encourages compliance by giving an award to the organizations that complete an audit. Another is that WCAG 1.0 is obsolete. The NDA monitors complaints and if a complainant is not satisfied with the results of an investigation by the government's Enquiry Office, then he or she may then bring the complaint to the office of the Ombudsman [14].

FRANCE

France follows the welfare model approach to disabilities, not the ADA model, which creates statutory rights under federal law. Going back to the end of World War I, when French society was faced with caring for its disabled veterans, the French system has required private employers in certain areas to give priority to people with disabilities when hiring employees. The first major French law was passed in 1975 with a major amendment to the Labor Code in 1987 [34].

As described in the 2003 International Disability Rights Compendium Report, in France, a person with disabilities is one "for whom the possibility of obtaining or retaining employment is effectively reduced due to a deficiency or diminution of physical or mental capacity" [35]. Status as a person with a disability is given by the Commission Technique d'Orientation et de Reclassement Professional (COTOREP), which classifies a person into one of three categories based on the severity of the disability. France has a quota model, which requires employers with over twenty employees to have people with disabilities as six percent of their workforce and must report to the government on their satisfaction of these requirements [35].

In the private sector, employees have the same rights as other employees but have the right to earlier advance notice of termination [35]. The International Compendium of 2003 explains that if overall productivity of a private business is diminished by the employment of a person with disabilities, then the employer may be authorized to diminish the disabled worker's wage, but the difference is provided by government funds allocated for this purpose [35]. Relevant to this book's focus on technology, the French civil service is also required to fill six percent of its employment rolls with people with disabilities. "[A]n inter-ministry fund was set up in 1998 to enhance the integration of disabled persons into the civil service. The fund is used to contribute towards experimental equipment and the adapting of workstations" [35].

GERMANY

In Germany, the Federal Ordinance on Barrier-Free Information Technology applies to "(1) web sites and webpages, (2) web sites and webpages which are publicly accessible, and (3) graphical user interfaces created on the basis of information technology which are publicly accessible." The act then states that "intention of the design of IT and internet facilities [as described above] in accordance with this ordinance shall be to enable disabled persons within the meaning of section 3 of the Act on Equal Opportunities for Disabled Persons, who can only use information technology to a limited extent unless additional conditions are fulfilled, to access it" [36]. This regulation is in keeping with the German constitution, which provides that "no person may be discriminated against because of his or her disability" [37]. The *Behindertengleichstellungsgesetz* outlaws discrimination, addresses the needs of women with disabilities specifically, and requires the federal government to provide barrier-free access to buildings, administrative procedures, access to information technology, restaurants, and public transportation [38].

One limit of the Federal Ordinance on Barrier-Free Information Technology is that it requires entities only "to conduct negotiations, not necessarily to come to a result" [14]. The regulation requires that "internet appearances and publicly accessible graphic program surfaces shall all be accessible … but applies to the private sector in a more limited way—mandating negotiations between private companies and registered organizations" [14]. The ordinance also creates a mechanism for review that accounts for technological development and creates a position of a Commissioner for the Interests of Persons with Disabilities [14].

ITALY

There have been three main legal pronouncements in Italy relating to access for people with disabilities. Law 4/2004, the "Stanca Act," is a detailed national law specifically addressing online access [39]. The law applies to public administrators and to "private firms which are licensees of public services, to regional municipal companies, to public assistance and rehabilitation agencies, to transport and tele-communication companies in which the State has a prevalent shareholding and to ICT (Information and Computer Technology) services contractors" [39]. The Act is named after Lucio Stanca who served as the Minister of Information Technology when the law was passed. The substance of the Act is inspired by the WCAG 1.0 guidelines and Section 508 of the Rehabilitation Act. The subsection entitled Accessibility Obligations is reproduced here in full:

1. [Public administrators and others to whom the law applies, as described above], when carrying out procedures to buy goods and to deliver services, are obliged, in the event that they are adjudicating bidders which all have submitted similar offers, to give preference to the bidder which offers the best compliance with the accessibility requirements provided for by the decree mentioned in article 11. Not taking in consideration the accessibility requirements or the purchase of goods or supplied services that are not accessible has to be adequately justified.
2. [Public administrators and others to whom the law applies, as described above], cannot draw up contracts for the implementation and modification of INTERNET web sites, if they fail to respect the accessibility requirements provided for in the Decree article 11; any stipulated contract failing to respect such requirements will be considered null and void. All existing contracts signed before the Decree article 11 comes into effect must adhere to the provisions relating to accessibility requirements of the same law, in the event of the contract's extension, modification or renewal; any extended, modified or renewal contract which fails to respect such requirements will be declared null and void, while upgrading to meet such requirements should be carried out no later than twelve months from the date the Decree comes into force.
3. The provision of public funds to private subjects for the purchase of computer goods and services to be used by disabled workers or by other users, also in the event of the installation of telework equipment, is only legitimate if goods and services conform to the accessibility requirements provided for by the Decree article 11.
4. Public and private employers must provide disabled employees with hardware equipment, software tools and assistive technologies which are suitable for their needs and enable them to carry out their duties; this also applies in the event of teleworking. The private employers are subject to the provision as referred to in article 13, subsection 1, letter c) of the law n. 68 dated March 12, 1999.
5. Public employers must adhere to subsection 4, in the case that such funds are available in the budget [39].

The next important Italian regulation was the "Decree of the President of the Republic," March 1, 2005, No. 75, entitled "Enforcement Regulations for Law 4/2005 to promote the access of the disabled to information technologies." The decree "introduc[es] the key concept of usability. Web sites must not only be barrier-free but also simple, effective, efficient and they must satisfy the user's needs" [40].

Web sites that are the most usable and accessible may obtain an accessibility mark by applying for an evaluation from the National Centre for Informatics in Public Administration, which keeps a list of trusted evaluators [40]. The government may also independently grade a web site's compliance with the law.

The CNIPA (National Center for Information in Public Administration) and the Department for Information Technology are responsible for monitoring enforcement of the act. At the local level, regional and local government provide training to encourage adoption of accessible technology [40].

The next decree, handed down on July 8, 2005, provides for "Technical Rules of Law 4/2004," again referring to the Stanca Act, which gives the technical requirements to meet the required level of accessibility [41]. Working groups were established to create a list of requirements. The groups focused on those requirements that were measurable. For example Annex A to the 2005 Decree provides 22 technical requirements that, if complied with, guarantee a web site is compliant with WCAG 1.0 Level AA. Annex A explains how an evaluator can assess a web site [41]. For example, the evaluator should examine whether the following portions of a web site comply: the home page, all interactive pages, the first level of pages linked from the home page, whether the web site is accessible even when accessed by different web browsers, whether audio content is available as text, and whether the page is browsable using the keyboard only and not a mouse [40,41]. Commentators attribute some of the success of the Italian drive toward web accessibility to the "strong campaign of information, training and sensitization" in addition to the official legal approach taken by the government [40]. Note that Chapter 10, best practices, provides details on how automated accessibility tools were used by the Emilia-Romagna regional government in Italy, operating under the requirements of the Stanca Act.

HONG KONG

Hong Kong, which is not a sovereign state, but rather a Special Administrative Region of the People's Republic of China, is considered a leader in Asia in digital accessibility. Beginning in 1999, Hong Kong released the first version of its Digital 21 plan, a "blueprint for the development of information and communications technology (ICT) in Hong Kong" (similar to the Digital Agenda in many of the European Union countries) [42]. Regular updates to the plan are provided, and a new version is expected to be released in 2015 [42]. The office of the Government Chief Information Officer provides multiple documents containing guidance and advice for improving digital accessibility. Since 1999, clear guidance has been issued on government web site design in a document known as "Guidelines on Dissemination of Information Through Government Web sites" [43]. This document, the most recent version of which was issued in March 2012, covers all aspects of government web site design, includes requirements for web accessibility. Specifically, government web sites, as of January 1, 2013, must meet WCAG 2.0 AA (earlier versions of the document required compliance with earlier standards). The office of the Government Chief Information Officer has also started a publicity campaign, including seminars and workshops, awards for improving accessibility, and listing of those who are able to provide digital accessibility services [44]. Also, nearly all of the publicly funded universities in Hong Kong provide coursework on digital accessibility [45]. The 2010/11 budget of the Office of the Government Chief Information Officer allocated "a one-off funding of HK$3.6 million in 2010/11 to support the development of ICT-based assistive tools and applications for persons with disabilities." This was a grant competition for projects to assist people with disabilities in digital access, and nine projects were funded. These included smartphone apps for navigation and recognizing printed text and text input and software for rehabilitation and independent home living [46].

JAPAN

The Japanese Industrial Standard X 8413-3 is a revised version of Japan's non-mandatory guidelines on accessibility for people with disabilities and the elderly. As stated in the Centre for Internet and Society's report, "Japan does not have any legislation around accessibility but has specified its accessibility policies for both web and other electronic infrastructure in the form of industrial standards" [47]. The Industrial Standard is mandatory for governmental entities with web sites, but it is not mandatory for private industry—merely encouraged [48]. One challenge facing designers of accessible technology in Japan is the complexity the character-based Japanese language. The WCAG was developed in contemplation of alphabet-based languages. However, another challenge is the absence of data, from government or private sources, as to the degree of accessibility of Japanese web sites.

SUMMARY

Countries around the world use a variety of approaches to encourage digital accessibility, ranging from guidance and voluntary compliance with standards to regulatory enforcement with fines, as well as private lawsuits to require compliance. No country can yet claim significant success, and there is no indication, ultimately, that an approach that works for one country will work for another, due to the many differences in legal tradition and culture.

Because of the significance of the United States to the IT market, the failure, so far, of the United States to ratify the CRPD and the Marrakesh Treaty makes progress harder for the rest of the world. More multi-national coordination efforts, however, such as the coordination between the EU Mandate M 376 and the refresh of Section 508 in the United States can help bring progress. For countries that have "digital agendas," long-term plans for digital technology and infrastructure, it is important that accessibility become a core piece of the country's digital agenda. Some countries have no public data about their digital accessibility, or no transparency about compliance or enforcement, and increasing the amount of publicly available data will highlight the importance of digital accessibility. Ultimately, if nations that are significant licensees of digital technology insist on buying truly accessible technology, there will be a strong business imperative to market accessible technology and, thus, make digital accessibility a necessary part of the "conversation" as technology developers design new products, software, and web sites.

REFERENCES

[1] Monitoring eAccessibility Consortium. (2011) 2011 Annual report. Available at: http://www.eaccessibility-monitoring.eu/researchResult.aspx.

[2] Blanck P, Hill E, Siegal C, Waterstone M. Disability Civil Rights Law and Policy § 22-3. St. Paul, MN: West; 2004.

[3] Stein, M., and Stein, P. (2007). Beyond Disability Civil Rights, 58 Hastings L.J. 1203, 1203–04.

[4] Normand, L. (Sept.–Oct. 2012). Understanding HCI Policy in Spain and in the Context of Accessibility. *Interactions,* 58-61. Available at: http://interactions.acm.org/archive/view/september-october-2012/understanding-hci-policy-in-spain-in-the-context-of-accessibility.

[5] Kanter, A. (2003). The Globalization of Disability Rights Law, *30 Syracuse J. Int'l L. & Com. 241.*

[6] G3ict & Centre for Internet and Society. (February 28, 2012). Web Accessibility Policy Making: An International Perspective. Available at: http://cis-india.org/accessibility/web-accessibility-policy-making-an-international-perspective/web-accessibility.pdf.

[7] Quinn, G., and Degener, T., with Bruce, A., Burke, B., Castellino, J., Kenna, P., Kilkelly, U., and Quinlivan, S. (2002). Human Rights and Disability: The current use and future potential of United Nations human rights instruments in the context of disability. United Nations, N.Y. & Geneva. Available at: http://www.ohchr.org/Documents/Publications/HRDisabilityen.pdf.

[8] United Nations Enable, World Programme of Action Concerning Disabled Persons. Available at: http://www.un.org/disabilities/default.asp?id=23.

[9] United Nations General Assembly Economic and Social Council (May 5, 2000). Beijing Declaration of Rights of People with Disability in the New Century. Available at: http://www.un.org/documents/ecosoc/docs/2000/e2000-47.pdf (last visited March 11, 2015).

[10] United Nations Convention on the Rights of Persons with Disabilities. (2006). Full text treaty. Available at: http://www.un.org/disabilities/convention/conventionfull.shtml.

[11] United Nations. (2011). Treaty Series: Convention on the Rights of Persons with Disabilities, Dec. 13, 2006, Vol. 2515, p. 3. Available at: https://treaties.un.org/doc/Publication/UNTS/Volume%202515/v2515.pdf.

[12] Hunt, A. (Feb. 23, 2014). On Disabilities Treaty, the Right Fights with the Right, *New York Times.* Available at: http//nyti.ms/1e75Lee.

[13] Giannoumis G. Regulating web content: the nexus of legislation and performance standards in the United Kingdom and Norway. Behav Sci Law. February 6, 2014;32:52–75.

[14] The Centre for Internet & Society. (January 2012). Web Accessibility Policy Making, An International Perspective. Available at: http://cis-india.org/accessibility/web-accessibility.pdf.

[15] Franz, V. (June 28, 2013). The Miracle in Marrakesh: Copyright Reform to End the "Book Famine." Open Society Foundation. Available at: http://www.opensocietyfoundations.org/voices/miracle-marrakesh-copyright-reform-end-book-famine.

[16] World Health Organization. (August 2014). Visual Impairment and Blindness, Fact Sheet No. 282. Available at: http://www.who.int/mediacentre/factsheets/fs282/en/ (last visited March 11, 2015).

[17] Gardner, B.W. Black's Law Dictionary. 9th ed. St. Paul, MN: West; 2009, 1376.

[18] World Intellectual Property Organization. (June 30, 2014). India Is First to Ratify "Marrakesh Treaty" Easing Access to Books for Persons Who Are Visually Impaired. Available at: http://www.wipo.int/pressroom/en/articles/2014/article_0008.html.

[19] Cen-Cenlec. (February 19, 2014). New European Standard will help to make ICT products and services accessible to all. Available at: http://www.cencenelec.eu/news/press_releases/Pages/PR-2014-03.aspx.

[20] Martinez, L., and Pluke, M. Mandate M 376: new software accessibility requirements. Procedia Comput Sci 2014;27:271–80. Available at: http://www.sciencedirect.com/science/article/pii/S1877050914000325.

[21] ETSI-Cen-Cenelec. (February 2014). European Standard: Accessibility requirements suitable for public procurement of ICT products and services in Europe. EN 301–549, Vol. 1.1.1. Available at: http://www.etsi.org/deliver/etsi_en/301500_301599/301549/01.01.01_60/en_301549v010101p.pdf.

[22] European Commission. Digital Agenda for Europe: A Europe 2020 Initiative. Available at: http://ec.europa.eu/digital-agenda/en/digital-agenda-europe-2020-strategy (last visited March 11, 2015).

[23] Regeringskansliet Government Offices of Sweden. (November 2011). ITC for Everyone – A Digital Agenda for Sweden, 20-22. Available at: http://www.government.se/content/1/c6/18/19/14/70f489cb.pdf.

[24] The Electoral Knowledge Network, ACE Project. United Kingdom Equality Act 2010, Chapter 15, Section 20 (6). Available at: http://aceproject.org/ero-en/regions/europe/GB/united-kingdom-equality-act-2010/view (last visited March 11, 2015).

[25] Kelly, B., Hassell, J., Sloan, D., Lukes, D., Draffan, E.A., Lewthwaite, S. (July 2013). Bring Your Own Policy: Why Accessibility Standards Need to Be Contextually Sensitive. *Ariadne*, Issue 71. Available at: http://www.ariadne.ac.uk/print/issue71/kelly-et-al.

[26] Australian Human Rights Commission. (October 2010). World Wide Web Access: Disability Discrimination Act Advisory Notes, ver. 4.0. Available at: http://www.humanrights.gov.au/our-work/disability-rights/standards/world-wide-web-access-disability-discrimination-act-advisory#foreword (last visited March 11, 2015).

[27] Australian Human Rights Commission. (1992). Commonwealth Consolidated Acts: Disability Discrimination Act 1992 – Section 5. Available at: http://www.austlii.edu.au/au/legis/cth/consol_act/dda1992264/s5.html (last visited March 11, 2015).

[28] Australian Human Rights Commission. (1992). Commonwealth Consolidated Acts: Disability Discrimination Act 1992 – Section 6. Available at: http://www.austlii.edu.au/au/legis/cth/consol_act/dda1992264/s6.html (last visited March 11, 2015).

[29] *Maguire v. Sydney Organizing Committee for the Olympic Games* (No. H99/115) (2000) (Austl.). Available at: https://www.humanrights.gov.au/bruce-lindsay-maguire-v-sydney-organising-committee-olympic-games.

[30] *Jodhan v. Attorney General of Canada,* 2012 F.C. 161, paras. 151. (Can.).

[31] *Eldridge v. British Columbia (Attorney General),* [1997] 3 S.C.R. 624, para. 56 (Can., B.C.).

[32] Ontario, CA. (2009). E-Laws: Accessibility for Ontarians with Disabilities Act, 2005, S.O. 2005, Chapter 11. Available at: http://www.e-laws.gov.on.ca/html/statutes/english/elaws_statutes_05a11_e.htm.

[33] Accessibility for Ontarians with Disabilities Act Alliance. (February 25, 2015). Summary. Available at: http://www.aodaalliance.org/strong-effective-aoda/02252015.asp.

[34] Journal Officiel, J.O. (Official Gazette of France). (July 1, 1975) p. 6596.

[35] Center for International Rehabilitation. (June 2003). International Disability Rights Compendium Report, p. 169-173. Available at: wwda.org.au/wp-content/uploads/2013/12/discompendium1.pdf (last visited March 11, 2015).

[36] Federal Ordinance on Barrier-Free Information Technology. Based on ordinance on Creation of Barrier-Free Information Technology in accordance with Act on Equal Opportunities for Disabled Persons as of April 27, 2002 (Germany). Available at: http://www.einfach-fuer-alle.de/artikel/bitv_english/ (last visited March 11, 2015).

[37] Grundgesetz. (December 20, 1993). Basic Law of the Federal Republic of Germany, Chapt. 1, Art. 3. Available at: http://www.iuscomp.org/gla/statutes/GG.htm#3.

[38] Kock, M. (2004). Disability Law in Germany: An Overview of Employment, Education and Access Rights, *German L. J. Vol. 5, No. 11,* p. 1374. Available at: https://www.germanlawjournal.com/pdfs/Vol05No11/PDF_Vol_05_No_11_1373-1392_Private_Kock.pdf.

[39] Official Gazette of the Italian Republic. (January 17, 2004). Provisions to Support the access of information technologies for the disabled. Available at: http://www.pubbliaccesso.it/normative/law_20040109_n4.htm (last visited March 12, 2015).

[40] Sintini, S. Legislation on eAccessibility: The Italian Approach. *Centro Nazionale per l'Informaticanella Pubblica Amministrazione.* Available at: www.pubbliaccesso.gov.it/english/eAccessibility-Italy.doc (last visited March 12, 2015).

[41] Agenzia per l'Italia Digitale. (July 8, 2005). Ministerial Decree July 8, 2005, Annex A: Technical assessment and technical accessibility requirements of Internet technology-based applications. Available at: http://www.pubbliaccesso.it/normative/DM080705-A-en.htm (last visited March 12, 2015).

[42] Government of Hong Kong Special Administrative Region, Office of the Government Chief Information Officer. Digital 21 Strategy. Available at: http://www.ogcio.gov.hk/en/strategies/government/digital_21/ (last visited March 12, 2015).

[43] Government of Hong Kong Special Administrative Region, Office of the Government Chief Information Officer. (March 2012). Guidelines on Dissemination of Information through Government Web sites. Available at: http://www.ogcio.gov.hk/en/community/web_accessibility/doc/disseminationguidelines.pdf (last visited March 12, 2015).

[44] Government of Hong Kong Special Administrative Region, Office of the Government Chief Information Officer. Web Accessibility Campaign. Available at: http://www.ogcio.gov.hk/en/community/web_accessibility/campaign/ (last visited March 12, 2015).

[45] Government of Hong Kong Special Administrative Region, Office of the Government Chief Information Officer. (June 2014). Summary of Higher Education Institutions on Incorporating Web Accessibility into relevant ICT Curricula. Available at: http://www.ogcio.gov.hk/en/community/web_accessibility/doc/Summary_Of_Incorporating_WA_In_Education_Institutions.pdf (last visited March 12, 2015).

[46] Government of Hong Kong Special Administrative Region, Office of the Government Chief Information Officer. Development of Assistive Technologies for Persons with Disabilities. Available at: http://www.ogcio.gov.hk/en/community/disabilities/ (last visited March 12, 2015).

[47] G3ict: The Global Initiative for Inclusive ICTs. (2015). Web Accessibility Policy Making; An International Perspective: Japan. Available at: http://www.g3ict.org/resource:center/country_profiles/G3ict_White_Paper_-Accessibility_Policy_Making/Japan (last visited March 12, 2015).

[48] Even Grounds, Accessibility Consulting. (June 18, 2010). Web Accessibility in Japan. Available at: http://www.evengrounds.com/blog/web-accessibility-in-japan (last visited March 12, 2015).

Regulations

7

INTRODUCTION

Public policies may be specified at a high level by statutes or court rulings. Yet the specific details of implementing policies often take the form of regulations that are implemented by government agencies. Even in the late 1800s, Woodrow Wilson identified the difference between elected officials, who had responsibility for defining objectives of public policy, and government agencies and public administrators, who had the responsibility for technical implementation, of figuring out the details to meet those policy objectives [1]. That dualism is still with us today in the form of regulations, which help define the technical details of implementing a law.

Regulations may require specific actions; define obligations; set standards; and direct data collection activity. Within the US, these regulations are generally promulgated by executive agencies. Within the domain of IT accessibility, the principal federal agencies involved in the issuance of regulations are the Departments of Justice, Education, Health and Human Services, Transportation, and the Architectural and Transportation Barriers Compliance Board, known familiarly as the Access Board. Federal accessibility regulations define the obligations of entities subject to the Americans with Disabilities Act (ADA), those that receive federal funding and common carriers, as well as the government's own procurement process.

The process by which regulations are developed and promulgated allows all stakeholders the opportunity to voice their opinions as to the necessity, timetable, and scope of any proposed regulation.

In the United States, the Administrative Procedure Act specifies the process, which is displayed in Table 7.1.

In some instances, there is a first step called "Advance Notice of Proposed Rulemaking" (ANPRM), adding yet another round of hearings and comments prior to Step 1 above. Furthermore, once there is a final rule, an affected party who believes that the regulation was invalidly promulgated may attack it judicially.

When Congress enacts legislation that anticipates the promulgation of regulations, it often sets deadlines for the issuance of regulations—deadlines that are rarely honored. Agencies, when they issue an ANPRM or NPRM, will set deadlines, not only for comments, but for anticipated dates through the end of the process. These are not enforceable and are rarely met. Moreover, proposed regulations often must pass through more than one entity. For example, anything proposed by the Access Board must thereafter be approved by the Department of Justice. The agency charged with

Table 7.1 The regulatory development process in the US (from [2])

The process by which regulations are developed in the US
1. An announcement of a proposed new regulation, called a "Notice of Proposed Rulemaking" (NPRM), must appear in the Federal Register
2. Hearings, research, and opportunities for stakeholders to provide feedback
3. Issuance of a proposed rule
4. Comments on the proposed rule
5. Issuance of a final rule

promulgating the regulations must submit an analysis of their economic impact to the Office of Management and Budget, an entity that must approve every regulation that is implemented. There are exceptions, notably the FCC's largely on-time implementation of regulations pursuant to the Communications and Video Accessibility Act.

This process, designed to ensure fairness, may occasionally produce a fair result, but it also gives maximum leverage to lobbyists who have many opportunities to persuade a government agency to do nothing with a regulation their clients do not like. Sometimes this can mean that a proposed regulation may sit, unacted upon, throughout an entire administration, even though the hearings have been held, the comment period is over, and the proposed final rule has been announced. Current examples of regulations consigned to political purgatory are those applying Titles II (state and local government) and III (public accommodations) of the ADA to the Internet (as described in Chapter 5) and applying Title II to emergency planning. Even when all stakeholders agree on a regulation, however, the gestation period will always be multi-year.

Once a final rule is promulgated, various government agencies may be empowered to enforce it, through administrative process or litigation. In many instances, private parties affected by a regulatory breach may sue to enforce compliance as well.

Regulations are more appropriate than legislation for providing detailed guidance. The legislative process is ill-suited for deciding the necessary turning radius in a wheelchair-accessible bathroom, and both the construction industry and the wheelchair industry need regulatory guidance. Legislation sets the norm, in this case equal access, and the regulation sets forth the details of what access will comprise.

The statutory obligation created by the ADA persists even when no regulations have been enacted. Thus, in *Fortyune v. City of Lomita* (2014 WL 4377467, --- F.3d ---, 9th Cir. 2014), the City of Lomita has thus far unsuccessfully claimed it had no obligation to provide accessible on street parking, since no regulation defined the requirements. The court dismissed this argument, saying "the lack of specific regulations cannot eliminate a statutory obligation." The City of Lomita, as of the time of writing, is seeking review by the U.S. Supreme Court. The Department of Justice has taken a like view, filing a Statement of Interest in *New v. Lucky Brand Dungarees Stores, Inc.* (http://www.ada.gov/briefs/lucky_brand_soi.pdf), asserting that the absence of a specific regulation governing the accessibility of point of sale machines did not eviscerate the requirement that places of public accommodation offer equal access to their services.

Designing effective regulations governing accessible technology requires an acknowledgment of the dynamic nature of technology development. Prescriptive or checklist regulations, such as the current Section 508 regulations, will necessarily become obsolete, while performance-oriented regulations, such as those in the current version of the proposed Section 508 "refresh," should allow new technological solutions to evolve to satisfy the regulatory requirements. Prescriptive technical details tend to focus on a specific technology or a specific approach to access, so when technology changes, these technical details no longer are appropriate or, in some circumstances, may actually limit access.

HOW REGULATIONS ARE INFLUENCED BY INTERNATIONAL TECHNICAL STANDARDS

Regulations often specify a number of different aspects of implementing a public policy. For instance, regulations may specify timelines, coverage (e.g., only companies with at least 50 employees are subject to this regulation), appeal processes, penalties, and evaluation mechanisms. Most of these details are focused on managing the process of compliance with the regulation. However, regulations often must specify technical details. Relating to IT accessibility, regulations must specify what it means to be accessible. Defining accessibility, from a technical point of view, is not primarily a policy definition, but a technical definition. It's a question that is often asked: what is the legal threshold for IT accessibility?

There are typically two approaches to defining IT accessibility in a regulation: technical guidelines and performance standards. Performance standards will be discussed in the next section, but technical guidelines will be addressed in this section. A technical guideline is, at the broadest level, a set of rules. Because technical guidelines are often created by international non-government organizations, often known as standards bodies, these guidelines are often called international guidelines or standards. The Web Accessibility Initiative, part of the World Wide Web Consortium, sets technical standards relating to the web, including standards for HTML and XML. Chapter 4 describes all of the technical standards in detail. These technical guidelines offer much guidance, in terms of not only understanding why a certain guideline is important, but also offering specific coding suggestions for implementation of the guideline. Because these international technical standards are widely adopted, well-known, and well-documented, these can form the basis for technical guidelines within a regulation and, when they do, avoid the risk of competing standards. Because these standards guide multiple communities, regulatory adoption further enhances uniformity. Moreover, technical experts are often already familiar with these standards, resulting in a body of expertise and documentation for implementation. In some cases, software tools for testing for the technical standards may also exist.

In an ideal world, international technical standards, when they exist and are current, should be incorporated, by reference, into a regulation if the standards will satisfy the statutory commands the regulations are to further. This means that the regulation should specify which set of technical guidelines are most appropriate. It is superior, when possible, to refer to the technical standard rather than include it verbatim within a regulation. If a technical standard is referenced, then whenever the technical standard is updated, the new standard applies in the regulation. If a verbatim copy of the technical standard is included in the regulation, even when there's a new technical standard, the older technical details are still a part of the regulation, which can confuse stakeholders in various communities.

When a regulation incorporates technical guidelines, then should not deviate from any existing international standard, except to the extent that the standards fall short of what the statute requires. When a government agency modifies an existing international technical standard, the burden of compliance on those regulated increases. New documentation must be created, new software tools developed, and everyone affected must be re-trained. As an example, in the original implementation of Section 508 in the US, the regulation required a modified version of WCAG 1.0, so that if a technology met WCAG 1.0 requirements, it still would not meet Section 508 requirements. Thus, there was a need for new training and new testing tools. Critics of IT accessibility often cite the burden instituted by requiring IT accessibility. However, the burden should be minimal when familiar technical standards pre-exist the design phase and are followed. Using existing technical standards is also encouraged by U.S. Federal policies. The U.S. Office of Management and Budget Circular A-119 specifically "directs agencies to use voluntary consensus standards in lieu of government-unique standards except where inconsistent with law or otherwise impractical" [3].

There is also a trickle-down effect to international technical standards, first to national/federal regulations and then to state/provincial/local laws and regulations. Often, state and provincial laws and regulations are patterned on similar laws at a national or federal level. For example, Section 508 of the Rehabilitation Act has regulations defining digital accessibility to guide federal purchasing requirements. Eighteen states have enacted "little 508s" to guide accessible technology procurement for state governments. Table 7.2 displays a list of U.S. state laws related to technology accessibility. Those states that have adopted existing Section 508 regulations as state regulations, rather than by referencing existing technical standards, will necessarily encounter an additional delay in updating once new Section 508 regulations are promulgated.

THE ROLE OF PERFORMANCE STANDARDS

Because most interface standards (including interface accessibility standards, as discussed in Chapter 4) focus on meeting technical criteria in code, meeting a set of technical standards for people with disabilities is one potential definition of accessibility [4]. However, an interface may meet a set of technical standards but still be hard to use. For example, a 2012 study of 32 blind users on the web from Power et al. found that only half of the problems encountered by blind users were actually addressed in WCAG 2.0 [5]. It's also important to note that compared to WCAG 1.0, WCAG

Table 7.2 U.S. state laws related to technology accessibility

State	Regulation
Arizona	Ariz. Rev. Stat. Ann. § 41-3532
Arkansas	Ark. Code Ann. §§ 25-26-202 *et seq.*
California	Cal. Gov't Code § 11135(d)(2)
Colorado	Colo. Rev. Stat. Ann. § 24-85-102 *et seq.*
Connecticut (relating to Health Records)	Conn. Gen. Stat. Ann. § 19a-25d(b)(2)
Florida	Fla. Stat. Ann. § 282.601 *et seq.*
Idaho	Idaho Code Ann. § 67-6701 *et seq.*
Indiana	Ind. Code Ann. § 4-13.1-1-3 *et seq.*
Kentucky	Ky. Rev. Stat. Ann. § 61.980 *et seq.*
Louisiana	La. Rev. Stat. Ann. § 39:302
Maryland	Md. Code Ann., State Fin. & Proc. § 3A-311
Minnesota	Minn. Stat. Ann. § 16E.03 *et seq.*
Missouri	Mo. Ann. Stat. § 191.863
Montana	Mont. Code Ann. § 18-5-602 *et seq.*
Nebraska	Neb. Rev. Stat. § 73-205
Oklahoma	Okla. Stat. Ann. tit. 62, § 34.28 *et seq.*
Virginia	Va. Code Ann. § 2.2-3500 *et seq.*
West Virginia	W. Va. Code Ann. § 18-10N-3 *et seq.*

2.0 places less of an emphasis on specific technical solutions. Another example of technically accessible but very hard to use interface features is audio CAPTCHAs, which are theoretically accessible for blind users, but many of the audio CAPTCHAs have task success rates below 50% [6].

Conversely, it is possible that an interface might be easy for people with disabilities to use but not meet a set of technical standards. For instance, current interface technical standards in regulations may not allow for the possibility that blind people can use touch screens. However, touch screens with the accessibility features found on newer devices are effective and well-liked by blind people. The technical standards neither predicted nor allowed for the development of such technologies, because the technical standards were more focused on specific technologies, rather than performance or functionality. Often, the best solution is a combination of technical standards and performance standards.

Performance standards in regulations may help bridge the gap, allowing a way for technologies not envisioned in a set of technical standards to emerge that could afford effective alternative methods of achieving accessibility. This approach avoids or at least reduces the risk of regulatory obsolescence—a problem that not only can affect the disabled consumer but also can restrict technological advance. One might expect, therefore, that industry would prefer performance standards, but this has not historically been the case.

Automated teller machines provide an example of the complexity at the intersection of performance standards and technical standards. The original Americans with Disabilities Act Accessibility Guidelines (ADAAG) regulation governing nonvisual accessibility of ATMs provided merely that all functions of the ATM available to sighted users should be available to blind users and did not specify whether to achieve this by voice guidance technology or otherwise (see Table 7.3). Banks and ATM manufacturers complained that they did not understand what this standard required and lobbied for more prescriptive approaches that would define, among other things, the need for speech output, uniformity in the order of keys, and their size and distance (see the newer standards from 2010 in Table 7.3). These keys must be tactilely discernable, even though accessible touch screens are now a feasible option. An ATM built according to these technical standards (specifying prescriptive

Table 7.3 A comparison of technical standards and performance standards for automated teller machines

Example	
Technical standard for an automated teller machine	Machines shall be speech enabled. Operating instructions and orientation, visible transaction prompts, user input verification, error messages, and all displayed information for full use shall be accessible to and independently usable by individuals with vision impairments. Speech shall be delivered through a mechanism that is readily available to all users, including but not limited to, an industry standard connector or a telephone handset. Speech shall be recorded or digitized human, or synthesized Exceptions: 1. Audible tones shall be permitted instead of speech for visible output that is not displayed for security purposes, including but not limited to, asterisks representing personal identification numbers 2. Advertisements and other similar information shall not be required to be audible unless they convey information that can be used in the transaction being conducted 3. Where speech synthesis cannot be supported, dynamic alphabetic output shall not be required to be audible (from [7])
Performance standard for an automated teller machine	Instructions and all information for use shall be made accessible to and independently usable by persons with vision impairments (from [8])

approaches) will be nonvisually accessible and would have been accessible under the previous ADAAG performance standard. The difference lies in the future—with specific technical standards, ATMs cannot change methods of being accessible without a change in the technical standards. Furthermore, there are separate technical standards for wheelchair access to ATM machines, for which detailed technical specifications are necessary, and which don't change based on new technologies.

Performance standards—whether users can accomplish tasks utilizing an interface—focus on user-defined criteria, not technically defined criteria. It would be wrong to distinguish technical standards as addressing technical accessibility and performance standards as addressing usability. Performance standards in regulations do not often specify a threshold for where performance must be. So, within structured usability testing, it might be typical to say, "usability testing and iterative design will continue until user performance reaches the 90% level," but that is not how most performance standards are written. A regulation will rarely state HOW user performance will be evaluated or what level of user performance to complete tasks within an interface will be acceptable. So, from a usability point of view, the threshold would be a specific level of user success and description of the method for measurement, but from a regulatory point of view, the threshold is often something simpler like "can be effectively used by a person who is blind." Even with the stated limitations, ideally, regulations should incorporate performance criteria and relegate technical approaches based on current technology to technical guidelines, except, arguably, with respect to physical accessibility, where continuity of design outweighs the potential for design changes.

EXISTING REGULATIONS RELATED TO DIGITAL ACCESSIBILITY
SECTION 508 OF THE REHABILITATION ACT

Section 508 of the Rehabilitation Act was signed into law in 1998, with a focus on ensuring that technologies developed, procured, maintained, or used by the federal government were accessible for people with disabilities. The regulatory standards promulgated pursuant to that statute went into effect in June 2001 and focused on 6 different categories of technology: (1) Software applications and operating systems: (2) Web-based intranet and Internet information and systems, (3) Telecommunication products, (4) Video and multimedia products, (5) Self-contained, closed products, and (6) Desktop and portable computers (all contained in 36 C.F.R. §§ 1194.21-26). These standards were generated by the US Access Board, a small governmental agency that deals with architectural and technical accessibility. The original technical standards were, for the section on web-based intranet and Internet information and systems, a modified version of WCAG 1.0.

The Section 508 regulations also addressed functional performance standards in 36 C.F.R. § 1194.31, addressing functional performance criteria that require that the technology must provide or support assistive technology that makes it possible for there to be "at least one mode of operation and information retrieval" that will work for people who are blind, low vision, Deaf or hard of hearing, use assistive hearing devices, or have limited mobility or manual dexterity However, compliance with functional performance standards does not excuse failure to comply with the technical standards. The regulation in addressing its application states: "Products covered by this part shall comply with all applicable provisions of this part" (36 C.F.R. § 1194.2 (a)). Fortunately, some flexibility is provided by the section on "equivalent facilitation," which states, as follows: "Nothing in this part is intended to prevent the use of designs or technologies as alternatives to those prescribed in this part provided they result in substantially equivalent or greater access to and use of a product for people with disabilities" (36 C.F.R. § 1194.5).

Over time, these technical standards have become significantly obsolete. Furthermore, the six categories of technologies listed above have started to blend. For instance, a smartphone invokes each of the first four categories. A number of products (iPhones, tablet computers, e-book readers) did not exist when the regulations came out. So, because they did not exist at the time, mobile telecommunications devices without buttons (utilizing touch screens) were not addressed.

The regulatory process to update the rules (known informally as the "508 Refresh") began in 2006 with the formation of the Telecommunications and Electronic and Information Technology Advisory Committee (TEITAC), which presented a report to the U.S. Access Board in 2008. In 2010, the first proposed rule was released by the U.S. Access Board (as an Advanced Notice of Proposed Rulemaking) and opened for public comment. A second proposed rule was released in 2011 (again, as an Advanced Notice of Proposed Rulemaking), which incorporated WCAG 2.0 AA, referred to the Web Accessibility Initiative (WAI) document on applying WCAG 2.0 to non-web-based technologies, and then added additional requirements. The proposed rule's additional requirements take a functional performance approach. The 2011 proposed rule was also in line with U.S. Federal Office of Management and Budget Circular A-119 (also currently under revision), encouraging the federal government to utilize existing industry and international technical standards in public policies whenever possible [3]. The Access Board issued its proposed rule (not an ANPRM but an actual proposed rule) on February 18, 2015 and is holding hearings in March 2015. It remains uncertain how much further time will transpire before the Access Board sends a final rule for review to the Department of Justice or how long the review will take at the Department of Justice. However, there is a strong desire from significant portions of the technology developer sector for standards that may create a consensus for moving forward. In the meantime, some U.S. Federal agencies, such as the Departments of Justice, Transportation, and Health and Human Services, have already adopted WCAG 2.0 AA as their agency standard, ahead of the 508 Refresh.

SECTION 503 OF THE REHABILITATION ACT

Section 503 of the U.S. Rehabilitation Act prohibits federal contractors and subcontractors from discriminating in employment against individuals with disabilities. Unlike other parts of the Rehabilitation Act described in this chapter (which are coordinated by the U.S. Access Board or Department of Justice), Section 503 regulatory processes are managed by the U.S. Department of Labor, which is also in charge of enforcement. Online employment applications relate to Section 503 of the Rehabilitation Act of the US, which requires all employers that have federal contracts or subcontracts of at least $10,000 "must take affirmative action to hire, retain, and promote qualified individuals with disabilities" (41 CFR 60-741.1).

The Office of Federal Contract Compliance Programs at the U.S. Department of Labor issued an ANPRM in July 2010 to strengthen and update the regulations relating to Section 503 of the Rehabilitation Act [9]. Among the new requirements was the establishment of hiring goals by government contractors of persons with disabilities.

The ANPRM included a question (#13) relating to the accessibility of online employment applications. Specifically, the ANPRM asks

> What impact would result from requiring that Federal contractors and subcontractors make information and communication technology used by job applicants in the job application process, and by employees in connection with their employment fully accessible and usable by individuals with disabilities? What are the specific costs and/or benefits that might result from this requirement?

On August 27, 2013, the U.S. Department of Labor's Office of Federal Contract Compliance Programs (OFCCP) announced the Final Rule, modifying the regulatory changes to Section 503 of the Rehabilitation Act of 1973 [10]. The proposed change as described in the ANPRM in 2010 had required the contractors to ensure that their electronic or online job application systems are compatible with assistive technology. In the final rule, the requirement was softened to be a reasonable accommodation, rather than requiring that the technology actually be accessible. The new requirement is that the federal "contractor shall ensure" that applicants and employees with disabilities have "equal access to its personnel processes, including those implemented through information and communication technologies." From the text of the regulation:

> the reasonable accommodation obligation extends to contractors' use of electronic or online application systems. A contractor using such a system must provide necessary reasonable accommodation to ensure that qualified individuals with disabilities who are unable to fully utilize the system are provided equal opportunity to apply and be considered for all jobs.

Ironically, OFCCP has instructed that while the voluntary self-identification form, used to invite employees to self-identify as disabled and that employers must give their employees, may be provided in electronic format, the e-form must "use at least 11-pitch for font size (with the exception of the footnote and burden statement, which must be at least 10-pitch in size)." OFCCP explains that "though it may seem that specifying the size and type of font is unnecessary, OFCCP is doing so to ensure the consistency of appearance, ease of reading, and accessibility of the form." In fact, since it is not possible both to set a specific font and allow low-vision employees to increase the font, this requirement works against the accessibility of this form for low-vision employees. This is noted as a reminder that accessibility decisions need to be knowledgeably made at every stage of the process.

THE AMERICANS WITH DISABILITIES ACT

The ADA has had a major impact on the lives of people with disabilities in the US, and its coverage is broad. What is the application of the ADA to web sites and digital technology? The answer with respect to public-facing technology deployed by governmental entities (Title II) is easy. Persons with disabilities are entitled to equal access to programs and activities, so when a governmental entity (including public schools and universities) offers a program or activity that involves web technology or digital content, it must be accessible. Technology provided by government entities, for the public use, must be accessible. With respect to workplace technology used by public entities, the courts have so far been silent, and there has not been regulatory guidance. However, Title II does not distinguish between internal and external obligations, and it would make little sense to require, for example, physically accessible public spaces while failing to provide physical accessibility to employees. The same logic argues for accessible workplace technology.

With respect to private employers, the statutory obligation for accessibility comes from Title I of the ADA, which provides in part that an employer may not use methods of administration that have the effect of discrimination on the basis of disability, a command that would appear to require accessible workplace technology. Again, neither regulations or courts have spoken on this important point. Pending cases—such as one posing whether IBM may wait to caption training and other employment-related videos only when the employee requests it as a reasonable accommodation, since that practice would ensure that the Deaf employee will always be the "last to know"—will flesh out the scope of employer obligations.

With respect to Title III of the ADA, requiring public accommodations not to discriminate in the provision of their services, it appears clear from the Target case (discussed in Chapter 5) that at a minimum the web site of a physical place of public accommodation must be accessible. It is the reach of Title III to businesses in which transactions occur entirely on line (e-commerce) about which the courts have yet to speak clearly. The Netflix case (again, discussed in Chapter 5) holds that an online video store is subject to Title III, while the district court in Target was bound by the appellate court's limitation of Title III to physical places. The US Department of Justice has taken the consistent view that the web sites that function as a public accommodation are covered by Title III of the ADA and said so in an amicus filing in the Netflix litigation. In 1996, the head of the Civil Rights Division at the Department of Justice, Deval Patrick, wrote Senator Thomas Harkin, in response to the Senator's inquiry, and stated that entities covered under the ADA must have accessible web sites, but did not address whether a virtual business was a covered entity [11].

In 2010, the US Department of Justice issued an ANPRM to start a regulatory process for defining specific regulatory requirements for web sites as public accommodations, including virtual places of public accommodation (Title III of the ADA), as well as for the web sites of state and local government (Title II of the ADA) [12]. The regulations associated with the original implementation of the ADA had been issued in 1991, before the introduction of the web to the general public.

The regulatory advance has been glacial. The original ANPRMs for Title II and Title III proposed a public comment period that would close in January 2011. The rulemaking processes for Title II and Title III were subsequently split into two separate regulatory processes. An NPRM for Title II (state and local government) was expected to issue in August 2014, but it had not been issued as of publication of this book. The NPRM for Title III (public accommodations) has been repeatedly postponed and it is unknown when it will be issued [13].

Despite the lack of existing regulatory guidance, the U.S. Department of Justice has made it clear that entities covered under the ADA must provide accessible technology, even without existing regulations with specific requirements. In the *New v. Lucky Brand Jeans* case, the U.S. Department of Justice filed a statement of interest documenting the legal reasoning. David New, a blind individual, tried to purchase items at a Lucky Brand Jeans store, but was unable to use the point of sale terminal because it did not provide any tactile or audio feedback, only a touch screen (despite many touch screens being accessible), and therefore filed under the ADA. Lucky Brand argued for dismissing the case specifically because the regulations and standards under Title III of the ADA do not have specific requirements for point of sale (POS) terminals to have tactile key pads. The DOJ indicated that the interpretation provided by Lucky Brand is incorrect, since "its suggestion that the ADA Standards alone establish a public accommodation's obligations under Title III is incorrect" [14, p. 6]. The DOJ noted that there are many instances where "… the Department has found physical and communication barriers not specifically identified in its regulation or the ADA Standards to be covered under Title III" [14, p. 7]. In addition, U.S. Federal courts have also taken similar positions in multiple cases in multiple circuits, holding that web sites and digital technologies are covered under Title III's requirement to provide appropriate auxiliary aids and services and to ensure effective communication. The DOJ mentioned in the statement of interest that other types of technologies (medical equipment, e-readers, and interactive multimedia) have been covered by Title III even though they are not specifically mentioned in the regulations. Furthermore, there is an existing regulatory process that would provide specific detailed requirements for point of sale terminals, and the DOJ summarized the point by noting, "Until the process of establishing specific technical requirements for POS devices is complete, public accommodations have a degree of flexibility in complying with Title III's more general requirements of nondiscrimination and effective communication—but they still must comply" [14, p. 8–9].

NONDISCRIMINATION ON THE BASIS OF DISABILITY IN AIR TRAVEL: ACCESSIBILITY OF WEB SITES AND AUTOMATED KIOSKS AT U.S. AIRPORTS

The U.S. Department of Transportation (DOT) issued regulations related to airline web sites on May 13, 2008, as a part of the Air Carrier Access Act and under the heading "Nondiscrimination on the Basis of Disability in Air Travel." These regulations, in effect since May 13, 2009 (a year after the regulations were issued), required that if an airline web site was inaccessible, users with disabilities must be able to get the same airfare price over the phone as on the web, and may not be charged extra for using the call center. At the time, the U.S. Department of Transportation noted that some decisions, related to requiring airlines to make their web sites and airport kiosks accessible, would be decided in a future regulatory process.

The specific text of the regulation from 2008 is as follows (from § 382.31):

If a carrier charges people who make reservations by phone or in person more than people who make reservations on the website, this surcharge cannot be applied to persons with disabilities who must make reservations by another means because the website is inaccessible to them. Likewise, if there are "web only" discounts or special offers made available to passengers on the carrier's website, passengers with disabilities who cannot use the website must be offered the same terms when they seek to book a flight by other means. [15, p. 81]

This specific rule was a stop-gap measure, to limit the existence of pricing discrimination, until more permanent regulatory measures could be taken. However, a 2010 research study, as well as a follow-up study from 2012, found that pricing discrimination was frequent against people with disabilities when web sites were inaccessible [16,17].

In December 2012, DOT finally promulgated a new regulation, titled "Nondiscrimination on the Basis of Disability in Air Travel: Accessibility of Web Sites and Automated Kiosks at U.S. Airports." The regulations require US and foreign air carriers that have at least one aircraft with a capacity of 60 seats to make their web sites accessible in accordance with the WCAG 2.0 AA standard. By December 2015, core air travel services and information (e.g., booking or changing a reservation) must be made accessible, and the entire web site must be accessible by December 2016. One of the more interesting aspects of the regulation is that it requires that airlines "test the usability of their accessible primary Web sites in consultation with individuals or organizations representing visual, auditory, tactile, and cognitive disabilities." This focuses the regulation more on performance requirements, rather than only technical standards (as discussed in other portions of this chapter). Rules prohibiting pricing discrimination for airline tickets, similar to the previously existing regulations, still exist and have been expanded to ticket agents who are not airlines (and are not small businesses). So, even if a ticket is not being purchased directly from an airline, third parties such as travel agents must also refrain from pricing discrimination against people with disabilities when the third party web sites are inaccessible.

Furthermore, airline check-in kiosks installed starting in December 2016 must be accessible, and 25% of all check-in kiosks, no matter their age, must be accessible by December 2022. Because of the long time delay involved, this portion of the regulation was publicly criticized by disability advocates who note that, by 2022, a different type of technology will likely be utilized rather than the existing kiosk model at airports. As a side note, disability advocates criticized the regulatory process itself for being, at times, inaccessible. As the final rule notes,

By early November 2011, members of the disability community and advocacy organizations were also requesting that we delay the closing of the comment period until accessibility issues concerning the comment form available at www.regulations.gov could be resolved. In response, we sought expedited action from the Regulations.gov workgroup to correct the accessibility problems with the form and issued a notice in the Federal Register on November 21, 2011, outlining alternative methods for submitting comments until the comment form could be made fully accessible. [18]

In January 2014, the National Federation of the Blind and certain blind air travelers sued the DOT, alleging that the regulation governing kiosks is unlawful in that (1) DOT is not authorized to regulate the accessibility of airport kiosks, because the Air Carrier Access Act ("ACAA") only gives DOT authority over embarkation through de-embarkation; (2) that, if the ACAA is applicable, it does not authorize DOT to consider the cost to the airlines of engaging in nondiscriminatory behavior; (3) that if DOT may consider "cost," it must do so in the context of the overall resources of the industry, which it failed to do; and (4) DOT relied on the undisclosed report of a contractor received after the close of the comment period in crafting the time limits. The DOT has challenged the jurisdiction of the district court to hear this case. In response, the district court has transferred the case to the United States Court of Appeals for the District of Columbia, where it is pending at the time of this writing.

COMMUNICATIONS AND VIDEO ACCESSIBILITY ACT AND E-BOOK READERS

The Communications and Video Accessibility Act (CVAA) of 2010 is one of the newest laws related to digital accessibility. The CVAA was designed to update the telecommunications laws to ensure that the newest technologies and communications devices and transmission media are accessible for people with disabilities. For instance, text-based communication, such as e-mail, Internet browsing, and text messaging, were outside the scope of Section 255 of the Communications Act. Unlike those broad-based civil rights statutes that define the civil right at issue and then define a broad scope where that right is exercised, the CVAA is entirely focused on accessibility in the context of telecommunications. Whereas many of the provisions of the disability rights laws cover the purchasers of technology (such as government and higher education), the CVAA covers manufacturers of communications devices and providers of communications services. Under disability rights laws such as the ADA and Sections 504 and 508 of the Rehabilitation Act, companies can choose to manufacture inaccessible devices, they may just lose a lot of potential sales. Under a telecommunications law, the manufacturing of inaccessible devices itself is regulated.

The CVAA modified the original Communications Act of 1934 and also added Sections 715-719 to the Communications Act. Section 715 specifies that Voice Over IP (VOIP) providers shall contribute to the telecommunications Relay Services Fund. Section 716 relates to ensuring the accessibility of advanced communications services (hardware and software relating to networking). Section 717 relates to recordkeeping requirements for manufacturers and enforcement procedures. Section 718 requires that smartphones designed for public usage, including a web browser, must ensure that the web browser is accessible to people who are blind or low vision. Section 719 authorizes for federal funding "those programs that are approved by the Commission for the distribution of specialized customer premises equipment designed to make telecommunications service, Internet access service, and advanced communications, including interexchange services and advanced telecommunications and information services, accessible by low-income individuals who are deaf-blind" [19]. Following the CVAA's enactment, the FCC further extended the scope of its rules under Section 255 to cover Internet service providers [20]. (https://apps.fcc.gov/edocs_public/attachmatch/DA-08-821A1.pdf at paragraph 472)

Rather than adopting substantive changes to its rules, the FCC covered broadband providers by expanding the scope of "telecommunications services" covered under Title II of the 1934 Act in the 2015 *Protecting and Promoting the Open Internet* order to include Internet service providers. While the precise application of the rules to ISPs and Internet services is not yet clear, the Commission's Section 255 rules require that telecommunications services be accessible and that telecommunications equipment be designed, developed, and manufactured to be accessible in collaboration with people with disabilities [21]. (http://www.ecfr.gov/cgi-bin/text-idx?SID=c072052085084a57812c42c18fe6ee09&mc=true&tpl=/ecfrbrowse/Title47/47cfr6_main_02.tpl) It is likely that the contours of the rules as applied to Internet service providers will become more clear following the resolution of litigation over the order on issues not related to accessibility.

CVAA Waivers

The topic of e-book reader accessibility, and the regulations associated with the CVAA, has been in the news within the last few years, due to one provision of the CVAA: "The FCC is empowered to grant waivers to qualifying entities in two situations: (1) where a device or service capable of advanced communications services is designed for multiple purposes, but is designed primarily for purposes other than using advanced communications services; and (2) for small entities" [19]. Because most e-reader devices contain advance communication services, they become, in the legal sense, communications devices, subject to the CVAA. The requirements under Section 716 (and the associated regulations) would require equipment used for advanced communications services to be accessible as of October 8, 2013.

On May 6, 2013, the Coalition of E-Readers Manufacturers (a group of companies that manufacturer e-reader devices) filed a petition with the Federal Communications Commission for a waiver of Sections 716 and 717 of the Communications Act and Part 14 of the FCC's regulations. Its main argument was that e-reader devices are designed for the primary purpose of reading text, not communicating [19]. The Coalition specifically defined devices that are primarily for e-reading as those devices with no camera and no LCD screen, to separate them from tablet computers.

A larger coalition of consumer, advocacy, and library groups fought against this waiver. Their comments, as reported in the waiver granted by the FCC, noted that earlier obsolete e-readers had included accessibility features that were not found in the newer products and went on to say, in part, as follows:

> *that the ACS features of e-readers, including the ability to access books on the Internet through web browsers, the ability to connect with others, and to share and discuss content with friends over social media, are the very features that set e-readers apart from print books ... granting a waiver would undermine other federal nondiscrimination laws that direct educational institutions not to use electronic book readers or other technologies that are not accessible to people who are blind or visually impaired.*

> *... in response to the [e-reader manufacturer] Coalition's assertion that other accessible alternatives to basic e-readers are available, Consumer Groups assert that having to purchase costlier devices, such as tablets and smartphones, with "many more features than they would want to use, just to be able to read digital books" would result in a "disability tax" and a "separate but equal" standard of access that is inconsistent with the spirit of the CVAA.* [19]

While the Coalition of E-Reader Manufacturers asked for a permanent waiver, the FCC originally granted a one-year waiver until January 28, 2015, and an extension was recently granted, until January 28, 2016. Furthermore, there were more stipulations added to the waiver, aside from devices not having a camera or LCD screen. The waiver granted by the FCC also requires that waived devices not be "(3) ... offered or shipped to consumers with built-in ACS client applications and the device manufacturer does not develop ACS applications for its respective device, but the device may be offered or shipped to consumers with a browser and social media applications." Furthermore, "The device is marketed to consumers as a reading device and promotional material about the device does not tout the capability to access ACS." It is unclear what the future status of this specific regulatory waiver will become. However, what is clear is that, regardless of the outcome within telecommunications laws, the requirements under the ADA and the Rehabilitation Act of 1973 still apply. As previously stated in previous chapters and this chapter, on June 29, 2010, the Civil Rights Division of the US Department of Justice, and the Office of Civil Rights of the US Department of Education, issued a collaborative letter to presidents of all colleges and universities in the US. This letter warned the universities against requiring the use of inaccessible e-book readers (which do not allow for text-to-speech or do not have accessible menus) in higher education coursework. The letter noted that requiring the use of e-book readers that are inaccessible to students who are blind or low vision, without providing accessible alternatives, would violate both the Americans with Disabilities Act of 1990 and Section 504 of the Rehabilitation Act of 1973. The U.S. Department of Education noted that these rules also applied to K-12 education. Other legal settlements about e-book readers related to public libraries, and more details about all of these agreements are provided in Chapter 5 about US Laws and Lawsuits.

REGULATIONS IN OTHER COUNTRIES

Regulations tend to play a more prominent role in the United States and countries that are part of the Commonwealth (the UK and 52 other countries that were primarily former British colonies). The key aspects of regulations that are present in other countries, are (1) usually the focus on providing more technical details that are outside of the scope of legislation, and (2) providing a public comment period. For instance, Canadian laws are translated from the legal statute into the "Common Look and Feel for the Internet 2.0" regulation which contains specific technical guidelines for web accessibility for Canadian government web sites, and is provided by the Treasury Board of Canada Secretariat. For the Disability Discrimination Act in Australia, there are "advisory notes" which provide guidance and interpretation of the law. See Chapter 6 on International Disability Law for more information on both Canadian and Australian examples.

Perhaps the most significant example of a multi-national regulatory process is the European Union's efforts with EU Mandate 376. The European Commission issued a mandate, titled Mandate 376, in 2005. Three European standards organizations (CEN, CENELEC, and ETSI) were charged with the development of functional accessibility requirements for technology procurements by governments [20]. Phase 1 involved background research to evaluate existing accessibility requirements and evaluation approaches. Phase 2, which it is hoped will result in a final standard being adopted by the end of 2015 (at publication time, the standard had not been issued), includes the development of online toolkits and supporting documents [21]. In the current draft, WCAG 2.0 AA is supported as the technical standard, but priority is placed on the functional performance standards (similarly to current regulatory drafts of Section 508 in the US). The WCAG2ICT, the guidelines for translating WCAG for use in non-web technologies, was also adopted in the documents (again, similarly to the Section 508 regulatory process).

As discussed in Chapter 9 on compliance monitoring and procurements, among the drafts available as a part of EU Mandate 376 is Draft TR 101551,"Guidelines on the use of accessibility award criteria for publicly procured ICT products and services in Europe," which that documents specific methods related to procurement to be used in tandem with the EU-wide technical standards being developed. The EU 376 document suggests that procurements should specify the accessibility required, in terms of performance or functional requirements, rather than having a general statement such as stating that a technology "must meet EU 376." The EU 376 document discusses what to do, for example, in situations in which multiple bids are sought, but only one company has the expertise to provide the accessibility requirements. The document also notes how evidence to support the vendor claims of accessibility [22] should be required.

The EU 376 mandate documents are in draft form, but the technical specifications are designed to harmonize with the Section 508 requirements in the United States so that an IT that meets the accessibility requirements of one would also meet the accessibility requirements of the other. The draft report "TR 101550: Documents relevant to EN 301549 accessibility requirements for public procurement of ICT products and services in Europe" specifically notes that the goal of EU Mandate 376 is to harmonize technology and procurement requirements

> ... to reduce the burden on manufacturers by providing a common set of public procurement requirements for accessibility which as far as possible could apply to markets both in Europe and in the rest of the world. [23, p. 7]

It is important to note that while a priority was placed on functional performance criteria, the draft TR 101550 noted "It is not possible to have 'Usage with limited cognition' as a testable FPC because the range of cognitive impairments is broad and the ways to address these different impairments are so diverse that no single test of success in meeting such an FPC could be devised" [23, p. 10]. This echoes the sentiments in our introductory chapter, that accessibility for cognitive impairment is currently still a challenging goal.

SUMMARY

Regulations play an important role in digital accessibility, bridging the gap between broad statutes setting normative standards and technical advice and definitions. Past regulations have placed more of an emphasis on technical guidelines than user performance criteria, but in the US and Europe, the trend in current regulatory processes is to place more of an emphasis on user performance criteria. The good news for all involved is that the trend in regulation is to harmonize with both international and inter-governmental technical standards. Weaknesses of a regulatory regime include the slow process for regulatory approval and the influence that corporate interests can have on the regulatory process. Finally, the regulations often leave out policies for implementation and monitoring, a topic to be discussed in more detail in Chapter 9.

REFERENCES

[1] Gupta D. Analyzing public policy: concepts, tools, and techniques. Washington, DC: Congressional Quarterly Press; 2001.

[2] Dye T. Understanding public policy. Boston: Pearson Education; 2013.

[3] Office of Management and Budget (1998). Circular No. A-119—Federal Register (Federal Participation in the Development and Use of Voluntary Consensus Standards and in Conformity Assessment Activities). Available at: http://www.whitehouse.gov/omb/circulars_a119_a119fr.

[4] Petrie H, Kheir O. The relationship between accessibility and usability of websites. In: Proceedings of the ACM conference on human factors in computing systems (CHI); 2007. p. 397–406.

[5] Power C, Freire A, Petrie H, Swallow D. Guidelines are only half the story: accessibility problems encountered by blind users on the web. In: Proceedings of the ACM conference on human factors in computing systems (CHI); 2012. p. 433–42.

[6] Sauer G, Lazar J, Hochheiser H, Feng J. Towards a universally usable human interaction proof: evaluation of task completion strategies. ACM Trans Access Comput 2010;2(4):1–32.

[7] U.S. Department of Justice (2010). 2010 ADA Standards for Accessible Design. Available at: http://www.ada.gov/regs2010/2010ADAStandards/2010ADAstandards.htm.

[8] U.S. Access Board (2002). Americans with Disabilities Act Accessibility Guidelines. Available at: http://www.access-board.gov/guidelines-and-standards/buildings-and-sites/about-the-ada-standards/background/adaag#4.34.

[9] Lazar J, Olalere A, Wentz B. Investigating the accessibility and usability of job application web sites for blind users. J Usability Stud 2012;7(2):68–87.

[10] U.S. Department of Labor (2013). Affirmative Action and Nondiscrimination Obligations of Contractors and Subcontractors Regarding Individuals with Disabilities. Available at: http://www.dol.gov/ofccp/regs/compliance/section503.htm.

[11] U.S. Department of Justice (1996). Letter to Senator Tom Harkin from Assistant Attorney General Deval Patrick. Available at: http://www.justice.gov/crt/foia/readingroom/frequent_requests/ada_tal/tal712.txt.

[12] U.S. Department of Justice (2010). Nondiscrimination on the Basis of Disability; Accessibility of Web Information and Services of State and Local Government Entities and Public Accommodations. Available at: http://www.ada.gov/anprm2010/web%2020anprm_2010.htm.

[13] Regulations.gov (2014). Nondiscrimination on the Basis of Disability; Accessibility of Web Information and Services of Public Accommodations. Available at: http://www.reginfo.gov/public/do/eAgendaViewRule?pubId=201404&RIN=1190-AA61.

[14] U.S. Department of Justice (2014). Statement of Interest in *New v. Lucky Brand Jeans*. Available at: http://www.ada.gov/briefs/lucky_brand_soi.pdf.

[15] U.S. Department of Transportation (2009). Nondiscrimination on the basis of disability in air travel. 14 CFR 382. Available at: http://airconsumer.ost.dot.gov/rules/Part%20382-2008.pdf.

[16] Lazar J, Jaeger P, Adams A, Angelozzi A, Manohar J, Marciniak J, et al. Up in the air: are airlines following the new DOT rules on equal pricing for people with disabilities when websites are inaccessible? Gov Inf Q 2010;27(4):329–36.

[17] Lazar J, Jaeger P, Olalere A, Algarne M, Augustine Z, Brown C, et al. Still up in the air: government regulation of airline websites and continuing price inequality for persons with disabilities online. In: Proceedings of the 13th annual international conference on digital government research; 2012. p. 240–5.

[18] Regulations.gov (2014). Nondiscrimination on the Basis of Disability in Air Travel: Accessibility of Web Sites and Automated Kiosks at U.S. Airports. Available at: http://www.regulations.gov/#!documentDetail;D=DOT-OST-2011-0177-0111.

[19] U.S. Federal Communications Commission (2014). Coalition of E-Reader Manufacturers' Petition for Waiver of ACS Rules. Available at: http://www.fcc.gov/document/coalition-e-reader-manufacturers-petition-waiver-acs-rules.

[20] Martinez L, Pluke M. Mandate M 376: new software accessibility requirements. Procedia Comput Sci 2014;(DSAI 2013):271–80.

[21] European Union (2013). Draft EN 301549: Accessibility requirements for public procurement of ICT products and services in Europe. Available at: http://www.etsi.org/deliver/etsi_en/301500_301599/301549/301501.301500.301500_301520/en_301549v010000c.pdf.

[22] European Union (2013). Draft TR 101551: Guidelines on the use of accessibility award criteria for publicly procured ICT products and services in Europe. Available at: http://www.mandate376.eu/doc/TR%20101%20551v20008.doc.

[23] European Union (2013). Draft TR 101550: Documents relevant to EN 301549: accessibility requirements for public procurement of ICT products and services in Europe. Available at: http://www.mandate376.eu/doc/TR%20101%20550v008.doc.

Evaluation methods and measurement

8

INTRODUCTION

Because no specific guidance exists in technical standards or policies for how to evaluate accessibility, evaluation is one of the most challenging steps for policymakers and developers. Once a developer has built a technology following all the guidelines, how does one evaluate it to make sure it is as accessible as was intended? The interface standards (discussed in Chapter 4) provide technical guidance on design, but not on evaluation. The laws (discussed in Chapters 5 and 6) have broad reach and high-level goals that do not address evaluation. Nor is this treated at present in regulations (discussed in Chapter 7). The evaluation methods (discussed in this chapter) are different from the compliance monitoring policies (discussed in Chapter 9).

Evaluation methods (user testing, expert review, automated evaluation) are at a more technical level and correspond to identifying specific flaws in design and coding. Evaluation methods address the accessibility of specific interfaces. The aggregated results of evaluation methods—specific technical improvements needed in specific interfaces—inform developers, designers, and engineers. Evaluation methods are a human-computer interaction activity.

Compliance monitoring (discussed in Chapter 9), is a policy activity. Compliance monitoring focuses not on specific technical details, but instead focuses on policies and processes. For instance, compliance monitoring (at a macro level) might specify how often certain evaluation method activities take place or what trigger event (such as updating to a new version of software) would require an evaluation method to take place. Unlike the aggregated results of evaluation methods, which inform those involved with technical design, the aggregated results of compliance monitoring inform policymakers and managers.

The interface standards, discussed in Chapter 4, must be utilized in combination with the evaluation methods in the current chapter. Getting users involved with the design process and utilizing the interface standards discussed in Chapter 4 are the first step. Design is an iterative process in which the imagination of design is subject to the experimental application of science. Technical interface standards are written for an entire field and for every possible situation, not for a specific design and a specific situation. Therefore, interface standards may not address every need and may be hard to apply for a particular situation. Or the people who are charged with applying the interface standards may not have enough expertise to do so. Or, because of time pressures, interface standards may not have been applied consistently throughout design. Mechanically applying technical standards will not necessarily mean that an interface will be accessible in every possible situation.

Furthermore, a technology may be consistent with a set of interface standards, and therefore should be accessible to someone with a disability, but empirically prove difficult to use. For instance, visual CAPTCHAs are inaccessible to people who are blind. This is a clear accessibility violation, if a web site requires a CAPTCHA but has no audio equivalent. Imagine that an audio CAPTCHA was added to the site, as required by WCAG (Web Content Accessibility Guidelines) 2.0. The site is then accessible, right? But what happens if the audio CAPTCHA is incredibly hard to use for blind people? Task success rates for blind users attempting audio CAPTCHAs often are less than 50% [1–3]. So there are situations where a site might meet technical accessibility guidelines but still be very hard to use and, therefore, not provide equal access. Researchers have found that commonly used web accessibility guidelines do not ensure easy web site usage for someone with a disability [4,5]. For instance, a web site might state that it is in compliance with WCAG 2.0, but blind users may still find aspects of the site very hard to use [6].

THE ROLE OF EVALUATION METHODS

For maximum efficacy and efficiency, evaluation should be performed before implementation, but where the technology is dynamic, such as a web site, it should also be done on an ongoing basis to ensure that changes and updates have not created unintended accessibility barriers. Because adding accessibility features earlier in development is easier and less expensive than retrofitting existing interfaces, evaluation should take place from the beginning of the design process [7,8]. Because technologies, documents, and web content change, evaluation must be ongoing. Thus, the challenge in devising a good evaluation protocol is not only the determination of the degree and extent of sampling and the evaluation methodology, but also the frequency with which to evaluate.

THE NEED FOR ONGOING EVALUATION

Software and content updates require ongoing evaluation. Some devices, primarily hardware devices, are often "fixed in time." If a device is built using accessibility standards and, after evaluation for accessibility is found to be accessible, re-evaluation would be needed only if the operating system or other software is updated. For instance, phones, office copiers, and voting machines do not need to be repeatedly evaluated for accessibility. By contrast, because web-based technologies have features and content that are modified on a daily, and in some cases an hourly, basis, they must be monitored on an ongoing basis. A web site that is accessible one day can be inaccessible the next. An online course management system can have an accessible software shell, but content is uploaded on a regular basis, and some of the new content may not be accessible. While e-book devices may themselves be accessible, book publishers unfortunately can choose to disable the text-to-speech options on their book content or fail to label graphics adequately. Some prophylactic steps are possible, such as requiring new content or new web pages to be entered through an accessible template or requiring a label before one can upload a graphic. Nonetheless, for these technologies, evaluation must be ongoing, even daily, to ensure that accessibility is maintained.

DISTINCTION BETWEEN ACCESSIBILITY AND USABILITY

Usable technology is accessible, but the converse is not always true. The International Standards Organization (ISO) explains usability as having users achieve their task goals effectively, efficiently, and in a satisfied manner within a context of use [9]. ISO then incorporates usability into its definition of accessibility: "the usability of a product, service, environment, or facility by people with the widest range of capabilities" [10]. However, other definitions of accessibility may focus less on ease of use and more on theoretical access [10]. Chapter 7, on regulations, has a deeper discussion of the difference in regulations between technical design and performance measurements.

An arid approach to accessibility that ignores the critical importance of ease of use and satisfaction ignores the end goal of accessibility: *equality of access*. If the disabled user must have greater expertise than the average nondisabled user or can only accomplish in two hours a task doable in five minutes by the nondisabled user, then accessibility has been an academic exercise of little practical value. If disabled users have a 30% success rate, one could argue that it is 100% accessible for those who succeeded, but the sophistic nature of such a claim is apparent if nondisabled users experience a 90% success rate. The distinction between access and ease of use, has led to distinct evaluation methods, with usability testing focusing more on ease of use by actual users and expert inspections and automated testing focusing more on technical accessibility.

The idea of building interfaces that can be used by a broad majority of users appears under different names in different disciplines. Both Lazar and Shneiderman have championed "universal usability," a term popular in the human-computer interaction community. Universal usability is interface design that is easy to use across diverse populations, including ones with differences in ability/disability, computing experience, and network connectivity speed [11,12]. The terms "universal design" and "inclusive design" originated in the product design and home design communities, are both related to universal usability, but have a different focus. Universal design focuses on designing for a wide range of abilities. Inclusive design focuses on including a wide range of people in the design process (similar to user-centered design in the human-computer interaction community) [13]. These terms share a common thread: to ensure ease of use by a wide range of users, potential users should be included, as early as possible, in the design, development, and evaluation processes. Evaluation methods are in no way meant to replace user involvement. Evaluation methods are a confirmation that, indeed, user needs are being met.

METRICS FOR ACCESSIBILITY?

While it might seem desirable to assign one score to a technology as a clear accessibility "rating," the diversity of technologies, users and disabilities, and evaluation methods makes impossible a single metric or score that completely defines the accessibility and/or usability of a product or interface. Such a global statistic would neither be accurate or useful. Metrics are used, but all suffer from biases. For instance, usability testing, a core approach for evaluation, often involves the metrics of task performance (number of tasks successfully completed as a percentage of tasks attempted), time performance (length of time required to successfully complete tasks), and user satisfaction (subjective measure of how much a user liked interacting with a technology). Although these are international standards for measuring usability [9], they are still subject to bias regarding which tasks were attempted and which users (with which disabilities) took part in the usability testing. Metrics might be easiest to determine for automated evaluations; however, because of the confusing results often given by automated evaluations (described later in this chapter), these metrics are questionable.

Authors have attempted to create accessibility metrics using automated evaluation tools for web sites. These web accessibility metrics include the failure rate (percentage of violations of the total potential violations) [14], web accessibility barrier score (which incorporates the importance of a specific violation) [15], and a web accessibility quantitative metric (which attempts to eliminate the bias inherent in a system that determines web page accessibility based on a large number of potential violations not occurring) [16]. Rather than just focus on a point-in-time metric, other metrics focus on longitudinal studies, looking at improvement (or decline) of accessibility over time. The benefit of using such a time-related metric for accessibility is that, regardless of the bias a metric uses, that bias is present over time [17]. Almost all of these metrics are related to web accessibility, not other types of technologies, and they all have weaknesses.

CORE METHODS FOR EVALUATION

The three core methods for accessibility evaluation are user testing (involving users with disabilities), expert reviews/inspections, and automated software tools. These methods are not exclusive; they can be used together. The only limitations (which occur frequently) are time and money. These three approaches investigate different aspects of accessibility, and each has strengths and weaknesses. When used together, they sometimes should be used in a specific order. For instance, when usability testing and expert inspections are used, the expert inspections should be done first because they find the more obvious accessibility-related interface flaws, allowing users taking part in usability testing to detect less-obvious problems. These three methods are not equally useful for different technologies. Automated evaluations are useful primarily for web pages; they are available for few applications or operating systems and do not exist at all for hardware devices. As previously mentioned in this chapter, evaluations using these three methods are not a substitute for getting people with disabilities involved in the development process. Ideally, people with disabilities are involved in multiple stages of development, informing the design, providing suggestions, and perhaps, even, doing user testing of early prototypes and designs.

Table 8.1 provides an overview of the strengths and weaknesses of usability testing, expert inspections, and automated reviews. Usability testing, which involves representative users with identified disabilities performing representative tasks, is most useful for determining true ease of use, but because the tasks used in usability testing do not cover all aspects of the interface, they will not reveal all accessibility barriers to all disabled users [18]. Expert inspections are good at determining legal compliance [19] and identifying accessibility problems for a wide range of users [18] but may not identify issues related to ease of use for a series of inter-related tasks. Both usability testing and expert reviews are ideal; however, neither scales well if hundreds and thousands of screen designs must be evaluated. If usability testing or expert inspections are used, some type of sampling method often must be applied to determine which screens, devices, and tasks are fully evaluated for accessibility [20].

Table 8.1 A basic comparison of the strengths and weaknesses of usability testing, expert inspections, and automated reviews

Method	Strength	Weakness
User testing	Most accurate method for determining true usability; also most accurate for determining usability of multi-step processes (such as purchasing an item online) or multi-screen interactions	Users with disabilities may find only interface problems that relate to their own disability; complexity of planning usability testing limits the number of times that it can occur
Expert inspection	Most accurate for determining strict compliance with legal requirements or technical guidelines	May miss aspects of the interface that relate more specifically to ease of use, rather than technical compliance; experts may not be able to incorporate the limited amount of technical or domain knowledge of users
Automated review	Unlimited scale, thousands or tens of thousands of interfaces can be evaluated	Only code-based interfaces (such as screen layout or web pages) can be evaluated; automated reviews determine the presence of features such as ALT text or labels but cannot determine the effectiveness or appropriateness of those labels; reports from tools can be confusing

The Web Accessibility Initiative has a working draft of an evaluation methodology that describes a framework for doing accessibility evaluations (for more information, see http://www.w3.org/TR/WCAG-EM/). In its draft evaluation framework, the need to select a representative sample of web pages is highlighted as an important step. Only automated reviews (software tools) work well over thousands of screen designs, but the results are often misleading, with many false positives, and will fail to detect labels of graphics, links, and edit boxes that contain inadequate information.

Furthermore, expert inspections and usability testing can be used for any type of technology, but automated software tools typically work only for web pages, not operating systems, applications, or hardware devices. Regardless of the evaluation methods used, evaluation should occur as early in development as possible. Discovering accessibility flaws early in development lowers the cost of remediation and shortens the repair time. The more fully a technology (hardware or software) is built before the detection of accessibility barriers, the greater the cost and effort to fix. Retrofitting is much more expensive than building accessibility features into initial design [7].

USER TESTING

As a first step, usability testing can involve having representative users attempting representative tasks, at any stage of development, from early prototypes of interfaces, to fully mature products [21]. The representative users help identify the flaws as they interact with the interface and attempt to complete tasks [22]. Observers monitor the usability testing to note when users are having problems interacting with an interface or device [23]. Conceptually, this is similar to product focus groups, where feedback is given about consumer products while they are under development. In the context of users with disabilities, usability testing helps bridge a specific gap: the gap between an interface that technically might be accessible for people with disabilities but in reality is impossible to use [24]. Testing by people with disabilities gives real-world feedback on how a device or interface would be used by real users.

Usability testing involves giving users a list of tasks to perform on a new technology. The users are asked to attempt these tasks without outside assistance. Observers (often usability experts or the interface designers) watch as the users attempt the tasks, noting where there are areas that are problematic. Task performance (how many tasks are successfully completed) and time performance (how long it takes to successfully perform a task) are recorded as the two most typical metrics [22]. See Table 8.2 for an example of quantitative data from usability testing. Users are also sometimes asked to comment on the interface as they use it (the "think aloud" protocol), provide feedback, and note problems. Finally, users are asked to comment on the interface after the session has completed, often through a satisfaction survey. As in any type of usability testing, it is important to protect the anonymity of participants with disabilities, ensuring that any data or videos resulting from the usability testing do not identify the participants in any way.

Table 8.2 An example of quantitative usability testing data for blind users performing usability testing of a specific e-mail task on five different web-based, e-mail applications (from [25])

Application	Users with experience	Experienced users (task performance/ average time performance)	Inexperienced users (task performance/ average time performance)
Outlook 2007	2 of 5	82% 89.5 seconds	71% 103.6 seconds
Outlook Express	3 of 5	97% 43.5 seconds	88% 88.9 seconds
Gmail	3 of 4	49% 101.7 seconds	24% 133.5 seconds
Hotmail	1 of 3	65% 222.5 seconds	56% 164.3 seconds
Yahoo Mail	3 of 4	47% 144.2 seconds	60% 91 seconds

Formal usability testing can involve a laboratory with two separate rooms, one for the user and one for an observer who watches the user through a one-way mirror [22]. However, such settings are rarely necessary. Portable lab equipment, remote usability testing (utilizing applications that can collect data remotely), and even having an observer sit next to a user during testing are all considered valid forms of usability testing. Usability testing adapts some of the techniques from experimental design; however, there are different goals: usability testing focuses on identifying and fixing flaws in interfaces, whereas experimental design focuses on identifying statistical differences between treatment groups that can be generalized to other situations [22]. Usability testing can take place at multiple stages: paper prototypes, partially working prototypes, or fully working prototypes.

Usability testing can be done for screen designs or hardware devices. The overall goal is to improve the quality of an interface design by identifying flaws that need to be improved. When simply "identifying interface flaws so that they can be improved" is the goal, rather than "generalizing findings to other categories of research," there is a capability for flexibility that often doesn't exist in more traditional research methods. For instance, in a controlled experiment, it is important that multiple factors be controlled. Everyone in the same treatment group must receive exactly the same treatment. However, in usability testing, the interface can be modified after every few users so that the interface design is continuously improved, and interface changes are immediately evaluated to see if they are effective [26]. This is known as iterative usability testing, in which the interface is changed repeatedly, often after every user or every few users.

One of the biggest challenges in usability testing is determining the number of users sufficient for valid results. There is disagreement within the human-computer interaction community regarding the number of participants required. The classic saying is that "five users will find a majority of the interface flaws," but the research literature has pointed to 10-15 users being a more appropriate testing group [22,27,28]. Furthermore, while more users are better, for most interfaces, having 30, 50, or 70 users test an interface just isn't realistic. Usability testing isn't experimental design, where the goal is to have large enough samples to statistically test theories [22]. With usability testing, there is a diminishing marginal return once you have more than 15 or 20 users. After even a few users, you will typically begin to see the same patterns emerge. Rather than have many users perform usability testing at one stage for one interface, it's important to have smaller groups attempt usability testing on a range of interfaces, on a regular basis. Furthermore, the reality is that, regardless of how many users test an interface, ALL of the flaws will not be found, and even if all of the flaws were found, they probably couldn't all be fixed [26]. Therefore, the goal of usability testing should be to include as many users as possible, given the budget and timeline, to guide the interface design toward usability.

Usability testing focuses on improvement, not perfection. Within the disability/accessibility context, this may mean that it is important to get users with a variety of disabilities. Unless the interface/technology is being designed specifically for one population of users (such as a web site designed specifically for people with Down syndrome) [29], users with different disabilities should be used in the testing of the interface. Blind people often are the focus of usability testing on web-based interfaces simply because they face more challenges on web sites, as compared to many other user groups. Similarly, Deaf people often face more challenges with telecommunications products such as phones (although blind people also face challenges with telecommunications products). Thus, although a population with a specific disability may be the focus of testing of a certain product, it is a best practice to perform usability testing with users who have a variety of disabilities, including ones who are blind, Deaf, or have motor impairment. This was done with the usability evaluation of the recovery.gov web site [30]. It is also good to have a few users with cognitive impairments; however, this does not occur as often as it should.

Like any evaluation method, usability testing has strengths and weaknesses. The strengths of such testing with regard to people with disabilities include the most obvious: when people with disabilities perform a usability test, they utilize the tools that they are most comfortable and familiar with. There are certain tools that they naturally prefer. This helps reveal whether the interface is accessible the way that a person with that specific disability will typically use it. The distribution of computer skills (and communication skills) is often wide in the community of people with disabilities [31]; some users are expert, but others are novice. Having a few users with disabilities evaluate an interface often serves as a "reality check."

The feedback provided by users with disabilities is useful, helpful, and important, because how developers envision users with disabilities and the skills and experience levels of such people often are different. Usability testing is also most useful for ascertaining the usability of multi-step transactions, where users must go through a series of steps (such as purchasing an item online, registering for classes, reading, responding, and sending an e-mail message, or configuring a new hardware device) [25]. Expert reviews are good at checking for the accessibility of a single step, but user testing is helpful in understanding how users go through the entire process [32].

There are a number of weaknesses of usability testing involving people with disabilities. Usability testing of an interface by someone with a specific disability may yield results that are specific to the user, his or her disability, and his or her technical setup [33]. Blind testers should not be testing for usability by Deaf people, and those with motor impairments should not evaluate the usability of an interface by someone with a cognitive impairment. Furthermore, a single blind person will not be able to determine if an interface is easy for ALL blind people to use, because ease of use sometimes is affected by whether the blind person uses low vision techniques, is completely blind, and uses a refreshable Braille display, as well as whether the person is newly blind and thus new to experience with nonvisual technology. Or a blind individual might have years of expertise utilizing the JAWS screen reader, but if asked to attempt a usability test with the VoiceOver screen reader, the results may be misleading. In addition, factors such as years of experience, technology environment, and quality of network connection come into play. Thus, having one person with a specific disability evaluate a technology will not allow you to determine if the technology will work well for all people with disabilities or even for all people with the same disability [33].

There are challenges in coordinating usability testing involving users with disabilities. One challenge is that often there are threshold accessibility barriers that prevent a user from getting past entry-level tasks. For instance, if the search engine on a job posting web site won't allow for blind users even to search for jobs (due to a clickable image map requiring a pointing device), then the blind user is stymied at the outset and cannot take the next step toward applying online for a job [32]. When this occurs, some type of intervention is required, in which researchers/evaluators must perform a task for a user with a disability that the user cannot independently perform. Absent intervention, such a usability testing session would simply grind to a halt. After intervention, the user can move on to other areas of the interface and attempt to perform other tasks. This intervention approach has been used in having blind people test automated teller machines [34] and online employment applications [32]. Because of the high likelihood of barriers and frustrations occurring, it is especially important to tell the users that they are NOT being tested; rather, they are testing the interface, and their feedback is important and will result in changes to the interface design.

LOGISTICS OF USABILITY TESTING INVOLVING PEOPLE WITH DISABILITIES

Preparing logistics for the testing is critical. It is helpful to hold pilot studies that test materials (printed, verbal, and audio), equipment, and physical setup at the testing location [35]. Appropriate assistive technology, including properly configured updated versions, is critical [10]. Thought must be given as to how information will be presented. For instance, if Deaf users are performing the usability testing and you are not fluent with sign language, an interpreter will be needed. You need to e-mail to blind users any forms that must be signed (such as informed consent), in advance, in an accessible electronic format, one that is savable, fillable online, and which can be signed with an e-signature or facsimile signature. You also need to give instructions in verbal format, and if materials are provided in Braille format, ensure that all participants are fluent enough in Braille to find the materials useful. People with autism may not feel comfortable expressing their thoughts during usability testing using the "think aloud" technique [31]. Modifications may be needed for users with cognitive impairments who do not have reading skills sufficient for understanding complex written task instructions [36]. For such people, it may be a good idea to have a version of the instructions written in simpler language [37]. People with memory-related limitations may need to be asked to bring a written copy of their passwords if their own passwords are required for the usability testing [35]. It's a tricky balance to both prepare appropriately for the specific group of users, while at the same time not making generalizations. For instance, some populations with cognitive impairments (specifically computer users with Down syndrome) have no problems following written instructions for usability testing [35]. People with Down syndrome also have visual strengths, so it's more effective to present satisfaction scales, such as Likert scales, using a visual method rather than an audio method [35]. For people with cognitive impairments, it also may be useful to have a trusted friend or companion come with the user for the duration of the test, especially if testing is done in an unfamiliar location (this is not necessary for someone with a perceptual or motor impairment) [37].

It is important to know the typical strengths and weaknesses of the people who will take part in the usability testing. Ideally, individuals moderating the usability testing will also have experience working with people with the specific disability involved because typical parts of a usability test, such as having users think aloud as they are performing tasks, may need to be modified, or the testing may result in lower amounts of feedback from users with disabilities than from users without disabilities [38]. More time should be included in the schedule than with usability testing involving people without disabilities. Despite being given a set amount of time, users with disabilities often are persistent and will refuse to give up on a task until they have successfully completed it, regardless of the schedule [22,37].

It sometimes is hard to find participants with disabilities locally, either because not many are available with a specific disability, or transportation challenges make it difficult for the people with disabilities to come to a centralized location. Do NOT simulate disabilities or perform testing with proxy users, such as by putting a blindfold on a person with vision and considering the results equivalent to those of a blind user (they are not equivalent) [10,22]. If you are asking users with disabilities to come to your location for usability testing, it is important to make sure that the location is accessible, meaning that the building, offices, desks, and bathrooms are wheelchair accessible and Braille signage is available [37]. Depending on the situation, it may be best to go out into the user's environment (home, workplace, or school). For instance, visiting people in their own environment might be the best option for usability testing involving people with autism, who may be anxious in new settings [31], or children with disabilities, who may get tired or upset simply by traveling a long distance to a usability lab [39]. Another factor to consider is that using a non-controlled setting such as a school or workplace may lead to a greater likelihood of intrusions by people not involved in the testing [37]. On the positive side, if you visit a user's home or office environment, it is likely that any required assistive technology is already in place. Furthermore, conducting usability testing where the tasks normally take place (where the user is located) has greater ecological validity.

Another option is remote usability testing. In remote usability testing, data are collected on the usability of a system without researchers or observers being present [40]. This can either be done using webcams and conference software like Skype or specialized remote usability testing software such as UserZoom. This may be more effective if a usability test is more summative, with quantitative metrics, because more formative tests, for which qualitative user feedback is the goal, may yield less information when done remotely [40]. However, one study found that remote usability testing performed with users with disabilities was relatively ineffective [41]; a number of contextual factors may affect the usefulness of remote usability testing involving people with disabilities. Another option might be to do a preliminary usability test (such as on one web site) in a controlled setting, interacting with participants so that they understand the type of data that need to be collected, and then follow-up usability tests (say, on 10 other web sites) can be done remotely [40].

It is ideal for usability testing to take place in conjunction with another type of evaluation, such as expert reviews. Expert reviews and user testing complement each other well; however, if the two are done in conjunction, it is important that the expert reviews be done first. Expert reviews will find the more obvious accessibility problems, enabling removal of the biggest barriers before users point out problems less obvious to interface experts (such as those inherent to the task domain) and limiting the problem of needing "interventions," as described previously in this chapter.

EXPERT INSPECTION (ALSO KNOWN AS EXPERT REVIEWS)

At the core, an expert inspection differs from a usability test in two main ways. An expert is not a representative user; the expert knows interfaces well but may not be well-versed in the domain knowledge of the task. Conversely, users know tasks, not interfaces. An expert inspects the interface for flaws, regardless of the typical task instructions [22,42]. There are multiple types of expert inspections. In a heuristic evaluation, a short set of heuristics are applied to interfaces in a search for problems related to accessibility; such a review covers only the most common problems. A full guidelines review is comprehensive, addresses full compliance with legal requirements, and covers multiple types of disabilities. Such reviews are time-consuming. A consistency inspection involves experts reviewing a series of screens, interfaces, or devices for consistency in layout, color, terminology, or language [22]. Consistency inspections are common, but do not address anything specific to accessibility. A little-used alternate is the barrier walkthrough method [18] in which the expert, not a user, pursues task scenarios [10].

It is common to have interface experts go through an interface using an assistive technology and checking for compliance. For instance, accessibility experts often inspect a web page using a screen reader, comparing what they hear with the screen reader to what they see on the screen as they inspect the web page, and then check for compliance with each guideline of WCAG 2.0 or a government law [43,44]. Screen readers are very useful tools for expert inspections, because they also help ascertain problems for people with motor impairments, who may be unable to use a pointing device, and therefore, like blind users, primarily use the keyboard for input. Research has found that the most effective type of expert review for accessibility (and possibly more effective in certain circumstances than a user test) is an interface expert using a screen reader to inspect a web page [41]. At the core of effective expert inspection is usually (1) the expert's experience; and (2) a set of guidelines (such as WCAG 2.0) that are being used to evaluate the interface as part of the inspection. Multiple experts performing individual evaluations and combining their results can lead to a higher level of validity of the inspection results.

Because they focus on a list of heuristics or a checklist, and such lists can be a list of requirements under the law [19], expert inspections are often more effective than only usability testing in determining compliance with laws. As mentioned, expert inspections tend to cover a broader range of problems than do user-based evaluations, which tend to focus on the barriers faced by the specific user or those related to the specific tasks in the task list. A voluntary product accessibility template (VPAT) is a form of expert review that documents an interface's compliance with Section 508 of the Rehabilitation Act in the United States. Table 8.3 provides an example of a VPAT from Microsoft for Word 2013 for Windows (from http://www.microsoft.com/government/en-us/products/section508/Pages/default.aspx).

Expert reviews will find only the types of accessibility problems indicated in the guidelines used. Therefore, if the guidelines don't address a certain user population, the expert inspection won't address that aspect of interface accessibility. One option for an expert review is to choose at the outset the type of barrier you are most interested in ascertaining (such as barriers for blind users or Deaf users) [45]. There are a number of different interface guidelines from the human-computer interaction community (such as Apple or Microsoft interface guidelines for applications), but the most important standards or guidelines related to accessibility are from the Web Accessibility Initiative (see Chapter 4). Furthermore, the Web Accessibility Initiative has provided information on applying WCAG 2.0 to non-web information and communications technologies (see http://www.w3.org/TR/wcag2ict/ for more information), so WCAG 2.0 can be applied to operating systems, software applications, and mobile apps.

For an expert review to be successful the experts must truly be experts in accessibility; having new developers perform an expert review will probably not lead to

Table 8.3 A VPAT, which is a form of expert review, documenting compliance of Microsoft Word 2013 with Section 508 of the Rehabilitation Act (Section 1194.21 Software Applications and Operating Systems)

Criteria	Supporting feature	Remarks and explanations
(a) When software is designed to run on a system that has a keyboard, product functions shall be executable from a keyboard where the function itself or the result of performing a function can be discerned textually	Supported with minor exceptions	All scenarios are feasible, although there are some instances where minor issues may occur. All issues have workarounds but may require additional effort on the part of the user Some examples of issues with workarounds are • When closing the co-authoring conflict resolution pane, focus unexpectedly returns to another open task pane • While in conflict resolution mode, the F6 key may become trapped in certain UI—ribbon keyboarding and other shortcuts can be used to navigate elsewhere or to close the pane • When a document is marked as not editable (for example, read only, protected), users cannot access text inside a floating textbox. Users can work around this issue by making the document editable
(b) Applications shall not disrupt or disable activated features of other products that are identified as accessibility features, where those features are developed and documented according to industry standards. Applications also shall not disrupt or disable activated features of any operating system that are identified as accessibility features where the application programming interface for those accessibility features has been documented by the manufacturer of the operating system and is available to the product developer	Supported	
(c) A well-defined on-screen indication of the current focus shall be provided that moves among interactive interface elements as the input focus changes. The focus shall be programmatically exposed so that Assistive Technology can track focus and focus changes	Supported	

(Continued)

Table 8.3 A VPAT, which is a form of expert review, documenting compliance of Microsoft Word 2013 with Section 508 of the Rehabilitation Act (Section 1194.21 Software Applications and Operating Systems)—cont'd

Criteria	Supporting feature	Remarks and explanations
(d) Sufficient information about a user interface element including the identity, operation, and state of the element shall be available to Assistive Technology. When an image represents a program element, the information conveyed by the image must also be available in text	Supported	
(e) When bitmap images are used to identify controls, status indicators, or other programmatic elements, the meaning assigned to those images shall be consistent throughout an application's performance	Supported	
(f) Textual information shall be provided through operating system functions for displaying text. The minimum information that shall be made available is text content, text input caret location, and text attributes	Supported	
(g) Applications shall not override user selected contrast and color selections and other individual display attributes	Supported	
(h) When animation is displayed, the information shall be displayable in at least one non-animated presentation mode at the option of the user	Supported	
(i) Color coding shall not be used as the only means of conveying information, indicating an action, prompting a response, or distinguishing a visual element	Supported	
(j) When a product permits a user to adjust color and contrast settings, a variety of color selections capable of producing a range of contrast levels shall be provided	Supported	
(k) Software shall not use flashing or blinking text, objects, or other elements having a flash or blink frequency greater than 2 Hz and lower than 55 Hz	Supported	
(l) When electronic forms are used, the form shall allow people using Assistive Technology to access the information, field elements, and functionality required for completion and submission of the form, including all directions and cues	Supported with minor exceptions	When form protection is enabled, Tab will not cycle from the last content control to the first. Instead, Shift+Tab must be used to recycle back through the existing content controls

useful feedback. Experts with more web accessibility experience can more accurately find accessibility barriers and do so in less time than can individuals with less experience in web accessibility [45]. However, even with high levels of expertise, human accessibility inspections can lead to false-positive results, and experts can miss true accessibility problems [46]. There can also be disagreement among experts about whether a certain instance is an accessibility violation [47]. Any human-performed inspection is likely to be imperfect [46]. Just as multiple users are needed to find problems, multiple experts are needed to identify different accessibility-related problems; multiple experts, working independently, can increase the validity of the accessibility inspection [43,47].

AUTOMATED REVIEW

Automated reviews are based on software tools that check a screen design (usually a web page) for compliance with a set of technical guidelines. There are a number of different software tools, including free ones, such as A-Checker and WAVE, and fee-based tools, such as WorldSpace, InFocus, Compliance Sheriff, and ComplyFirst (see http://www.w3.org/WAI/RC/tools for more information about tools). The main strength of automated reviews is that they can quickly and repeatedly ascertain accessibility on a large number of web pages. Because of that fact alone, automated tools are likely to have a role in the web accessibility plans of any large organization. However, even though automated accessibility evaluation tools will likely be a part of any large-scale organizational accessibility plan, there are a number of concerns regarding relying solely on automated tools for understanding accessibility.

Automated tools for evaluating web accessibility are imperfect. They often provide results that are confusing at best. WCAG 2.0 splits evaluation into items that can be reliably tested by machines versus those that can be reliably tested by humans [17,47]. Some accessibility aspects cannot be evaluated by an automated tool. For instance, automated tools will indicate that a specific feature is present on a page, such as the use of color, but the tool may not be able to determine if there is sufficient contrast between the text and the background color, which may require a manual check [42]. Similarly, an automated tool can check for the presence of alt tags and table headings, but the automated tool cannot determine if these tags are meaningful and useful. Human, manual checks are still required. These manual checks require human interpretation; often these potential problems are inappropriately flagged as being accessibility violations or ignored with no follow-up by human experts. In addition, many automated tools are not transparent about which aspects of each WCAG guideline are checked and how they are checked, so interpreting the results is challenging [10]. The Australian government's document "Web Accessibility National Transition Strategy" says, "Agencies are reminded that automated tools provide incomplete conformance information, and human assessment is also required" [48], and "It must be borne in mind, however, that automated testing tools can only interpret a limited range of criteria, which means that human judgment will also be needed in carrying out the tests. This will require staff skilled in web accessibility who can understand and apply the guidelines" [48].

Automated reviews do not in any way check for ease of use; they check only for technical compliance, even if that compliance is not useful to real users. In many cases, automated reviews check for the *presence*, not usefulness, of a feature in code. In reality, the accessibility feature may be of limited use; for instance, automated reviews can check for the presence of alternative, descriptive text of a graphic but not its usefulness [17]. Any ALT text for a graphic that indicates "jibberjabber" would pass an automated test (since there is ALT text present), even though it would be of limited use to a person with a disability. Another potential weakness of automated tools is that they often do not check how web pages will appear in different browsers, versions of browsers, operating systems, or mobile devices [49]. A skeptic of that criticism may say that automated tools are not supposed to check for compatibility with every single potential circumstance, just compliance with standards like WCAG 2.0.

Automated tools are best at determining the presence of accessibility features in code on a large-scale. These automated tools are good at ascertaining the presence of alt tags, headers, and keyboard-friendly event handlers. For instance, in JavaScript, an OnMouseOver event handler directs what occurs when a user moves a mouse over an object on the screen. If an OnMouseOver event handler is present, a JavaScript OnFocus event handler also needs to be present for users who may not use a pointing device. Automated tools can check for the presence of equivalent event handlers. This shouldn't be minimized; it IS important to determine whether hundreds or thousands of web pages include these features. For instance, although an automated tool cannot determine if the ALT text or the header names are appropriate and useful, it can detect the absence of ALT text or headings. Thus, an automated tool can assist developers or managers in identifying potential accessibility problems on an organizational scale. Automated tools may be best at providing a large-scale overview: a snapshot of compliance across tens of thousands of web pages. Expert reviews and user-based testing cannot provide broad overviews of an organization's web site accessibility, but automated tools can. It's not surprising that the largest-scale web accessibility evaluations, such as those of 100 web sites over a 14-year period [17] or those of 192 countries that are members of the United Nations [50], use automated tools. Automated tools are really most effective at doing long-term, large-scale trend analysis for web accessibility [49].

While automated tools can be most useful for large-scale trend analysis, they can also be useful at a very basic technical level. For decision makers/developers who are not deeply familiar with web accessibility concepts, some automated tools can help in understanding where potential problems lie and also assist in fixing the problems. Useful automated tools do the following: (1) provide a clear description of the problem; (2) if a manual check is required, guide developers through the process of determining if a potential problem is in reality a problem; and (3) provide advice and a wizard or tutor to guide the developer through the process of fixing the accessibility problem. A number of automated tools provide these features, assisting programmers, designers, or developers in identifying and fixing the problem.

WHAT TO DO WITH ALL OF THE EVALUATION DATA

Evaluating the accessibility of various interfaces, by itself, is not enough; the results of those evaluations need to be communicated to the appropriate decision makers, in a useful format. The evaluation methods performed—user testing, expert reviews, and automated inspections—are determined by the goals of evaluation (such as determining legal compliance), target disability user group, cost, timeline, and availability of participants. Performing evaluations alone does not ensure that change will occur. Communicating results of accessibility and usability evaluation is important to influence the design. The key is to provide summarized information in a useful format, presenting the information in a manner that developers, programmers, systems analysts, and software engineers can understand and use [8] (the specific job classification of the person making the fixes will depend on the organizational structure). All of the accessibility problems identified should be prioritized to ensure that the highest impact problems are addressed first [42]. Problems should be identified and explained, and potential solutions should be explained. It should be noted which modifications are easy and which are more complex [8].

As an example of communicating results within the accessibility context, most automated evaluation tools provide long lists of potential accessibility violations on the web pages that have been evaluated. Rather than give a list of the 500 potential violations reported, it is more useful to note that a specific type of problem exists (e.g., missing headers), explain the problem (e.g., why headers are important, how they are used, and how they can be implemented), and provide a few examples, along with a reminder that the problem occurs throughout the site (without enumerating all 500 potential violations) [8]. Not only is it easier for the programmer/developer to understand, but the number of guidelines violated is considered to be a more accurate metric for determining the level of accessibility, as compared to listing the number of instances of violation of one guideline (i.e., it is easier to fix 30 instances of the same violation than 30 different types of violations) [51,52]. In addition, sharing any videos of users attempting tasks or problems identified in the expert inspections may be useful in communicating the accessibility problems [42]. The specific target level of accessibility (task performance goals or meet specific guidelines or laws) should be clear in the summary report [8].

As previously discussed in this chapter, it is important to influence design as early as possible. Therefore, reports and feedback should be sent to the relevant stakeholders (developers, programmers, software engineers, systems analysts) on an ongoing basis. Daily reports, providing feedback, and suggestions on minor changes that can be made are far more useful than a final, 30-page long report, sent after an entire series of usability evaluations. Think of it another way: students need ongoing feedback on how they are doing in a university class. Therefore, there are assignments throughout the semester. Similarly, the feedback about IT accessibility, going to the various stakeholders, needs to be ongoing, so that the feedback will be more likely to influence the design, and changes and tweaks may be made on an ongoing basis. Positive collaborations and working partnerships are most likely to lead to success.

SUMMARY

There are three core evaluation methods for evaluating accessibility and usability: user testing, expert reviews, and automated inspections. The methods used, and to what extent, will be determined by the goals of evaluation (such as determining legal compliance), target disability user group, cost, timeline, and availability of participants. A plan for evaluation is needed: knowing why to perform specific evaluation tasks improves the chance to gain useful insights on specific technical improvements. Regardless of which evaluation activities are performed, no interface will be perfect, and the evaluation activities most likely will result in a prioritized list of the most serious accessibility problems. Communicating the accessibility problems to the web developers and software engineers in an easy-to-understand format and on an ongoing basis is important to ensuring that changes are made.

REFERENCES

[1] Bigham J, Cavender A. Evaluating existing audio CAPTCHAs and an interface optimized for non-visual use. In: Proceedings of the ACM conference on human factors in computing systems (CHI); 2009. p. 1829–38.
[2] Lazar J, Feng J, Adelegan O, Giller A, Hardsock A, Horney R, et al. Assessing the usability of the new radio clip-based human interaction proofs. In: Proceedings of the ACM SOUPS symposium on usable privacy and security; 2010. p. 1–2.
[3] Sauer G, Holman J, Lazar J, Hochheiser H, Feng J. Accessible privacy and security: a universally usable human-interaction proof. Univ Access Inf Soc 2010;9(3):239–48.
[4] Petrie H, Kheir O. The relationship between accessibility and usability of websites. In: Proceedings of the ACM conference on human factors in computing systems (CHI); 2007. p. 397–406.
[5] Romen D, Svanaes D. Evaluating web site accessibility: validating the WAI guidelines through usability testing with disabled users. In: Proceedings of the NordiCHI 2008; 2008. p. 535–8.
[6] Power C, Freire A, Petrie H, Swallow D. Guidelines are only half the story: accessibility problems encountered by blind users on the web. In: Proceedings of the ACM conference on computer-human interaction (CHI); 2012. p. 433–42.

[7] Wentz B, Jaeger P, Lazar J. Retrofitting accessibility: the inequality of after-the-fact access for persons with disabilities in the United States. First Monday 2011;16(11). Available at: http://firstmonday.org/htbin/cgiwrap/bin/ojs/index.php/fm/article/view/3666/3077.

[8] Law C, Jacko J, Edwards P. Programmer-focused website accessibility evaluations. In: Proceedings of the ACM conference on accessible technologies (ASSETS); 2005. p. 20–7.

[9] Bevan N. International standards for usability should be more widely used. J Usabil Stud 2009;4(3):106–13.

[10] Petrie H, Bevan N. The evaluation of accessibility, usability, and user experience. In: Stephanidis C, editor. The universal access handbook. Boca Raton: CRC Press; 2009. p. 201–14.

[11] Lazar J, editor. Universal usability: designing computer interfaces for diverse user populations. Chichester, UK: John Wiley & Sons; 2007.

[12] Shneiderman B. Universal usability: pushing human-computer interaction research to empower every citizen. Commun ACM 2000;43(5):84–91.

[13] Langdon P, Clarkson J, Robinson P, Lazar J, Heylighen A, editors. Designing inclusive systems. London: Springer; 2012.

[14] Sullivan T, Matson R. Barriers to use: usability and content accessibility on the web's most popular sites. Proceedings of the ACM conference on universal usability; 2000. p. 139–44.

[15] Hackett S, Parmento B, Zeng X. Accessibility of Internet websites through time. In: Proceedings of the ACM conference on assistive technology (ASSETS); 2004. p. 32–9.

[16] Brajnik G, Lomuscio R. SAMBA: a semi-automatic method for measuring barriers of accessibility. In: Proceedings of the ACM conference on accessible technologies (ASSETS); 2007. p. 43–50.

[17] Hanson V, Richards J. Progress on website accessibility? ACM Trans Web 2013;7(1):1–30.

[18] Brajnik G. A comparative test of web accessibility evaluation methods. In: Proceedings of the ACM conference on accessible computing (ASSETS); 2008. p. 113–20.

[19] Lazar J, Wentz B, Almalhem A, Antonescu C, Aynbinder Y, Bands M, et al. A longitudinal study of state government homepage accessibility in Maryland and the role of web page templates for improving accessibility. Gov Inf Q 2013;30(3):289–299.

[20] Brajnik G, Mulas A, Pitton C. Effects of sampling methods on web accessibility evaluations. In: Proceedings of the ACM conference on accessible computing (ASSETS); 2007. p. 59–66.

[21] Lewis J. Sample sizes for usability tests: mostly math, not magic. Interactions 2006;13(6):29–33.

[22] Lazar J, Feng J, Hochheiser H. Research methods in human computer interaction. Chichester, UK: John Wiley and Sons; 2010.

[23] Nielsen J. Usability engineering. Boston: Academic Press; 1994.

[24] Theofanos M, Redish J. Bridging the gap: between accessibility and usability. Interactions 2003;10(6):36–51.

[25] Wentz B, Lazar J. Usability evaluation of e-mail applications by blind users. J Usabil Stud 2011;6(2):75–89.

[26] Wixon D. Evaluating usability methods: why the current literature fails the practitioner. Interactions 2003;10(4):28–34.

[27] Nielsen J, Landauer T. A mathematical model of the finding of usability problems. In: Proceedings of the ACM conference on human factors in computing systems (CHI); 1993. p. 206–13.

[28] Lindgaard G, Chattratichart J. Usability testing: what have we overlooked? In: Proceedings of the ACM conference on human factors in computing systems (CHI); 2007. p. 1415–24.

[29] Kirijian A, Myers M, Charland S. Web fun central: online learning tools for individuals with Down syndrome. In: Lazar J, editor. Universal usability: designing computer interfaces for diverse user populations. Chichester, UK: John Wiley & Sons; 2007. p. 195–230.

[30] Lazar J, Green D, Fuchs T, Siempelkamp A, Wood, M. (2011). Ensuring Accessibility and Section 508 Compliance for the Recovery.gov web site. Available at: http://www.id-book.com/casestudy_14-11_12.php.

[31] Bahiss K, Cunningham S, Smith T. Investigating the usability of social networking sites for teenagers with autism. Proceedings of the conference of the New Zealand chapter of the ACM special interest group on human-computer interaction; 2010. p. 5–8.

[32] Lazar J, Olalere A, Wentz B. Investigating the accessibility and usability of job application web sites for blind users. J Usabil Stud 2012;7(2):68–87.

[33] Shelly C, Barta M. Application of traditional software testing methodologies to web accessibility. In: Proceedings of the 2010 international cross disciplinary conference on web accessibility (W4A); 2010. p. 4–7.

[34] Oswal S. How accessible are the voice-guided automatic teller machines for the visually impaired? In: Proceedings of the ACM conference on systems documentation (SIGDOC); 2012. p. 65–70.

[35] Kumin L, Lazar J, Feng J, Wentz B, Ekedebe N. Usability evaluation of workplace-related tasks on a multi-touch tablet computer by adults with Down syndrome. J Usabil Stud 2012;7(4):118–42.

[36] Lepisto A, Ovaska S. Usability evaluation involving participants with cognitive disabilities. In: Proceedings of the 2004 Nordic conference on computer-human interaction (NordiCHI); 2004. p. 305–8.

[37] VanDerGeest T. Conducting usability studies with users who are elderly or have disabilities. Tech Commun 2006;53(1):23–31.

[38] Chandrasheker S, Fels D, Stockman T, Benedyk R. Using think aloud protocol with blind users: a case for inclusive usability evaluation methods. In: Proceedings of the ACM conference on accessible technology (ASSETS); 2006. p. 251–2.

[39] Raisamo R, Hippula A, Patomaki S, Tuominen E, Pasto V, Hasu M. Testing usability of multimodal applications with visually impaired children. IEEE MultiMedia 2006;13(3):70–6.

[40] Petrie H, Hamilton F, King N, Pavan P. Remote usability evaluations with disabled people. In: Proceedings of the ACM conference on human factors in computing systems (CHI); 2006. p. 1133–41.

[41] Mankoff J, Fait H, Tran T. Is your web page accessible? A comparative study of methods for assessing web page accessibility for the blind. In: Proceedings of the ACM conference on human factors in computing systems; 2005. p. 41–50.

[42] Lazar J. Web usability: a user-centered design approach. Boston: Addison-Wesley; 2006.

[43] Lazar J, Wentz B, Akeley C, Almulhim M, Barmoy S, Beavan P, et al. Equal access to information? Evaluating the accessibility of public library websites in the State of Maryland. In: Langdon P, Clarkson J, Robinson J, Lazar J, Heylighen A, editors. Designing inclusive systems: designing inclusion for real-world applications. London: Springer; 2012. p. 185–94.

[44] Lazar J, Beavan P, Brown J, Coffey D, Nolf B, Poole R, et al. Investigating the accessibility of state government web sites in Maryland. In: Langdon P, Clarkson P, Robinson P, editors. Designing inclusive interactions—Proceedings of the 2010 Cambridge workshop on universal access and assistive technology. London: Springer-Verlag; 2010. p. 69–78.

[45] Yesilada Y, Brajnik G, Harper S. How much does expertise matter? A barrier walkthrough study with experts and non-experts. In: Proceedings of the ACM conference on accessible technology (ASSETS); 2009. p. 203–10.

[46] Brajnik G, Yesilada Y, Harper S. Testability and validity of WCAG 2.0: the expertise effect. In: Proceedings of the ACM conference on accessible technologies (ASSETS); 2010. p. 43–50.

[47] Brajnik G, Yesilada Y, Harper S. Is accessibility conformance an elusive property? A study of validity and reliability of WCAG 2.0. ACM Trans Access Comput 2012;4(2):1–28.

[48] Australian Government Department of Finance. (2013). Web Accessibility National Transition Strategy. Available at: http://www.finance.gov.au/publications/wcag-2-implementation/.

[49] Paterno F, Schiavone A. Public policies and accessibility: the role of tool support. ACM Interact 2015;22(3).

[50] Goodwin M, Susar D, Nietzio A, Snaprud M, Jensen C. Global web accessibility analysis of national government portals and ministry web sites. J Inf Technol Polit 2011;8(1):41–67.

[51] Loiacono E, McCoy S, Chin W. Federal web site accessibility for people with disabilities. Inf Technol Prof 2005;7(1):27–31.

[52] Lazar J, Greenidge K. One year older, but not necessarily wiser: an evaluation of homepage accessibility problems over time. Univ Access Inf Soc 2006;4(4):285–91.

Compliance monitoring policies and procurement

INTRODUCTION

The evaluation methods described in Chapter 8 need to be used to understand whether specific interfaces and technologies are accessible, but the policies and processes in place for compliance monitoring will specify when those evaluations are performed, which evaluation methods are used, who performs those evaluations, and what criteria for violations are used. The compliance monitoring policies also will specify, if violations are discovered, what actions are taken and how the information is presented and shared.

How does compliance monitoring differ from evaluation methods? Compliance monitoring involves a determination of when to invoke evaluation methods to ensure that accessibility barriers have been eliminated and that new ones have not been created. Put another way, compliance monitoring is an overall policy-level activity (either for a specific organization or an entire government), whereas evaluation methods (user testing, expert review, automated evaluation) are at a more technical level. Compliance monitoring is about policy and law. Evaluation methods are about human-computer interaction.

Compliance monitoring is about implementing procedures to ensure effective adherence to laws, policies, or regulations in achieving a higher level of information technology (IT) accessibility. Evaluation methods address the accessibility of specific interfaces. The aggregated results of compliance monitoring inform policymakers and managers, whereas the results of evaluation methods, which are specific improvements needed in specific interfaces, inform developers, designers, and engineers.

Compliance monitoring is a policy. Compliance monitoring is sometimes instituted in response to accessibility complaints from advocates or the government, which seeks to have the web developer/manager or software vendor take on self-monitoring. Thus, compliance monitoring is a process of proactively investigating, monitoring, and ensuring accessibility by being "out in front," rather than responding to crises after they occur.

REASONS WHY COMPLIANCE MONITORING IS NECESSARY

Because ever-changing content and technologies are the very nature of information technology, proactive compliance monitoring for accessibility is important. Often, when companies, organizations, or universities are told their IT is inaccessible for people with disabilities, they first express shock: "We didn't know!" One of the most common responses is "Can you tell us what we are doing wrong?" Organizations simply don't know what they are doing wrong, and they look to government agencies or disability advocacy groups to tell them. **There's a core logical problem with that approach**: if you count on outsiders to tell you what you are doing wrong related to IT accessibility, it's not likely that your organization will acquire/develop the expertise to understand the causes of the problems. When outside complaints drive accessibility changes, accessibility improvements will be transitory because the organization will not have the necessary knowledge of IT accessibility to prevent the creation of new barriers. By developing a compliance monitoring approach, the organization takes proactive responsibility for assessing and understanding IT accessibility. Performing compliance monitoring means that an organization KNOWS how it is doing.

A second reason proactive compliance monitoring is necessary is that when IT is discovered to be inaccessible, if it can be made accessible (and in some cases, it must simply be replaced with other technology) there is a time delay while the technology is made accessible. One-at-a-time accommodations introduce a time delay in access to the technology and/or content for the individual with disabilites. This time delay is a form of societal discrimination: people without disabilities have access to technology and information, but people with disabilities are placed in a "holding pattern," receiving unequal access to information and potentially being excluded from educational or social situations that use the technology (see Chapter 3 for more about the societal effects of delayed access to information). Moreover, without compliance monitoring while remediation is underway, new barriers may come into being, thus leaving the web site or technology no closer to accessibility.

A third reason proactive compliance monitoring is necessary is that it is always easier and less expensive to make IT accessible during the early stages of design, when doing so may add only 1-2% to the budget [1]. When accessibility changes need to be made at a later time, after initial design stages are complete, costs may be higher. In addition, if a software product or hardware device that is inaccessible is procured (purchased), what can be done to make it accessible? It is possible that the procured technology must simply be cancelled or tossed out, which is a waste of money. An organization knows whether technology is accessible or not, only by being proactive in investigating the accessibility. Another potential factor related to cost is avoiding the potential of legal investigations or lawsuits that result from unequal access to technology in violation of the law. (Table 9.1 provides a summary of reasons why compliance monitoring is necessary.)

Table 9.1 Why proactive compliance monitoring is necessary

If an organization doesn't know which technologies are accessible and which are not, there's no way to have a permanent solution
Reactively responding to inaccessible IT causes a time delay and unequal access
Reactively responding to inaccessible IT is more expensive
Reactively responding to inaccessible IT may lead to lawsuits

COMPLIANCE MONITORING IS OFTEN MISSING FROM REGULATIONS

There is a core problem with accessibility regulations in many countries: regulations may specify technical interface guidelines (from Chapter 4) but often leave out the entire process of compliance monitoring. One of the greatest weaknesses of IT accessibility laws internationally is that they typically have provided no compliance monitoring. Laws and regulations are the first step, but compliance monitoring ensures that regulations are followed. Compliance monitoring is especially important because a study of web sites in Germany, Italy, the Netherlands, Spain, and the United Kingdom found that most web sites claiming to be fully accessible are not accessible [2]. However, in terms of government-funded IT and technology provided by public accommodations, compliance monitoring often is limited or nonexistent in developed countries (as described in the next sections). Compliance monitoring has also been absent in developing countries, such as Thailand, where there is no compliance monitoring for web accessibility [3], and Brazil, where there is no compliance monitoring for web accessibility and a majority of developers are not familiar with the law related to web accessibility [4]. Many Asian countries are economically developed, but Asian countries are frequently left out of discussions about IT accessibility. Limited studies also report problems with IT accessibility and compliance monitoring and enforcement in South Korea [5] and China [6].

COMPLIANCE MONITORING IN CANADA

In Canada there are laws at the national and provincial levels that guarantee equality and accessibility for people with disabilities. The Canadian Constitution includes a Charter of Rights. Section 15 of the Charter requires governments at all levels to respect the right to equality of all, including equality for people with a mental or physical disability. Each province, as well as the federal government, has enacted a law called a "Human Rights Code," which bans discrimination in jobs, housing, and access to services and facilities (and in some cases, goods) on grounds such as disability. There are national Canadian web accessibility standards from the Treasury Board of Canada Secretariat, yet a Charter of Rights lawsuit was filed and won against the Government of Canada under the Charter of Rights, due to federal website inaccessibility [7].

The provinces of Ontario and Manitoba have gone further, by enacting a disability rights law requiring proactive government action to lead each province to become fully accessible to people with disabilities. However, a recent external evaluation by an independent reviewer to evaluate the effectiveness of the Accessibility for Ontarians with Disabilities Act (AODA) noted multiple problems related to technology. For instance, the Ontario government posts many inaccessible PDF files online. Furthermore, there are no technology-related accessibility requirements in the Ontario government's 10-year infrastructure plan [8]. In a related example, within Ontario, private businesses with at least 20 employees are required to file an "Accessibility Compliance Report" with the provincial government, detailing how customer service is made accessible for customers with disabilities [9]. As of the end of 2014, 33,097 of the 53,181 private sector organizations in Ontario with at least 20 employees have violated the AODA by failing to file a mandatory accessibility self-report with the government [10].

COMPLIANCE MONITORING IN THE UNITED STATES

At the US federal level, compliance monitoring of IT accessibility is required by Section 508 of the Rehabilitation Act but rarely occurs. Section 508 requires that the US Department of Justice (DOJ) must prepare and submit a report to the President and Congress every two years. The DOJ did not collect data from 2004 until 2010 [11]. In 2010, a memo was released by the Office of Management and Budget, indicating that compliance monitoring by the DOJ would begin again [12]. In 2012, the DOJ released a compliance report, noting that compliance with Section 508 continued to be a problem [13]. The data were collected by survey from federal agencies; some agencies indicated they were not in compliance with Section 508 and had no plans to become compliant [13]. In January 2013, the White House released a memo with a comprehensive plan for improving Section 508 compliance [14]. Planned improvements include adding a clear accessibility statement on all web sites (with a method for providing feedback), a standard government-wide template for measuring compliance with Section 508, and required baseline assessments of compliance with Section 508. The plan does not clearly state whether any of the results will be made public, but the information is to be shared with the CIO (Chief Information Officer) Council Accessibility committee [14]. The plan states that from 2014 on, US federal agencies will be required to "share progress in improving baseline assessment measures with OMB" [Office of Management and Budget] [14]. In the next few years, these actions may improve compliance monitoring, but this is not a certainty given the 10-year track record of Section 508 enforcement.

Because of the continuing problem of compliance with Section 508, disability advocates filed a series of Freedom of Information Act (FOIA) requests to multiple US federal agencies in 2010 seeking to determine which agencies were and were not performing compliance activities related to Section 508. Some of the findings from the FOIA requests are in the sidebar below.

FOIA REQUESTS AND SECTION 508 COMPLIANCE

Compliance monitoring needs to be consistent. In 2011-2012, FOIA requests related to Section 508 compliance were filed by disability advocates at more than 100 US federal agencies. The authors of this book analyzed the documents and found some troubling patterns in compliance monitoring throughout the US federal government. Here are some of the troubling patterns:

Agencies use a variety of automated software tools from different vendors without any validation or confidence in the results. The automated accessibility tools used include A-Checker, WAVE, Deque RAMP or Worldspace, WatchFire, Bobby, Maximine, Inspect32, InspectObject, FireBug, InFocus, Leaderboard, AccVerify/AccRepair, Functional Accessibility Evaluator (FAE), cynthiasays, Compliance Sheriff, Thunder/WebbIE (a screen reader-like simulator), VisCheck, and SSB AMP. No one in the federal government has compared these tools to determine which are the most effective. The choice often is made based on which tools are cheapest (read "free"). There is no confidence in the validity of any of the tools. Furthermore, it is likely that standardizing on fewer tools would lead to scales of economy: larger contracts with lower overall costs per user.

Each agency creates its own "Section 508 documents" on how to make web pages, applications, and office automation documents (e.g., MS Word and PowerPoint) accessible. This is clearly wasted effort. There should be one standard set of documents. Having standard guides would ensure that everyone was working on Section 508 compliance using the same documentation and understanding. In addition, in the provided FOIA documents, there were often questions from employees about simple 508 questions. For many of these questions, documented answers exist, but they are not publicly posted where employees can find them in their own agency. As an example, there were multiple discussions about the use of Flash, whether it is accessible, and if not, how to create an equivalent version of the content that is accessible. Answers should be centrally posted and available to all.

Agency officials often do not know whether their web sites are in compliance with Section 508. Sometimes they rely on complaints to inform them of noncompliance; sometimes they hire outside consultants to check; and other times they simply trust that the website is compliant because the contractor said it would be. In an example from the Chemical Safety Board, on April 29, 2011, an employee from the CIO's office asked the contractor whether the web site developed by the contractor met all Section 508 requirements; in general, the answers was yes, except the web site was not in compliance with paragraph B (equivalent alternatives for multimedia). In another example, a 2009 purchase contract for $12,000 was to make all portions of the abilityone.gov site compliant with Section 508 (abilityone is a government program to employ people with disabilities). The documents note that all pages must be checked, prior to posting, for Section 508 compliance. However, in September 2011, SSB Bartgroup (not the contractor) did a high-level audit of the abilityone web site for Section 508 compliance and found that the site was not compliant. In a third example, in 2012 the Federal Mine Safety and Health Review Commission asked the Bureau of Public Debt (which runs the FMSH web site) whether the Commission's site was Section 508 compliant. No compliance studies had been done, and it was unknown whether the Commission's site was compliant. Finally, the survey responses of the Commission for Fine Arts to the DOJ noted that Commission personnel ".... evaluate and remediate only when notified of accessibility problems."

COMPLIANCE MONITORING IN ADA SETTLEMENTS

Even when IT accessibility is discovered to be a problem, and compliance monitoring has been absent, the monitoring solutions specified are often general. For instance, in a settlement between the US DOJ and Montgomery County, Maryland, related to government services and the Americans with Disabilities Act (broader than just technology), a portion of the settlement required that the county improve web accessibility. The specific settlement language is as follows:

1. *WEB-BASED SERVICES AND PROGRAMS*
2. Within one month of the effective date of this Agreement, and on subsequent anniversaries of the effective date of this Agreement, the County will distribute to all persons—employees and contractors—who design, develop, maintain, or otherwise have responsibility for content and format of its website(s) or third party websites used by the County (Internet Personnel) the technical assistance document, "Accessibility of State and Local Government Websites to People with Disabilities," which is Attachment H to this Agreement (it is also available at www. ada.gov/websites2.htm).

3. Within six months of the effective date of this Agreement, and throughout the life of the Agreement, the County will do the following:
   A. Establish, implement, and post online a policy that its web pages will be accessible and create a process for implementation;
   B. Develop and implement a plan for making existing web content more accessible;
   C. Provide a way for online visitors to request accessible information or services by posting a telephone number or e-mail address on its home page; and
   D. Periodically (at least annually) enlist people with disabilities to test its pages for ease of use.

Within 24 months of the effective date of this Agreement and throughout the life of the Agreement, the County will ensure that all new and modified County web pages and content are accessible to individuals with disabilities.

(source: http://www.ada.gov/montgomery_co_pca/montgomery_co_sa.htm)

The language used is generally vague and based on what has existed before (distribute information, establish a policy and implement a plan for improvement, and provide a method for requesting accessible versions or making complaints). Only one stipulation is specific: at least annually, enlist people with disabilities to test pages for ease of use. The vagueness for how compliance is performed, which often is said to be a necessity for the large variety of technologies and contexts, instead often leads to limited or no compliance monitoring or enforcement.

DIFFERENT TYPES OF TECHNOLOGY AND HOW COMPLIANCE MONITORING DIFFERS

There are potentially many different approaches to compliance monitoring. For web sites, online course content for universities, or other IT for which the interface or content (and potentially the accessibility) changes rapidly, compliance monitoring must be ongoing, and policies must be in place that encourage compliance by providing resources to assist those responsible (such as having training classes and the assistive technology needed to test software).

For hardware or off-the-shelf software that doesn't change often once it is built, procurement processes are the best enforcement mechanism; the procurement contract can provide details on accessibility requirements and enforcement. A third category is application software and operating systems, which are upgraded infrequently but are upgraded to new versions. These upgrades are not made by content contributors, and financial procurements often are not involved, past the initial time of purchase. Versioning controls need to be used to ensure accessibility of those types of technology.

The overall goal for any type of compliance monitoring is to be proactive, identifying when technologies are accessible or not, rather than having an outside group or monitoring body identify the problem. Government agencies, universities, nonprofit organizations, and corporations often cannot answer these questions: How accessible is your web site? Your corporate intranets? Your internal database systems? Your office technology? Frequently, when IT is not accessible, a company, organization, or government agency will become aware of the inaccessibility only when an outside individual or group files a complaint. Ensuring IT accessibility is a process. It's not a one-time event. Compliance monitoring for accessibility needs to be built into designer, developer, and software engineering practice [15,16].

In general, compliance needs to be split into three different types of compliance monitoring:

1. Those for which spending money is the trigger for evaluation;
2. Those for which updating content is the trigger for evaluation; and
3. Those for which updated versioning is the trigger for evaluation.

SPENDING MONEY AS THE TRIGGER

In many ways, ensuring accessibility of technology purchased is the easiest type of accessibility compliance to enforce, because of existing financial control mechanisms [17]. In most organizations (companies, universities, government agencies, nonprofit groups), an infrastructure exists for determining when funds can be spent, what approvals must be in place, and what terms must be met. In most cases, this process is known as "procurement," "acquisitions," or "purchasing" and is an ideal monitoring process for IT accessibility. Documentation can be required to specifically address how any type of technology procurement (copier machine, telephone, hardware device, contract to build a web site) will be accessible for people with disabilities. Procurements are an appropriate way to enforce accessibility of hardware of any type, as well as software and operating systems. Procurement approaches are at the forefront of compliance monitoring in many countries and multinational governments, including Australia [18] and the European Union, because procurement efforts use existing financial controls to enforce accessibility compliance. For instance, the use of inaccessible course management system software has been a problem at Canadian universities [19], but that is the type of situation that procurement controls can address.

European Union Mandate 376 is one of the best-known procurement efforts for improving accessible IT. This multinational effort, which involves three European standards organizations, started in 2005. Phase 1 involved background research to evaluate existing accessibility requirements and evaluation approaches. Phase 2, which it is hoped will result in a final standard being adopted by 2015, includes the development of online toolkits and supporting documents [20]. Among the drafts available is Draft TR 101551, "Guidelines on the use of accessibility award criteria for publicly procured ICT products and services in Europe," which documents specific methods related to procurement to be used in tandem with the EU-wide technical standards being developed. The EU 376 document suggests that procurement documents, rather than simply stating that a technology "must meet EU 376," should specify the accessibility required, in terms of performance or functional requirements. The EU 376 document discusses what to do, for example, in situations in which multiple bids are sought, but only one company has the expertise to provide the accessibility requirements. The document also describes how evidence that supports the vendor claims of accessibility [21] should be set forth. The EU 376 mandate documents are in draft form, but the technical specifications are designed to harmonize with the Section 508 requirements in the United States so that an IT that meets the accessibility requirements of one would also meet the accessibility requirements of the other.

At the federal level of US government, procurement efforts related to hardware and software purchased under Section 508 have sometimes been more effective than web site compliance measures [17]. There are multiple efforts related to accessibility compliance through procurement efforts. These efforts include the online web site http://www.buyaccessible.gov/, which provides a "wizard" to guide individuals through the process of procurement of accessible IT, and which also creates customized documentation related to accessibility. Since 2011, the General Services Administration has evaluated, on a quarterly basis, a sample of solicitations posted on FedBizOpps.gov to determine if the procurement materials (usually a request for quote or proposal) include the appropriate Section 508–related text [12]. The best-known effort related to IT accessibility and compliance might be the development of government product accessibility templates (GPATs) and voluntary product accessibility templates (VPATs) (an example of a VPAT is available in Chapter 8). With these templates, vendors provide details about the specific accessibility features and compliance of their software/hardware/IT products. For a VPAT, a company proactively completes the template before any contract solicitations are posted. For a GPAT, a company responds to specific government accessibility requirements included in a specific software/hardware/IT procurement [17]. States, provinces, and regional governments often use these procurement activities that originate at a federal government level. For instance, the Texas state government uses two approaches developed at the US federal level: the VPAT and the Buy Accessible Wizard [22]. Universities also use these tools; Loyola Marymount University requires VPATs in IT procurements (http://academics.lmu.edu/dss/forfaculty/technologyaccessibility/).

Someone in the procurement chain of command needs to be identified as responsible for accessibility. The language of the procurement contract needs to specify accessibility; and if an inaccessible technology is being procured, a waiver must be sought, documenting why an inaccessible technology is being procured and describing the research that was done to determine if accessible alternatives exist. A clear process needs to exist and be publicly posted.

At George Mason University, there is a web site that details all IT accessibility requirements. All technology procurements must be reviewed by the Assistive Technology Initiative, and all requests for procurement must fill out either an Accessibility Validation Statement, documenting the accessibility of a proposed procurement, or instead an exemption document, stating specific reasons why an accessible technology does not exist or cannot be procured. VPATs must be provided for the product that is potentially going to be procured (go to http://ati.gmu.edu for more information). The web site clearly presents the process for procurement and the compliance monitoring for accessibility that will take place.

The George Mason University process does not assume that the technology is accessible. Instead, the default is that documentation is necessary to prove that the technology is accessible. And if there is a need to procure an inaccessible technology, then those who want to procure it must make an argument for why there are no existing accessible options. These exception requests are starting to become more prevalent. For instance, in Texas, if state employees want to procure a technology that is not accessible, they must fill out an "Electronic and Information Resource Accessibility Exception Request" [22]. When accessibility compliance monitoring is built into procurement processes for government purchases, it can improve compliance for private purchasers as well, by increasing the amount of information available about the accessibility of a product. For instance, due to requests from government entities, major IT companies publicly post the VPATs from their IT products, and that information is helpful to private purchasers, as well.

All IT procurements need to include compliance with accessibility requirements. Part of ensuring compliance is to ensure that vendors are knowledgeable about and skilled in understanding IT accessibility concepts. Some contracts are offered to specifically cover accessibility-related services. Such services include auditing other technologies to determine accessibility and remediating accessibility problems on other IT systems. In one example of procurement methods being used to improve IT accessibility, the state of Massachusetts is trying an approach in which a set of vendors performing IT accessibility services are "pre-vetted" through a state contract to make acquiring such services easier (and ensuring that vendors have the needed IT accessibility skills). This state contract is specific to procuring IT accessibility services, not just general IT procurements (as is the case for the previously listed procurement tools, such as the VPAT). See sidebar for more details.

MASSACHUSETTS STATEWIDE CONTRACT FOR IT ACCESSIBILITY SERVICES

Massachusetts previously had a statewide contract for auditing IT to determine whether or not technologies were accessible. This approach brought more attention to IT accessibility issues and allowed for a higher quality of IT accessibility services provided to the state government (because in the past some agencies had hired contractors who claimed to have accessibility experience but did not). Executive branch agencies were required to use approved contractors, whereas towns and counties in Massachusetts had the option of using the state-approved contractors (which had been vetted and often had lower prices). The state has expanded the contract to include auditing and a variety of IT accessibility-related services. For the previous 5 years, the ITS34 contract prescribed which approved vendors could provide IT accessibility auditing services to Massachusetts executive branches.

The ITS34 contract (covering only IT accessibility auditing services) expired in March 2013, and the successor contract, ITS52, has been in place since 2013. The state contract was expanded in ITS52 to include accessibility audits, accessibility consulting (including planning, testing, design, remediation, and help desk services), document remediation (making PDFs, MS Office documents, and e-books accessible), accessibility training (classroom-based, remote, and on-demand), multimedia transcription captioning and video description, and assistive technology (custom) scripting. To be qualified as a vendor, companies must submit detailed documentation of how they are qualified to provide IT accessibility services. The call for vendors specifically mentions 11 federal and state laws, as well as technical standards, with which any potential vendor must be familiar. The potential vendors must provide a history of experience with IT accessibility services, including a minimum (in most cases) of 4 years' experience providing IT accessibility services (vendors for scripting services must have 6 years of experience). Letters of recommendation from previous customers are required. Documentation of specific employees who will work on IT accessibility projects and their knowledge, experience, certifications, and affiliations are required, and documentation of employee participation in advisory and working groups is encouraged. Vendors must be independent of any specific software/hardware providers or platforms. Potential vendors can be from any US state, Canada, or Mexico. Once a potential vendor submits qualifications paperwork, the vendor's documentation is evaluated; if qualifications are met, the vendor is declared an "approved" IT accessibility vendor for the state of Massachusetts under the ITS52 state contract. When a Massachusetts executive branch agency wants to procure IT accessibility services, the agency posts a "request for quotes" on the online procurement site, and approved IT accessibility vendors can provide a quote for services.

Furthermore, since December 1, 2006, solicitations for any type of IT services to be provided to the state of Massachusetts must include language that addresses IT accessibility. For instance, procurement contracts must include text such as the following:

I Compliance with Standards.

[Vendor] shall ensure that all deliverables that shall be used by end users delivered under this agreement adhere to the ITD Enterprise Information Technology Accessibility Standards (the "ITD Standards") issued by the Commonwealth of Massachusetts' Information Technology Division ("ITD"). For purposes of this Agreement, [Vendor] must test against the ITD Standards and the Supplemental Web Accessibility Testing Criteria Version 1.0, both of which are posted by ITD at www.mass.gov/itd. The ITD Standards and the Supplemental Web Accessibility Testing Criteria may be modified from time to time, and Vendor is responsible for compliance with the most current version in effect on the date that [Vendor] executes this Agreement.

More information about contract language for IT accessibility in Massachusetts is available at http://www.mass.gov/anf/research-and-tech/policies-legal-and-technical-guidance/tech-guidance/accessibility-guidance/it-acquisition-access-compliance-prog/accessibility-contract-language-faqs.html [23].

When existing contracts or partnerships are in place for providing IT accessibility services, it increases the likelihood of actual compliance with relevant laws. Often, in educational situations (both K–12 and higher education), course content is not made accessible because faculty and teachers do not know how to do so. Having a clear process or contract in place can help facilitate improved IT accessibility. For instance, at the University of Wisconsin-Madison, a statewide captioning/transcription contract is in place, allowing for quick, preapproved contracts for captioning content, such as course content, which not only makes the process easier, but also lowers the price and increases awareness of the need for captioning and transcripts. Chapter 10 contains other examples of best practices in the procurement of accessible IT, including a program in the California State University system. Another example of universities using procurement to improve IT accessibility is from Ohio State University (OSU) and is presented in the sidebar. OSU also took an important step in a specific procurement situation. In one situation, internal OSU testing indicated a technology was inaccessible, yet the vendor insisted the technology was accessible. OSU indicated it would procure the technology only if the vendor agreed to an indemnification clause in the contract. The clause would require the vendor to be responsible for costs if OSU was subject to a lawsuit or any penalties relating to the technology being inaccessible. The vendor agreed to the terms, and the procurement contract was signed.

SUGGESTED PROCUREMENT CONTRACT TEXT, FROM OHIO STATE UNIVERSITY

All content, interfaces, and navigation elements to be used by University faculty/staff, program participants, or other University constituencies must be compliant with the Americans with Disabilities Act, as amended. Compliance means that a person with a disability can acquire the same information, engage in the same interactions, and enjoy the same services as a person without a disability, in an equally effective and integrated manner, with substantially equivalent ease of use.

There are multiple approaches to providing equally effective and substantially equivalent ease of use. A product will be considered to have met this standard based on a review by the University or when the vendor demonstrates that the work clearly meets the applicable current portions of the Ohio State University's Minimum Web Accessibility Standards through documented accessibility testing.

The Ohio State University Minimum Web Accessibility Standards [MWAS] are implementation guidelines for its Web Accessibility Policy, adopted in 2004. They are based on Section 508 §1194.22 of the Federal Rehabilitation Act, the standard of legal compliance for US government institutions. The goal of MWAS is to ensure websites and web-based applications are functionally accessible to people with disabilities, as described in Section 508 §1194.31, Functional Performance Criteria. We understand that the 508 criteria are being revisited, and will likely come to harmonize with W3C WCAG 2.0 AA compliance. The criteria in the middle column of the table elaborate MWAS in an attempt to align it with current and emerging standards.

The accessibility testing process must be described in the proposal along with the completed chart (included below), and may include but is not limited to code reviews by internal or external experts, evaluations with accessibility checking software, vendor test bedding with assistive technologies, testing by users with disabilities, or testing by a third party organization.

Please answer the following questions:

1. Do you have clients who require accessibility (Federal govt., international, local company policies)? If so, in outline, how are they ensuring your product meets their requirement?
2. What standards are followed for coding of interfaces (if 508, what parts, if WCAG 2.0, which level)?
3. Do you do testing with users with disabilities? If so, can you explain the process and identify, roughly, the range of disabilities and access technologies used?
4. What experience do developers on your team have coding for accessibility?
5. What are your company's internal standards for developing with accessibility in mind? (Note: may have been answered by question 2.)
6. Does your company have a road map for accessibility going forward? If so, can you give us a general outline (goals, milestones)?
7. Have you tested and/or developed your mobile apps (especially iOS) with accessibility in mind?
8. If we find that there are changes that need to be made to web/mobile interfaces/apps, what guarantee can we have that these will be implemented to our satisfaction prior to go-live/going forward?
9. Would your company indemnify OSU against legal action related to accessibility?

Source: http://osu.edu/resources/accessibility/

The compliance approaches used in procurement could easily be applied to other types of funding mechanisms. For example, many universities and nonprofit organizations submit grant applications to both government agencies and private foundations to apply for funding. If these grant applications in any way involve building or acquiring technology or building electronic educational materials, both the submitting and receiving organizations could require accessibility in the grant process. For instance, when a member of the university faculty submits a grant application, the university could require that there be a line item in the budget for captioning any videos to be developed or for any other accessibility-related expenses. While we are not aware of any universities currently using this approach, some government agencies do use this approach. For instance, the U.S. Department of Labor, in some recent call for proposals, has used the following text:

> All online and technology-enabled courses developed under this SGA [Solicitation for Grant Applications] must incorporate the principles of universal design in order to ensure that they are readily accessible to qualified individuals with disabilities in full compliance with the Americans with Disability Act and Sections 504 and 508 of the Federal Rehabilitation Act of 1973, as amended.

When agencies receive grant applications, they could require that the grant proposals submitted include a statement on how the technology being built will be accessible or require when a grant is funded that the contract specifically list accessibility requirements. The key concepts of using the contract and procurement process for IT accessibility remain the same.

UPDATING CONTENT AS THE TRIGGER

For some types of technologies, primarily web sites and technologies related to web sites (such as online course content), updates occur frequently and are internal to the organization, without any financial expenditures. In these types of situations, the procurement process is ineffective because content updates do not require financial outlays, so no procurement requirements are triggered. In these situations, requirements are needed for updating of content. This is similar to how information is released from a government agency, university, organization, or company via a vetting process that ensures the information is appropriate for public release. In some cases, there is a "public information officer" or approvals occur through a "public relations office." Information posted on a web site is public information, so similar mechanisms should be possible, although the mechanisms should focus on the accessibility of the content, rather than the content itself. If a "shell" is being used for content, such as a content management system or a learning management system, there are two aspects that must be accessible: the software shell (such as Blackboard, Moodle, Drupal, Plone) and the posted content. Inaccessible PDF documents, PowerPoint files, and uncaptioned video are common problems related to inaccessible content at universities [19]. In the corporate context, updates to web sites will often get sign off from marketing, legal and other departments; in those instances, incorporating accessibility into the signoff process should be a minor procedural adjustment.

When considering the best way to improve compliance with content updates, it is important to determine if any approval mechanisms, not related to accessibility, are already in place. Is there any central gatekeeper who gets to approve content? For instance, for the US federal government web site recovery.gov, which tracks the funding spent by the American Recovery and Reinvestment Act (ARRA, known informally as the Stimulus Act), content is contributed by multiple sources, but all content is posted by web managers, who inspect each set of content and each PDF document for accessibility before it is posted. The web managers of recovery.gov often make minor fixes, but if major fixes are needed for accessibility, the content or documents are returned to the submitting agency, which is asked to make modifications before the document is posted [24].

If there is no organizational-level approval that occurs when content is updated, the policies will need to focus on the content providers, not the content. You can't control the content, but you can control the content providers and provide them with (1) information, (2) guidance, and in some cases (3) penalties.

INFORMATION ABOUT INACCESSIBLE CONTENT

How do content contributors receive information about inaccessible content? What are the triggers for finding inaccessible content updates when the content receives no approval beforehand? In some cases, complaints made by people with disabilities are the trigger for finding inaccessible content. Obviously, this is a reactive, not proactive, approach and thus is not preferred. A preferred approach is to do evaluations of content on a regular basis (say, quarterly), usually with a sample of content because it typically is impractical to evaluate all content on a web site or content management system. Accessibility reports should be provided to content owners or creators about inaccessible content discovered. Any of the methods described in Chapter 8 (evaluation methods and measurement), such as automated reviews, expert testing, and usability testing, can be used. For instance, in the recovery.gov web site, all content is evaluated quarterly for accessibility, using a combination of expert reviews and automated accessibility testing tools [24]. Chapter 10 describes how automated tools evaluate Swedish government web sites on a monthly basis [25]. Mirri et al. describe how reports of the automated accessibility evaluations performed regularly and trend analyses are provided to Italian government officials responsible for ensuring government web site accessibility [26]. At the US Census Bureau, an automated accessibility testing tool (Compliance Sheriff) is run on a monthly basis to evaluate 90% of the Census Bureau web sites for Section 508 compliance, and reports are forwarded to content owners [27]. Regular evaluations (also noted in the Montgomery County, Maryland, ADA settlement described previously) are important to keep the flow of information going to content contributors so they can understand how any content they post is inaccessible. Furthermore, it is hoped that sending reports about inaccessible content over time will lead to content being created accessibly because of increased awareness. The long-term goal is not remediation of inaccessible content but creation of accessible content without any delay or outside evaluation involved.

PROACTIVE GUIDANCE FOR CONTENT CONTRIBUTORS

All staff involved in contributing content must receive proactive guidance on how to make content accessible. Content contributors need to know how success is defined and should be provided with the informational resources to ensure that they can make content accessible. A great way to improve the likelihood of success is by making sure that content contributors are included in the development of technical standards and organization policies related to accessibility (as was done in Sweden) [25]. Content contributors are more likely to understand the guidelines and have a stake in success when they are included in the development of those guidelines. This is similar to how the use of increased involvement by stakeholders in IT systems development, using a method such as participatory design, leads to an increased likelihood of success because users find it harder to reject systems that they had a role in building [28].

All those responsible for accessible content should receive training and have resources available on demand (such as training videos and tech support) to assist them with remediating current IT content accessibility problems and avoiding problems in the future. For instance, at Oregon State University, free training seminars are available to all members of the community; these seminars teach the use of Drupal as a content management system and include information about accessibility. At the University of Wisconsin-Madison, any content contributor can ask for an accessibility review on request. At George Mason University, a checklist with instructions is provided for content contributors to perform a self-evaluation of their content accessibility. In the government sector, the US Food and Drug Administration provides video-based, training-on-demand for IT accessibility; in addition, information about IT accessibility is being added to new employee training, and annual training will be provided to help improve the visibility and awareness of the topic.

PENALTIES FOR NONCOMPLIANCE AND REWARDS FOR COMPLIANCE

Compliance policies calling for penalties can be the most challenging type to implement. What type of penalty could be put in place for posting inaccessible content? At the US Food and Drug Administration, no approvals are required before posting web content, which is done via a content management system (CMS). To receive an account on the CMS, content contributors must sign a contract stating they will post only content that is accessible and compliant with Section 508, with the expressed understanding that access to the CMS can be withdrawn for repeated posting of inaccessible content [27]. In a university setting, the web accessibility policy from Fresno State University provides a quick summary of how often evaluations will be performed, what actions will be taken, and what potential penalties can be in place:

> The designated university Accessibility Compliance Officer will perform annual audits for Web and accessibility standards. In addition, ongoing monitoring of site maintenance history and visitor activity will be performed. Site owners will be notified of the outcomes.
>
> Any website that is found to be noncompliant will be required to be brought into compliance. It is up to each school, college, division, administrative unit, department, program, institute or center to coordinate the remediation process with the designated university Accessibility Compliance Officer or designee.
>
> Stagnant sites with poor maintenance histories and low visitor activity may be identified as noncompliant and in need of a remediation plan or removal. The

designated university Accessibility Compliance Officer or designee will work with the site owner to establish a plan for renovating such sites.

**(from http://www.fresnostate.edu/advancement/ucomm/brand/documents/Fresno_
State_Web_policy_April2013.pdf).**

In the university setting, faculty may need to be reminded that posting inaccessible content is not an academic freedom issue (as some claim); it's a civil rights issue, and a failure to comply can be penalized using civil rights-related mechanisms. It is similar to providing classroom accommodations for students with documented learning disabilities. It is not the choice of the faculty member whether or not to do so; instead, the goal is to increase the number of students who can benefit from whatever the faculty member says or writes or assigns as a part of the course.

The penalties in place for inaccessible technology usually are that the content provider must remediate and make the content accessible. But one US state has gone as far as putting financial penalties in place. In Minnesota, Statute 363A.42 provides that all public records must be made accessible to people with disabilities. A violation of this statute "is subject to a penalty of $500 per violation, plus reasonable attorney fees, costs and disbursements." A related Minnesota statute, 363.43, provides a similar financial penalty for inaccessible continuing education or professional development courses (see http://mn.gov/oet/policies-and-standards/accessibility/accstatutory.jsp). It is unclear at this point who would be responsible for paying the financial penalties.

Even better than penalties are awards and recognition. Proactively recognizing individuals and offices that have been effective in posting only accessible content, or in improving the accessibility of content, is a great goal. Annual job evaluations for web content contributors or web editors could include a line item for posting accessible content. For instance, for university faculty, credit for posting only accessible course content could be included on faculty annual reports or applications for promotion and tenure as an area of success. University provosts, deans, and department chairs can include accessible IT content on annual departmental/college reports, accreditation reports, and reports to regional/provincial/state governments. Another approach, used at North Carolina State University, is to have a competition to see which offices can correct the highest number of accessibility violations (see http://accessibility.oit.ncsu.edu/blog/).

Government officials can note compliance and praise those who are doing a good job. Companies can note good accessibility compliance on annual employee reviews. People and organizations always prefer positive comments to negative appraisals. At an organizational level, companies that are well-known for their proactive accessibility (such as Apple) tend to receive praise in the accessibility community, including receiving many organizational awards.

UPDATED VERSIONING AS THE TRIGGER FOR EVALUATION

Version updates for software and operating systems can sometimes be a problem for IT accessibility. For some software applications and operating system software, major updates often do not involve a monetary cost and thus do not go through procurement processes. A new version of a software application or operating system is installed without prior notification to the users; the new version is suddenly inaccessible, whereas the previous version was accessible. This is a common problem that can be improved by leveraging existing infrastructure for testing of new versions. In this example, we are talking about version upgrades, not minor patches. Major upgrades that change the look, feel, or functionality of an application or operating system need to be evaluated for accessibility. The content and procurement triggers described previously often are not activated by software upgrades. Therefore, different triggers need to be used. This can be viewed as being similar to how alterations or renovations to a physical structure can trigger new requirements for physical accessibility under US laws and, therefore, must be considered as a part of the renovation plan.

Often, before new software versions are rolled out in an organization, they undergo a series of tests to ensure security, stability, and compatibility. Sometimes, applications are evaluated on a separate server, known as the test or development server. IT staff at the organization do not roll out the new versions of software or an operating system to the general organization until the versions have been fully evaluated to ensure stability and security. These types of versioning controls exist for new versions of software or operating systems; however, they rarely include accessibility evaluation. Within an organization, accessibility evaluation needs to be added before a software rollout, as a part of the testing process. Two examples of managing the accessibility evaluation in new versions of software (H&R Block and Peapod) are included in the sidebar on the next page, discussing recent legal settlements.

For web sites, there often is a complete site update, which may involve the modification of the look, feel, usability, content, and structure of the site. However, this is not a content update per se; it is a version update. Such an "update" to an entire web site is a perfect time to require improved accessibility [29]. Some laws specifically require it. For instance, when a nongovernment web site undergoes substantial change in Australia, it is required to be upgraded for accessibility [30].

ANNUAL REPORTS

One approach for compliance that is becoming more common is the annual report of IT accessibility. Within an organization, this annual report is a "snapshot" of progress made within the year related to technology accessibility. The report is often a sampling of the IT accessibility efforts going on in many different categories, including web content, software, and mobile devices. An annual report is simply a summary of IT accessibility compliance efforts occurring within an organizational or calendar year. As an example, the California State University system requires each campus to file an annual report of progress on campus IT accessibility (more info at http://ati.calstate.edu). Four recent legal settlements also require annual or semi-annual reports on IT accessibility, as well as detailing many other compliance monitoring requirements (see sidebar).

COMPLIANCE MECHANISMS IN RECENT US LEGAL SETTLEMENTS

Four recent legal settlements in the United States, with the University of Montana, Louisiana Technical University, H&R Block, and Peapod, included components related to compliance monitoring.

In July 2013, a settlement was reached between Louisiana Tech University and the US Department of Justice (DOJ), Civil Rights Division, relating to the use of inaccessible technology for a blind student. As a part of the settlement, all teaching faculty and instructors must receive training on the legal requirements of the Americans with Disabilities Act (ADA), including accessible instructional materials. An annual report must be filed with the DOJ Civil Rights Division, detailing the annual ADA training provided to faculty and staff and detailing any complaints received.

A March 2014 settlement between the US Department of Education Office for Civil Rights and the University of Montana (UM) went further. As a part of this settlement, UM is required to:

1. Include accessibility requirements in all technology procurement.
2. Perform a survey of current and former students about their experiences with barriers due to inaccessible technology at UM.
3. Perform an accessibility audit of all technologies on campus.
4. Create a remediation plan based on results of the audit.
5. Provide 15 specific reports to the US Department of Education, related to areas such as web accessibility, classroom technology, and grievance processes.
6. Provide a full report, due in March 2016, documenting how UM has met every required remediation action from the legal agreement.

In March 2014, a consent decree was filed to settle a lawsuit filed by the National Federation of the Blind against H&R Block (a company providing tax preparation services). As a part of the settlement, H&R Block must:

1. Ensure that the web site, mobile applications, and Online Tax Preparation Product conform to WCAG 2.0 AA.
2. Designate an employee as a web accessibility coordinator, who must report directly to the Chief Information Officer.
3. Publicly post an accessibility policy, as well as distribute the policy to all employees involved with either web content or customer service (call center agents).
4. Provide, on the H&R Block web site, an accessible form, e-mail address, phone number, and TTY contact, to allow customers to provide feedback on accessibility.
5. Perform, every three months, an automated accessibility test on the web site and mobile apps, and once a month until it is released, perform automated accessibility testing on the annual Online Tax Preparation Product.
6. Perform, once a year, usability testing with individuals with different disabilities, on the website, Online Tax Preparation Product, and mobile apps. In addition, any substantial changes to any of the three products must first undergo usability testing involving people with disabilities, before the changes can be implemented for public use.
7. Have an outside accessibility expert do an annual accessibility evaluation of the three products (web site, mobile apps, and Online Tax Preparation Product).
8. Require that all employees involved in web or mobile app development or content development must be given web accessibility training on an annual basis.
9. Evaluate, as a part of employee performance reviews, the effectiveness of implementing accessibility, for all who received the annual web accessibility training.

In November 2014, a settlement was reached between Peapod (the grocery delivery web site) and the U.S. Department of Justice. As a part of the settlement, Peapod must:

1. Ensure that the web site and mobile applications conform to WCAG 2.0 AA.
2. Designate an employee as a web accessibility coordinator, who must report directly to an executive.

3. Have an outside accessibility expert do an annual accessibility evaluation of the Peapod web site and mobile apps.
4. Perform, every six months, an automated accessibility test on the web site and mobile apps, and report the results to the US DOJ.
5. Perform, once a year, usability testing with individuals with different disabilities, on the website and mobile apps.
6. Perform automated accessibility testing and usability testing involving people with disabilities, when any major updates or changes to the web site or mobile app are made, before the changes can be implemented for public use.
7. Require mandatory accessibility training, on an annual basis, for all Peapod personnel involved with web content.
8. Publicly post an accessibility policy, as well as an e-mail address and toll-free phone number to report accessibility-related problems.

Note: These are brief and non-comprehensive summaries of the four settlements. The full settlements are available at:

http://www.ada.gov/louisiana-tech.htm
https://nfb.org/images/nfb/documents/word/agreement_university_of_montana_03_10_2014.doc
http://www.ada.gov/hrb-cd.htm
http://www.justice.gov/sites/default/files/opa/press-releases/attachments/2014/11/17/peapod_settlement_agreement.pdf

PUTTING AN IT ACCESSIBILITY PLAN IN PLACE

The first step to improving accessibility compliance is to put an organizational IT accessibility plan in place. Although an IT accessibility plan doesn't guarantee any type of implementation, creating the plan often is the first time many stakeholders and decision makers will face the challenges of figuring out the details of how to improve IT accessibility in an organization, company, or government agency. IT accessibility doesn't happen overnight, and it doesn't happen without planning. For example, a number of universities are trying to create an IT accessibility plan, but their plans cover the next 5-10 years.

IT accessibility plans may also occur at a national governmental level. The White House released a comprehensive Section 508 improvement plan in January 2013 [14], but the plan has yet to be implemented. For some countries, the governments have what is known as a "digital agenda," which is essentially a long-term plan for how to improve access to and use of ICT by the citizens of a country. A digital agenda often includes a section related to IT accessibility, which serves as the default national IT accessibility plan [25].The European Union also has a digital agenda [31], but again, these national IT agendas are very different from the more common, organizational IT accessibility plan.

These strategic organizational plans help lay out how improvements will be made in terms of IT accessibility. An IT accessibility plan should address at least five major points:

1. What technologies are covered?
2. Which "triggers" for evaluation are required?

3. Which evaluation methods should be used?
4. Who is responsible for implementation?
5. How do results get communicated?

Specific organizational context should drive the logistics of the organizational IT accessibility plan. For instance, in considering who is responsible for implementation, it is important to examine who in the organization has responsibility for diversity and disability issues because those offices should play a role. However, the offices that have responsibility for technology need to play the major role and have the major responsibility. This may include roles such as the chief information officer, director of information technology, or vice president for technology (again, the specific title and structure will depend on the nature of the organization). The gradual nature of a plan should be based on the specific nature of technology planning and turnover at an organization. Some organizations turn over technology quickly (installing new versions and hardware regularly), other organizations have longer delays between changes. Not all changes can be made rapidly, and there needs to be time for employee training and development, for buy-in to occur over time. Unless an organization is the subject of litigation or legal settlements, changes will tend to occur over time. The IT accessibility plan needs to specifically address how compliance monitoring will take place, the incentives for compliance, and the penalties for noncompliance. The IT accessibility plan also should be linked clearly with the mission of the organization. For instance, at Xavier University (a Roman Catholic university run by the Jesuits), the university IT accessibility plan is clearly explained within the context of the mission of Jesuit education [32].

The IT accessibility plan should be specific, not general. The specific technologies that are covered, the offices and roles involved, the evaluation methods, and the triggers should be described in detail. Proposed timelines should be presented. For instance, the following is a sample timeline for improving IT accessibility at a university:

6 Months: complete campus-wide IT accessibility audit
9 Months: ensure that IT procurement and purchasing processes include accessibility
12 Months: ensure that major web pages (university, department, college) are accessible
15 Months: have 95% of course content online accessible
18 months: major online student processes (library catalog, admissions, registration, payment, graduation) are all accessible

Once a plan is in place, it is important to communicate the plan and progress toward meeting the goal to multiple stakeholders. These stakeholders include individuals inside and outside of the organization. Most companies, universities, and government agencies hesitate to openly discuss their compliance monitoring process or the results, aside from posting a short statement that "our web site complies with disability-related laws" or "we procure only accessible information technology."

However, the results, good or bad, need to be communicated to the right decision makers, who can reward and highlight those doing a good job or, in other cases, improve the situation.

SUMMARY

When compliance mechanisms are in place, they can lead to a higher level of IT accessibility. Compliance mechanisms, which help clarify what technologies will be evaluated for accessibility, how often the evaluations will take place, and what other policies will lead to IT accessibility, are a policy-level activity. Different technologies may require the use of compliance triggers upon procurement, web content updates, and software/OS versioning updates. An organizational IT accessibility plan can help lay out a long-term strategy for improvement, and annual reports can help spotlight yearly progress and highlight areas that need improvement.

REFERENCES

[1] Wentz B, Jaeger P, Lazar J. Retrofitting accessibility: the inequality of after-the-fact access for persons with disabilities in the United States. First Monday 2011;16(11). Available at: http://firstmonday.org/htbin/cgiwrap/bin/ojs/index.php/fm/article/view/3666/3077.

[2] Keith S, Floratos N, Whitney G. Certification of conformance: making a successful commitment to WCAG 2.0. In: Proceedings of the W4A conference-Web for All; 2012. p. 1–5.

[3] Mitsamarn N, Gestubtim W, Junnatas S. Web accessibility: a government's effort to promote e-accessibility in Thailand. In: Proceedings of the i-CREATe '07: 1st international convention on rehabilitation engineering & assistive technology; 2007. p. 23–7.

[4] Freire A, Russo C, Fortes R. A survey on the accessibility awareness of people involved in web development projects in Brazil. In: Proceedings of the W4A conference-Web for All; 2008. p. 87–96.

[5] Hong S, Katerattanakul P, Lee D. Evaluating government web site accessibility: software tool vs human experts. Manage Res News 2008;31(8):27–40.

[6] Shi Y. E-government web site accessibility in Australia and China: a longitudinal study. Social Sci Comput Rev 2006;24(3):378–85.

[7] Accessibility for Ontarians with Disabilities Act. (2012). Federal Court of Appeals Reaffirms That Inaccessible Federal Government Websites Violate the Consitutional Rights of Blind People. Available at: http://www.aoda.ca/federal-court-of-appeal-reaffirms-that-inaccessible-federal-government-websites-violate-the-constitutional-rights-of-blind-canadians/.

[8] Moran, M. (2014). Second Legislative Review of the Accessibility for Ontarians with Disabilities Act. Available at: http://www.aodaalliance.org/strong-effective-aoda/Final-Report-Second-Legislative-Review-of-the-AODA.docx.

[9] Ontario Ministry of Economic Development, Trade, and Employment. (2013). Making Ontario Accessible. Available at: http://www.mcss.gov.on.ca/en/mcss/programs/accessibility/index.aspx.

[10] Duguid, B. (2015). Letter from Ontario Economic Development Minister Brad Duguid to the AODA Alliance. Available at: http://www.aodaalliance.org/strong-effective-aoda/02252015.asp.

[11] Olalere A, Lazar J. Accessibility of U.S. federal government home pages: Section 508 compliance and site accessibility statements. Gov Inf Q 2011;28(3):303–9.

[12] Office of Management and Budget. (2010). Improving the Accessibility of Government Information. Washington, DC: Office of Management and Budget. Available at: http://www.whitehouse.gov/sites/default/files/omb/assets/procurement_memo/improving_accessibility_gov_info_07192010.pdf.

[13] U.S. Department of Justice. (2012). Section 508 Report to the President and Congress: Accessibility of Federal Electronic and Information Technology. Available at: http://www.ada.gov/508/508_Report.htm.

[14] White House. (2013). Strategic Plan for Improving Management of Section 508 of the Rehabilitation Act. Available at: http://www.whitehouse.gov/sites/default/files/omb/procurement/memo/strategic-plan-508-compliance.pdf.

[15] Cooper M, Sloan D, Kelly B, Lewthwaite S. A challenge to web accessibility metrics and guidelines: putting people and processes first. In: Proceedings of the the the 9th international cross-disciplinary conference on web accessibility (W4A); 2012. p. 1–4.

[16] Law C, Jacko J, Edwards P. Programmer-focused website accessibility evaluations. In: Proceedings of the ACM conference on accessible technologies (ASSETS); 2005. p. 20–7.

[17] Lazar J, Wentz B. Ensuring accessibility for people with disabilities. In: Buie E, Murray D, editors. Usability in government systems: user experience design for citizens and public servants. Waltham, MA: Morgan Kaufmann Publishers; 2012. p. 191–204.

[18] Australian Government, Department of Finance (2013). Web Accessibility National Transition Strategy. Available at: http://www.finance.gov.au/publications/wcag-2-implementation/.

[19] Fichten C, Ferraro V, Asuncion J, Chwojka C, Barile M, Nguyen M, Klomp R, Wolforth J. Disabilities and e-learning problems and solutions: an exploratory study. Educ Technol Soc 2009;12(4):241–56.

[20] European Union. (2013). Draft: Accessibility requirements for public procurement of ICT products and services in Europe. Available at: http://www.etsi.org/deliver/etsi_en/30 1500_301599/301549/301501.301500.301500_301520/en_301549v010000c.pdf.

[21] European Union. (2013). Guidelines on the use of accessibility award criteria for publicly procured ICT products and services in Europe. Available at: http://www.mandate376.eu/doc/TR%20101%20551v20008.doc.

[22] State of Texas. (2013). Texas Workforce Commission Electronic and Information Resources Accessibility Compliance Plan. Available at: http://www.twc.state.tx.us/twcinfo/compliance:plan.html.

[23] State of Massachusetts. (2013). Request For Response for IT Accessibility Services. Available at: https://wiki.state.ma.us/confluence/display/assistivetechnologygroup/Request+For+Response+for+IT+Accessibility+Services.

[24] Lazar J, Green D, Fuchs T, Siempelkamp A, Wood M. (2011). Ensuring Accessibility and Section 508 Compliance for the Recovery.gov web site. Available at: http://www.id-book.com/casestudy_14-11_12.php.

[25] Gulliksen J, Axelson H, Persson H, Goransson B. Accessibility and public policy in Sweden. Interactions 2010;17(3):26–9.

[26] Mirri S, Muratoir L, Salomoni P. Monitoring accessibility: large scale evaluations at a geo-political level. In: Proceedings of the ACM conference on accessible computing (ASSETS); 2011. p. 163–70.

[27] Lazar J, Olalere A. Investigation of processes for maintaining Section 508 compliance in U.S. Federal web sites. In: Proceedings of the 14th international conference on human-computer interaction (HCII); 2011. p. 498–506.

[28] Schuler D, Namioka A, editors. Participatory design: principles and practices. Hillsdale, NJ: Lawrence Erlbaum Associates; 1993.

[29] Lazar J, Wentz B, Almalhem A, Antonescu C, Aynbinder Y, Bands M, Bastress E, Catinella A, Chan B, Chelden B, Feustel D, Gautam N, Gregg W, Heppding M, Householder C, Libby A, Melton C, Olgren J, Palestina L, Ricks M, Rinebold S, Seidel M. A longitudinal study of state government homepage accessibility in Maryland and the role of web page templates for improving accessibility. Gov Inf Q 2013;30(3):289–99.

[30] Australian Human Rights Commission. (2013). World Wide Web Access: Disability Discrimination Act Advisory Notes ver 4.0. Available at: http://www.humanrights.gov.au/world-wide-web-access-disability-discrimination-act-advisory-notes-ver-40-2010.

[31] European Union. (2013). Digital agenda for Europe: A Europe 2020 Initiative. Available at: http://ec.europa.eu/digital-agenda/.

[32] Crable E. (2013). A mission-driven effort to incorporate web accessibility into online courses. Available at: http://ajcunet.edu/connections-detail?ITN=MC-20130529063257 &Story=20130529061185.

Case studies of success

10

INTRODUCTION

This chapter provides multiple real-world case studies of success in ensuring information technology (IT) accessibility. These successes are in companies that manufacture hardware, companies that develop software, and government agencies, public libraries, and universities. Previously published examples and new case studies are included. Highlighting case studies of success is important because companies, educational institutions, software and hardware developers, and government agencies often aren't aware of what is possible when it comes to IT accessibility. It's important to learn how others have succeeded. In addition, when organizations are successful, they often do not publicly report that they are successful and accessible. For instance, multiple news stories have reported how the implementation of the US Section 508 regulations (which require accessible IT purchases and development for the federal government) has been unsuccessful. However, the success stories, such as those seen at the US Food and Drug Administration and the Department of Homeland Security, are not well-known and need to be brought to the attention of the public. Lawsuits against companies that have not been willing to electronically serve customers with disabilities are discussed in Chapters 5 and 6, but there ARE companies that are serving as role models, and their excellent work needs to be highlighted. Content in Chapter 9 presents real-world examples of successful policies and compliance monitoring procedures that have led to success. At a basic level, best practices (in this chapter) are efficient and practical processes or policies that can produce a certain result consistently over time.

Very often, when disability advocates complain about inaccessible technology, they are told by technology companies or universities that fixes "simply can't be done" or "aren't cost-effective, so no one can do them." An effective response is to point to companies, universities, and government agencies that are doing an effective job of ensuring that their interfaces and technologies are accessible. However, it's not enough to say that "others are doing it, so you can do it, too!" It's important to understand *how* other organizations are being effective with IT accessibility. Understanding the interface guidelines (Chapter 4), laws (Chapters 5 and 6), and evaluation methods (discussed in Chapter 8) alone isn't enough. What's needed is advice on *practices* [1]. For instance, the British Computing Society created British Standard 8878 (BS 8878), known as the "Web Accessibility Code of Practice," which provides guidance on how to operationally implement technical guidelines such as

WCAG 2.0. BS8878 provides specific guidance on creating and maintaining accessible web sites by providing 16 process steps [2]. Understanding these practices, at an organizational level, can help with understanding how to apply these approaches within a different organization.

Case studies of success often can show strategies that have been implemented and work. Although specific technologies can be patented, policy strategies or practices are not considered intellectual property (e.g., they cannot be trademarked, copyrighted, or patented), so they can be described in a published case study and the information used to implement them elsewhere. Because of this, many companies often hesitate to share publicly how they ensure accessibility because the strategies are not protected as intellectual property. Companies consider their practices a "competitive advantage" that they do not want to share with others. What is fascinating is that government agencies often act in the same way—it is understandable that agencies do not want to publicly acknowledge inaccessibility issues, but government agencies that have accessible technology often are reluctant to share their success openly. An example of this is the web site *disability.gov*—the web site was evaluated for accessibility in 2010 and deemed to be accessible [3], but multiple requests from disability advocates for information on the processes to ensure accessibility were refused. Lack of transparency in practices limits the ability of one government agency to learn about best practices from other agencies. As discussed in Chapter 9, government agencies often refuse to share their information with other government agencies, leading to inefficiencies and higher costs. It's important to have a set of best practices to highlight how IT accessibility has been successfully implemented. This chapter discusses some best practices in web accessibility, hardware, and application software in the corporate, education, library, and nonprofit sectors.

BEST PRACTICES IN LIBRARIES

Public libraries in multiple countries have a stated goal: to be information providers to the general public (e.g., [4]). In the past, separate libraries (e.g., the National Library Service of the Royal National Institute of Blind People (RNIB) in the United Kingdom, or the National Library Service of the Library of Congress in the United States) have existed for people with print-related disabilities when the only option was separate materials (large print, Braille, or audiobooks). However, as library materials have become increasingly digital, there is an opportunity for public libraries to provide e-books that are accessible and digital libraries and databases that are usable by all. So far, public libraries have been somewhat problematic in that they often have inaccessible web sites and digital databases and loan inaccessible e-book readers [5]. Public libraries, with their long tradition of public service and inclusion of underserved populations, should be a leader in providing accessible materials to the public. While the physical library buildings are often accessible, the digital materials are not accessible. The case study describes changes made in Maryland public libraries in the effort to be more inclusive in digital library materials.

SUMMARY OF MARYLAND STATE LIBRARY ACTIONS RELATED TO WEB ACCESSIBILITY

In January 2012, it was reported to the Maryland Association of Public Library Administrators (MAPLA) and the Division of Library Development and Services (DLDS) that a number of Maryland State public libraries had inaccessible web-based content, in violation of state and federal law. A DLDS administrator was assigned the task of putting plans and processes in place to improve the level of library web accessibility. It was noted that Goal 3 of the 2008 to 2012 DLDS Library Services and Technology Act (LSTA) Strategic Plan addresses accessibility as a support of an LSTA goal area: "Expanding services for learning and access to information and educational resources in a variety of formats, in all types of libraries, for individuals of all ages."

Increasing the knowledge level of library staff throughout the state on the topic of IT accessibility was identified as a key early need. To help meet that goal, a webinar on IT accessibility planning was provided to all library staff statewide in April 2012. In May and June 2012, two employees at the Maryland Library for the Blind and Physically Handicapped (LBPH), which is also a part of DLDS, offered seven in-person, one-day training sessions that focused on a review of the Federal Section 508 Regulations and Web Content Accessibility Guidelines. The training included time for discussions about modifying web sites and purchasing accessible software. Thirty-one people attended the training. Afterward, project representatives shared knowledge via a mailing list server. A goal was set to put plans or processes in place at each library system by the end of 2012 to improve IT accessibility. All public libraries submitted plans for what steps would be taken to improve IT accessibility. It was determined that LBPH would coordinate web site testing opportunities for participating libraries. Furthermore, arrangements were made by LBPH to make some library patrons available to test web sites for other library systems on an ongoing basis. While many actions were taken at the county level or to support the county level, some state-level actions were taken. For instance, a liaison has been assigned from the web accessibility working group (previously described) to the statewide group that is charged with negotiating purchases for library databases that are shared statewide. Vendors are now asked to send written statements to confirm accessibility compliance.

Examples of changes made by some county-level library systems:

Allegany County: The library converted all pages that were provided in PDF (library policies, library history, etc.) to html format, updated YouTube videos to include captions, updated all graphical elements to have a text equivalent, corrected issues with color contrast (darkened) on web pages, added a Web Accessibility Statement to their web site, and switched to an accessible web-based calendar for events.

Anne Arundel County: The library was in the process of re-designing its web site, so staff made sure that the re-design process included accessibility as a goal. Some actions included developing a web site accessibility policy, creating a focus group specifically geared for accessibility and usability, setting up the content management system (Drupal) with accessibility testing modules, and scheduling regular accessibility and usability testing, as well as staff training, on the topic of web accessibility.

Enoch Pratt Free Library (Baltimore City): (Note for readers: Baltimore City is not a part of Baltimore County, is a separate jurisdiction from Baltimore County, and therefore has its own library system, the Enoch Pratt Free Library.) The Enoch Pratt Free Library created a formal web accessibility plan to improve accessibility throughout the system. The plan has three stages: (1) Research and training on web accessibility; (2) Initial evaluation and handling existing issues; and (3) Long-term compliance. For stage 1, the web staff will review and get familiar with technical standards and best practices; select software, tools, and online resources to assist content creators; raise awareness of web accessibility with discussions at Web Editorial Board meetings; and provide training to content writers on web accessibility. For stage 2, the system's major public web sites will be evaluated, including the library's main web site,

Kids Buzz, Teen's Website, Maryland Digital Cultural Heritage, Sailor, SLRC.info, and the State Documents Repository Website, by sampling based on which pages are visited most often and by using manual and automated techniques. All videos posted on YouTube will be captioned. For the podcast collection, auto-transcribing software and equipment will be selected and purchased. The library will begin to evaluate the accessibility of services and products purchased from vendors, such as the library online public access catalog (OPAC) and databases. A web accessibility statement will be posted on all of the system's public web sites. For stage 3, a new policy will be created to clarify library staff responsibility and related maintenance processes. Going forward, staff will ensure that any new web page, application, or web site is accessible before it goes live, and web sites will be evaluated twice a year by people with disabilities. In addition, guidelines will be developed to ensure more accessible content from the library's partners, and accessibility will be incorporated into regular web training for all new web content writers.

Montgomery County: Montgomery County Public Libraries (MCPL) is working with the county's Department of Technology Services to ensure that the county's government and library web sites are accessible. In 2013, MCPL implemented new page templates that are compliant with Section 508. The county will run an accessibility scan each month and notify libraries of any issues found that need to be corrected.

Baltimore County: Baltimore County Public Library (BCPL) recognized that a large percentage of materials acquired are now in digital format, so this was an opportunity to start providing services to people who are blind or have low vision. BCPL partnered with students from Towson University in spring 2014 in a semester-long project to collect data and provide advice on how BCPL can improve services to people who are blind or have low vision. There were five areas of interest: (1) web accessibility and maintenance; (2) staff awareness and training; (3) physical environment of the library; (4) library offerings, including databases, materials, and equipment; and (5) marketing materials regarding what, how, and where to be more visible [6].

Wicomico County: The library contracted with an outside consultant to train and assist the computer services staff and launched an entirely new main web site that was designed with web accessibility as a goal. The redesigns of the other library web sites (children and teen sites) were completed in 2013. A web accessibility statement was drafted, outlining how the library will maintain this level of service and addressing the importance of such maintenance.

Public libraries often take the lead in providing access to underserved populations. However, research libraries, which often are located at universities, can also play a role in improving access for people with disabilities. For 2 years, the Association for Research Libraries (ARL), a North America-based group, has been working on developing a toolkit for improving IT accessibility, and their resources are now available at http://accessibility.arl.org. The toolkit was developed after an ARL task force discovered that research libraries could do much to improve the accessibility of their digital resources. The ARL Web Accessibility toolkit includes model language for database licensing, as well as resources for accessibility tailored to research libraries and best practices from the University of Michigan and Queen's University. A related project from Ontario, Canada, can serve as a best practice for how research libraries can play a role in improving IT accessibility.

IMPROVING ACCESSIBILITY IN CANADIAN RESEARCH LIBRARIES

The Ontario Council of University Libraries (OCUL) and the University of Toronto created the Accessible Content E-Portal (ACE) Pilot Project. The project has two goals: the creation of a centralized web application for the discovery and downloading of digital materials in accessible formats and the development of a toolkit to improve accessibility in both university and public libraries. All of this occurs within the framework of the Accessibility for Ontarians with Disabilities Act, which has more detailed requirements than do the laws of any other province in Canada. The centralized web application currently has more than 1250 texts (and growing) in five different formats that are accessible (two types of PDFs, Text, DAISY, and ePub). The toolkit is an 85-page report that documents requirements for communication with library patrons, accessibility of documents, accessibility of web sites, accessibility of instructional materials in university classes, and specifications for procurements of library materials. For example, the following text is suggested in procurement contracts for defining accessible materials:

Accessible Formats means content in a format that is perceivable and operable by persons with visual, perceptual or physical disabilities and be useable with assistive devices, such as screen readers and screen reading software. Such formats will comply with accessibility laws within Canada, including the Information and Communication Standards of Ontario Regulation 191/11 and the Accessibility for Ontarians with Disabilities Act, 2005 (as such laws may be amended from time to time). To address the requirements of such laws, web content must conform with the Web Content Accessibility Guidelines (WCAG) 2.0, initially at Level A and increasing to Level AA to the extent required to comply with such laws.

All information from http://www.ocul.on.ca/node/1698.

BEST PRACTICES IN EDUCATION

In general, public libraries have a longer history of providing access for people with disabilities (see Chapter 2 on the history of library services for people with disabilities), compared to education. The right for all children to have access to a free primary education was mentioned in the United Nations Declaration of Human Rights in 1948 [7], and specifically the right to education for children with disabilities was first mentioned in international policy by the UN 1971 Declaration on the Rights of Mentally Retarded Persons [8]. In the United States, only with the passage of the Education for All Handicapped Children Act in 1975 were children with disabilities guaranteed access to primary education, and it wasn't education that necessarily maximized their potential but education that was simply appropriate and beneficial [9].

Simply having access to an education isn't sufficient. More recent laws, such as the Individuals with Disabilities Education Act in the United States and the Social Educational Needs and Disability Act in the United Kingdom, require that students with disabilities be mainstreamed into local schools as much as possible [7]. In the 1980s and 1990s, the movement to include students with disabilities in the regular classroom setting increased across North America and Western and Central Europe [10]. Different countries provided "mainstreamed" classrooms at different rates and using different approaches. It is expected that the European Union, focusing on human rights and standardization across countries, will likely achieve over time similar, mainstreamed, educational policies across countries [7]. However, each EU country still has options to implement policies in unique ways and using country-specific policies. Although the laws and human rights documents might provide a high-level view (e.g., students with disabilities must have access to mainstreamed education), the specific details of providing equal access to the information and technology used in education often are presented in policies. Unfortunately, there are not many case studies of K–12 schools that are doing an excellent job with IT accessibility. The sidebar presents an example of one US state (Kentucky) that has taken a coordinated, statewide approach.

KENTUCKY ACCESSIBLE INFORMATION TECHNOLOGY IN SCHOOLS (AITIS) PROJECT

United States Federal law requires equal access to primary and secondary education for students with disabilities. Like many states, Kentucky has a state-level law that requires that school districts provide IT access for students with disabilities "that is equivalent to the access provided individuals who are not disabled." The Kentucky Accessible Information Technology in Schools (AITIS) project was launched to help schools "understand and fulfill their obligations under Kentucky's AIT law." These resources include a set of eight tutorials to aid in the understanding of technologies, policies, and procurement processes; the tutorials also include standard language to be used for developing policies and procurement documents. The web site includes a list of five county school systems in Kentucky that have taken a leading role in improving IT accessibility. A statewide survey was done in 2004 to assess the level of technology accessibility in school systems. Although the web page for this project is a bit out of date, the project highlights potential approaches that can be used at the statewide level to enhance IT accessibility in K–12 school systems. Kentucky also imposes liability on post-secondary textbook publishers who do not provide textbooks, upon request, in an accessible format in a timely manner. The statute subjects publishers to the same anti-discrimination obligations and remedies that apply to places of public accommodation [11,12].

All information from http://www.katsnet.org/publications/aitis/index.html.

As students with disabilities increasingly benefitted from primary and secondary education (through high school), an increasing number of them began seeking a post-secondary education, looking for access to the university curriculum. At this point, there is no guarantee that anyone, in countries such as the United States and United Kingdom, will have equal access to post-secondary education [13]. Federal law requires that universities may not provide less than equal access to students with disabilities and may offer separate solutions only when it is the only means by which to provide integration. This often means that if a student with a disability is admitted to a university, the student must also be provided with accommodations that allow him/her to partake in the curriculum. However, those accommodations often are not implemented properly.

Although universities have considered physical access to buildings as early as the 1980s and have addressed such concerns for students with learning disabilities for approximately the same amount of time, only recently have universities been examining how to address technology access for students with disabilities [14]. This same challenge applies not only to technology used in the classroom, but also to technology tools used for online learning [15]. Since the concept of online learning was introduced, there have been ongoing problems with the accessibility of online learning in the United States, United Kingdom, and Australia [16]. The recent lawsuits against Harvard and MIT for failing to caption their online courses highlight the problem of inaccessible online courses [17].

Chapter 5 discusses some of the recent legal cases related to technology accessibility in higher education. In addition, two separate advisory committees in the United States have recently published reports related to post-secondary education and accessible instructional materials. In December 2011, the Advisory Commission on Accessible Instructional Materials in Postsecondary Education for Students with Disabilities highlighted many of the current problems related to accessibility of instructional materials at universities [18]. In November 2012, a committee from the ARL issued the "Report of the ARL Joint Task Force on Services to Patrons with Print Disabilities," which highlighted the problems that students with print disabilities face in accessing library content at universities [19].

The previously mentioned publications and lawsuits highlight the major problems related to IT accessibility on university campuses. Very little is known about universities that are doing a good job. However, a number of universities are making strides, by taking certain policy and process steps that are best practices in specific areas. For these best practices, no single university excels at all aspects of IT accessibility, so the best practices are separated here into web accessibility, procurement, online learning, and curriculum.

BEST PRACTICES IN DIFFERENT CATEGORIES OF DIGITAL TECHNOLOGY AT UNIVERSITIES

Best Practices for Universities in Web Accessibility

Oregon State University uses Drupal to achieve a common infrastructure and branding for all university web sites and accessible page templates, which helps with enforcing accessibility. Free seminars on using Drupal are held frequently and are available to all members of the campus community; this training incorporates accessibility information. All new sites must be accessible, and existing sites must be made accessible as they are upgraded, complying with the WCAG 2.0 level AA. All web pages (new *and* legacy) must include a plain text link for reporting inaccessibility problems. All legacy web pages cannot immediately be made accessible, so the following is the prioritization approach taken by Oregon State University:

1. The top 20% of legacy Web pages most frequently used
2. Pages required for participation, funding, disability-related services, and other key pages needed by people with disabilities that are not already in the top 20% should be placed in the first priority
3. Any legacy web pages can be made accessible upon request

The University of Wisconsin-Madison has a web accessibility policy similar to that of Oregon State University (in terms of priority and requirements) and also has a statewide captioning/transcription contract, which lowers the price and increases awareness around the campus. Furthermore, any campus web site will receive an accessibility review upon request from the owner. Another example comes from the state of Oklahoma, where the Web Accessibility in Higher Education Project provides information and guidance to 26 institutions of higher learning in the state of Oklahoma on web accessibility. See http://www.ok.gov/abletech/IT_Accessibility/WAHEP/ for more information.

Best Practices for Universities in Procurement of Technology

Historically, requiring that government funds being spent must meet certain requirements has been a well-known technique for enforcing civil rights. In the United States, even before the Rehabilitation Act of 1973 required that recipients of federal funding not discriminate against people with disabilities in their programs, services, benefits, or opportunities, attaching requirements to how federal funding was spent had been used to enforce racial desegregation since the 1950s [20]. Because government funding is highly regulated and involves legal contracts, those legal contracts and processes, known as procurements, are an ideal place to enforce accessibility requirements.

The California State University (CSU) system has a formal process, known as the Accessible Technology Initiative, to improve IT accessibility across the entire CSU system. The California State University system, with 23 campuses, is the largest university system in the US, and the Accessible Technology Initiative is one of the earliest examples of a multi-campus system taking proactive actions. From the Coded Memorandum AA-2013-03, the goals of the Accessible Technology Initiative (ATI) related to procurement are:

> **Drive vendor improvements to product accessibility support**. *The CSU seeks to improve product accessibility through partnerships and by leveraging the procurement process.*

The specific stated goals from CSU related to procurement of IT are listed as:
Procurement Accessibility Goals

- **Procurement Procedures**: An ATI Electronic and Information Technology (E&IT) Procurement Plan, documents, forms, and other materials to support 508 procurements at the campus are created and published.
- **Staffing or Role Definition**: ATI procurement team is fully staffed with clearly defined roles for processing E&IT procurements.
- **Exemption Process**: A well-documented process has been established and is used for exemptions to E&IT procurements.
- **Equally Effective Access Plans**: Equally Effective Access Plans are created for E&IT products that are not fully 508 compliant.
- **Training**: All parties involved in E&IT procurement have been trained, and a continual training program is in place.
- **Outreach (Communications)**: All individuals on campus involved in the purchasing of goods are knowledgeable about Section 508 in the context of E&IT procurement.
- **Evaluation & Monitoring**: Campus has established a continual evaluation process with standard forms and procedures. Feedback from the process along with direction is provided to training, outreach, and other groups involved in E&IT procurements.
- **Experience/Implementation**: Campuses have sufficient experience and expertise in completing E&IT procurements [21].

As a part of the institution's procurement enforcement, CSU does accessibility evaluations, rather than trusting what companies say about the accessibility of their products. CSU negotiates with companies to make their IT accessible before CSU procures it. For instance, in the past, Apple, Google, and Blackboard were warned that their technologies were inaccessible and thus could not be adopted by CSU [22]. In 2011, the California State University ATI publicly warned the universities in the system that Google Apps for Education had been evaluated and was not accessible and thus should not be procured [23]. Although budget cuts may have scaled back some of the original goals of the initiative (tied to specific target dates), each campus is still required to document and show progress in IT accessibility on a yearly basis. Because of the large size of the California State University system, its actions in refusing procurements of inaccessible technology have made a major impression on companies that provide software and hardware. Note that the CSU ATI also includes components related to web accessibility and accessible instructional materials.

More information about the CSU ATI is available at: http://ati.calstate.edu/.

Note that other best practices in higher education, such as the compliance monitoring performed related to IT procurement at George Mason University, are described in Chapter 9 on compliance monitoring. More information is available at: http://ati.gmu.edu/.

Best Practices for Universities in Online Learning

The University of Washington could be considered as having best practice in the accessibility of online learning [24]. The University of Washington distance learning program is more than 100 years old; the institution first offered courses in an online format in 1995. Currently, the university has more than 300 courses with more than 10,000 students each year. The focus on accessibility in online learning greatly influences practices in course technology, development, and support. For instance, in course technology, accessible web page templates, which incorporate cascading style sheets, are used to maximize the likelihood of accessible course content. The cascading style sheet (CSS)-based pages include skip navigation, alternative text, and properly marked-up headers and tables.

In terms of training and support, all course developers receive training in accessibility, and ongoing support, specific to accessibility, is provided. Key members of the university's distance learning design team participate in an accessibility-related discussion list. When distance learning design staff provide a consultation with faculty members teaching a specific course, they always discuss the accessibility aspects of the content the faculty member wants to add. In terms of publicly posted policies, the distance learning web page says that the university strives to make online courses accessible to everyone and notes the proactive steps taken to ensure accessibility. Finally, the quality assurance and evaluation processes used to assess the quality of online programs include accessibility as a metric [24].

Best Practices for Universities in Including IT Accessibility Throughout the Curriculum

In the School of Computing at the University of Dundee (Scotland), all undergraduate computing courses include small components of accessibility. These are short modules on accessibility throughout the curriculum, which allows accessibility to be seen in *context*, rather than as a separate topic or presented as a component only within human-computer interaction. For instance, in the Introduction to Software Development course, it is mentioned that users with limited dexterity may mistype data entry. In Introduction to Data Structures and Algorithms, accessibility is presented within the context of user needs. The undergraduate program also features guest lecturers from industry, who discuss the importance of accessibility; simulations where students experience temporary limitations; and fourth-year projects that often involve accessibility. Accessibility is truly integrated throughout the entire undergraduate computing curriculum [25].

Best Practices for Universities in Grant-Funded Development of Educational Materials

No universities are doing this yet (it's the idea of the authors of this book). Ideally, when any grant proposals are submitted to federal or multinational agencies for funding student development or educational materials or infrastructure, universities should require a specific budget line item for IT accessibility. This would have multiple benefits:

- This raises awareness early in the process of the need to make sure that any educational materials being developed in the grant are accessible.
- Any costs of ensuring accessibility are included in the potential budget.
- If a grant is awarded, principal investigators (PIs) cannot say that there is no funding available for making materials accessible (e.g., captioning of videos that were developed)

This is a minor policy change that could easily be enforced by universities.

BEST PRACTICES IN GOVERNMENT

Government IT accessibility poses an interesting paradox. In general, the laws requiring accessibility for technology purchased or acquired using government funding are the earliest and most well-established laws relating to IT accessibility. Although some countries require IT accessibility for nongovernment agencies that are considered to be public accommodations, most developed countries establish the right of people with disabilities to access government information [26]. While the accessibility compliance levels often differ at the national (federal) and regional (state/local/provincial) level [27], the track record for government IT accessibility across the world is not an outstanding one [28]. However, there are some bright spots, where techniques have been used that have led to increased accessibility of technology. Furthermore, there are some signs of improvement on government web accessibility [29]. The next sections highlight some best practices in IT accessibility in the government sector.

IMPROVING GOVERNMENT WEB ACCESSIBILITY THROUGH TRANSPARENCY AND REGULAR AUTOMATED REVIEWS

Given that one of the world's oldest laws for government transparency is from Sweden (1766), it should not be a surprise that the Swedish national government attempts to improve IT accessibility through the use of transparency. When national guidelines for government web accessibility were developed, those in charge of implementing the accessibility guidelines on public administration web sites were included in the decision making process. Regular automated evaluations of government web sites are performed, and the results are publicly posted [30]. Regional governments in Italy have a similar approach, using a web-based automated tool called the Accessibility Monitoring Application (AMA), which was developed by a collaboration of the University of Bologna and the Emilia-Romagna regional government. The AMA tool regularly performs automated checking of publicly administered web sites, such as those for governments, schools, and public health institutions, that under the Stanca Act are required to be accessible for people with disabilities. The Emilia-Romagna regional government regularly checks 376 web sites (more than 4000 pages) and reports on their accessibility levels. Those responsible for web site accessibility can login to see trend reports, for instance, that accessibility of web sites has improved in 12 months in a certain region, or that one regional government has high levels of web accessibility while another regional government has low levels of accessibility [31].

BEST PRACTICES IN TRAINING

The Office of Accessible Systems and Technology of the US Department of Homeland Security created the "Trusted Tester" program in 2011 to train and certify individuals as being able to independently provide accurate assessment of compliance of technology with Section 508 of the Rehabilitation Act. One of the challenges mentioned in previous chapters (including Chapter 9 on compliance monitoring) is that there is no consistency in how different US federal agencies implement Section 508. As stated by the Department of Homeland Security in a presentation, "some agencies rely solely on VPATs [voluntary product accessibility templates]; some agencies use assistive technology (AT) only to test; some agencies rely solely on automated testing tools; some agencies use standards-based testing; some agencies mix it up; and some agencies do nothing." The stated goal of the Trusted Tester program is to have individuals who can perform reliable and repeatable test results with a focus on consistency. An individual who wants to become certified as a "trusted tester" must take a multi-day (as many as 5 days) training session, focusing on web technologies and software applications, and then pass a certification exam. Individuals must pass with a 90% grade to be a trusted tester; those with a grade between 80% and 90% can retake the exam; those scoring less than 80% must retake the entire training session. The training is based on techniques and compliance testing that have been vetted and approved by the Best Practices Subcommittee of the Federal Accessibility Community of Practice, and the sessions are not just lectures; they include hands-on experience and exercises. Part of the Trusted Tester program is following a consistent approach for documenting and reporting accessibility findings. For instance, the documentation includes an "impact guide," in which, for each evaluation, it is noted how the accessibility barriers specifically affect people who are blind, low vision, Deaf or hard of hearing, or with mobility impairments. The Department of Homeland Security recently completed development of an online version of the training course, and it will be made available on the Defense Acquisition University site so that the training is available online to government workers outside of the Department of Homeland Security, with the high-level goal of making the approach to accessibility evaluation unified and consistent throughout the federal government.

All material from the presentation "Trusted Tester Program," presented April 3, 2014, and archived at http://www.accessibilityonline.org/Archives/index.php?app=4&type=transcript &id=2014-04-03.

IMPROVING GOVERNMENT WEB ACCESSIBILITY THROUGH THE USE OF CONTENT MANAGEMENT SYSTEMS

The US Food and Drug Administration (FDA) is part of the Department of Health and Human Services (HHS), an agency in the executive branch, and is responsible for regulating, protecting, and promoting public health in the United States. The core strategy for web accessibility at the FDA is to use a content management system. More than 800 individuals contribute content for the FDA web site, so it would be logistically challenging to have each new piece of content approved before being posted! Before individuals receive an account on the content management system, they must sign a contract stating that if they post material that is not compliant with Section 508 multiple times, they will lose their account. If there is an immediate need to post emergency health information without ensuring Section 508 compliance, content contributors must first get an emergency waiver approved, describing how they will provide the information in alternative formats for people with disabilities and how soon the materials will be converted to Section 508 compliance. In addition, there is a panel of users with disabilities at the FDA, who meet bi-weekly to discuss usability and accessibility problems, and they perform testing on new content or technologies. Training sessions, available via video-on-demand, also assist FDA employees in making web content accessible.

One contribution that was made by the panel of users with disabilities is FDA's implementation of Microsoft SharePoint. The technology platform had specific challenges when using the accessibility mode built into the product. It was discovered that the mobile version of SharePoint was very accessible but lacked full functionality. The panel worked with the implementation team to leverage and enhance SharePoint's native mobile functionality to provide full functionality for all employees, while producing a platform that was accessible agency-wide.

All information from [32].

BEST PRACTICES IN CORPORATIONS

ACCESSIBILITY AT APPLE

One of the few IT hardware and software companies that takes a full-scale approach to accessibility is Apple. All of the newest Apple consumer appliances (such as the iPhone, iPad, and MacBook) include a bevy of accessibility features. These features include built-in speech recognition (speech-to-text) and screen readers (text-to-speech). Starting with the iPhone 3GS in 2009, Apple has made VoiceOver, the company's screen access program, available by default on every iPhone. Every "iDevice" released by Apple since then has had built-in accessibility features. However, Apple did not stop at providing speech access to the iDevices; with the release of the iOS4.2, Apple also provided Braille support, so that various refreshable Braille displays would interface properly with iOS by default. Siri and voice recognition are used not only by people with motor or dexterity impairments, but also by the general public. On Apple devices, gesturing using touch screens is designed in a way that can be used effectively by people who are blind and those with limited use of their fingers. All of these features are built-in, require no additional plug-ins or software, and are invisible to those who do not use them. Apple's move toward IT accessibility has been shrouded in secrecy, making it difficult for those who would have accessibility spread through the tech community to understand the dynamics of its success. Recently, and perhaps coincidentally, some of Apple's accessibility engineers have gone to other companies, while VoiceOver has developed problems. The speed and efficacy with which these issues are addressed may be telling as to how much of Apple's success is baked into its design processes and how much they are the product of individual advocates within the company. Nonetheless, Apple's actions have encouraged other industry leaders to include accessibility features, and as of 2012, all of the major operating systems for cell phones have some out-of-the-box accessibility features for people with print disabilities. Microsoft, following the lead of Apple having a no-cost screen reader, recently created a partnership with GW Micro to offer the Window-Eyes screen reader, free of charge, to users with a licensed version of Microsoft Office 2010 or later. Although Apple is an industry leader, the company could still make improvements. For instance, it would be helpful to have documentation on the iTunes App store stating which mobile apps are accessible and which are not.

ACCESSIBILITY AT DESIRE 2 LEARN
(WRITTEN BY JANNA CAMERON, DIRECTOR OF ACCESSIBILITY AT DESIRE 2 LEARN)

Desire 2 Learn (D2L) is an educational technology company and the creator of Brightspace, an integrated learning platform. Their technology supports online and blended learning environments for 15 million learners worldwide. They partner with thought-leading organizations that share their vision of improving learning by providing a personalized experience to every learner, regardless of geography or ability. By extension, ensuring accessibility for every individual is a critical part of their mission.

A lot of the internal advocacy for accessibility within D2L is spearheaded by their User Experience (UX) team. The UX team is a center of excellence within D2L's Product Development division. The UX team works with cross-functional teams to promote user-centered design practices, including universal design. The team brings a human-centered approach to accessible design. They start by learning how real assistive technology users would expect an interaction to work. They will consider questions like "does the system give appropriate visual and non-visual feedback when you ask it to do something?" They test concepts with real users and tailor them according to what they learn.

D2L's customers play an important part in this process. Each month, D2L staff talk with their "accessibility interest group," an open group of web accessibility experts and people with disabilities in organizations that use their software. The discussions often take the form of online focus groups, where D2L staff seek member opinions on broad accessibility topics.

While D2L takes a broad "functional" approach to accessibility, technical guidelines also play an important role. D2L's corporate standard is W3C's Web Content Accessibility Guidelines 2.0 level AA. This gives a clear benchmark for testing and reporting. This benchmark is well-supported by D2L's leadership. Usually, it's enough to say that an issue is a WCAG 2 failure to get it some quick attention, although that rarely happens. A major driver for D2L's staff is that they can see a connection between what they're doing, and making education more inclusive.

Accessibility is a collective responsibility. It's the responsibility of each Agile Product Owner to ensure that she is delivering accessible products. Accessibility testing is typically performed by developers and QA, although it isn't unheard of for designers to take on this duty. This testing is done as part of the acceptance criteria for features. D2L has built numerous warnings into their code check-ins, for developers to catch problems early. This includes checks for unique alt text, labels, and logical heading structures. Developers and QA do regular sanity testing with free browser-based tools. They also regularly do paired, use-case testing with D2L's in-house screen access technology expert in more advanced cases.

D2L has a number of job aids to help teams with testing, such as a wiki page called "the top 10 things to test before consulting one of the experts." This steps a novice through basic accessibility tests with detailed background on the rationale for the tests. D2L has found that providing rationale for the "rules" is essential. For example, instead of just saying "make links unique and descriptive," the "top 10 things" wiki explains that screen access software presents links out of context in a "links list."

D2L documents the accessibility of their products in both a WCAG 2 checklist and a Voluntary Product Accessibility Template (VPAT). The WCAG 2 checklist was created because WCAG 2 is well-accepted and is quite testable. Generally, this is what non-US buyers need. US prospects ask for VPATs. The D2L User Experience team updates VPATs when major user interface (UI) features are released. Creating and updating their VPATs is an exercise of going through their internal bug-tracking system, and seeing if there are any significant open issues from WCAG 2 testing. They aim to find a place for all open issues in their VPAT, rather than report just items that strictly meet the Section 508 criteria. The UX team spot-checks products when completing VPATs.

An accessibility advocate once said "vendors either understand their accessibility problems, and are working on them, or are in denial." D2L has made a concerted effort to be part of the first group through open reporting of issues and their dedication to continuous improvement. This approach has helped build trust and productive relationships with the larger community of individuals who want education to be more inclusive.

ACCESSIBILITY AT ORACLE
(WRITTEN BY PETER WALLACK, ACCESSIBILITY PROGRAM DIRECTOR, ORACLE)

Oracle Corporation is the world's leading provider of business hardware and software, with more than 400,000 organizations worldwide deploying their products and technologies to employees and customers. Oracle is committed to developing these products with accessibility in mind, for legal, business, and ethical reasons. Accessibility at Oracle starts with the commitment from executive management:

> *Oracle is committed to creating accessible technologies and products that enhance the overall workplace environment and contribute to the productivity of our employees, our customers, and our customers' customers.*

Safra Catz, President and CFO

The Oracle Accessibility Program Office, part of the central Corporate Architecture Group, is responsible for defining the corporate accessibility standards and serving as a central group of subject matter experts, including experts with disabilities. The office develops resources to educate the vast range of personnel involved with developing and maintaining Oracle products, including user experience engineers, developers, quality assurance testers, documentation writers, and support staff. This material is communicated in numerous ways, including formal training classes, moderated online forums, monthly newsletters, group meetings that include representatives of all the lines of business, and informal "brown-bag" sessions. Educating the product teams on accessibility enables them to incorporate accessibility into their product development lifecycle in the most effective way, both for new development and release updates. The Accessibility Program Office also acknowledges product teams or individual employees who go "above and beyond" to address accessibility, with the Oracle Accessibility Award.

Oracle is now focused on enhancing its products to conform to the Web Content Accessibility Guidelines (WCAG) version 2.0, developed by the Web Accessibility Initiative of the W3C (and for non-web products, Oracle follows the WCAG2ICT guidance). These internationally recognized standards create a high threshold for accessibility, and for complex enterprise-class applications such as Oracle's, they present a significant coding and testing challenge. Testing at Oracle involves multiple steps, including automated tools, tool-assisted tests that then require human judgment, manual operation, visual inspection, and testing with a variety of assistive technologies. Like any other vendor, Oracle strives to ship products that are "defect-free," but when it comes to conforming to these standards, it sometimes must be balanced with the other enormous demands placed on these products for functionality, security, cross-platform support, customization, internationalization, and numerous other capabilities. As a result, "accessibility" of extremely configurable, dynamic applications cannot be reported as an "all-or-nothing" response; doing so does not address the full complexity of all the component parts and their permutations.

In order to report the product degree of conformance with accessibility standards, Oracle uses the Voluntary Product Accessibility Template (VPAT®), which was developed jointly by the Information Technology Industry Council (ITI) and the General Services Administration (GSA) to assist US federal government contracting officials and other buyers in making preliminary assessments regarding the accessibility of IT products. The VPAT allows companies to report on a provision-by-provision basis how well a product conforms to each criterion, and to provide remarks to document detailed information, such as implementation and testing performed, and to describe known defects. Oracle publishes the VPATs on the corporate site (www.oracle.com/accessibility), and they are freely available to anyone. Oracle also specifies accessibility requirements when procuring products from other companies (note: the text of the procurement language is presented in Chapter 11).

The accessibility of Oracle products alone does not guarantee an "accessible IT solution." There are potentially numerous instances where products have been deployed and yet some users with disabilities struggled to use them. Some of the reasons for this include customizations done by the customer that did not keep accessibility in mind, deficiencies in the browser or assistive technology being used (often related to not addressing the newest accessibility standards), and insufficient training of users on their assistive technology. These "accessibility ecosystem" problems hint at the enormity of the challenge facing technology vendors, employers, and users when dealing with continually and rapidly changing IT systems. Oracle accessibility experts not only focus on the company's products, but also participate in organizations that create international technical standards, promote deployment best practices by working directly with customers, and testing solutions with the help of disability advocacy groups, such as the National Federation of the Blind (NFB). (Authors note: while Oracle is producing a number of accessible products, Oracle has recently acquired a number of software companies whose products have not yet been made accessible, but that Oracle continues to market.)

SUMMARY

The case studies in this chapter provide a diverse set of examples, in which companies, universities, libraries, and government agencies view digital accessibility as a key part of their organizational mission. By documenting examples and sharing with the greater community, these organizations are leading the way as role models, showing how process and policy can lead to improved digital accessibility. It is important to note that, regardless of what critics sometimes say, none of these organizations are financially suffering because of their focus on digital accessibility. Instead, these organizations are thriving, increasing their potential market share, and serving their citizens, customers, and students by ensuring that the greatest possible number of people have access to the digital technologies that are developed.

REFERENCES

[1] Seale J. The development of accessibility practices in e-learning: an exploration of communities of practice. ALT-J Res Learn Technol 2004;12(1):51–63.

[2] Lazar J, Abascal J, Davis J, Evers V, Gulliksen J, Jorge J, et al. HCI public policy activities in 2012: a 10-country discussion. Interactions 2012;19(3):78–81.

[3] Olalere A, Lazar J. Accessibility of U.S. federal government home pages: Section 508 compliance and site accessibility statements. Gov Inf Q 2011;28(3):303–9.

[4] Hawkins M, Morris A, Sumsion J. Socio-economic features of UK public library users. Libr Manage 2001;22(6/7):258–65.

[5] Danielsen C, Taylor A, Majerus W. Design and public policy considerations for accessible e-book readers. Interactions 2011;81(1):67–70.

[6] Lazar J, Briggs I. Improving services for patrons with print disabilities at public libraries. Libr Q 2015;85(2):172–84.

[7] Armstrong A, Armstrong D, Spandagou I. Inclusive education: international policy and practice. London: Sage Publishers; 2010.

[8] Peters S. A historical analysis of international inclusive education policy and individuals with disabilities. J Disabil Policy Stud 2007;18(2):98–108.

[9] Bagenstos S. Disability rights law: cases and materials. New York: Thompson Reuters; 2010.

[10] Ferguson D. International trends in inclusive education: the continuing challenge to teach each one and everyone. Eur J Spec Needs Educ 2008;23(2):109–20.

[11] Ky. Rev. Stat. Ann. § 164.477 (2006).

[12] Ky. Rev. Stat. Ann. § 344.200 (1996).

[13] Borland J, James S. The learning experience of students with disabilities in higher education. A case study of a UK university. Disabil Soc 1999;14(1):85–101.

[14] Wall P, Sarver L. Disabled student access in an era of technology. Internet Higher Educ 2003;6(3):277–84.

[15] Wattenberg T. Beyond legal compliance: communities of advocacy that support accessible online learning. Internet Higher Educ 2004;7(1):123–39.

[16] Seale J. E-learning and disability in higher education: accessibility research and practice. London: Routledge; 2006.

[17] Lewin, T. (February 12, 2015). Harvard and MIT Are Sued over Lack of Closed Captions, *New York Times*. Available at: http://www.nytimes.com/2015/2002/2013/education/harvard-and-mit-sued-over-failing-to-caption-online-courses.html?_r=2010.

[18] US Department of Education. (2011). Report of the Advisory Commission on Accessible Instructional Materials in Postsecondary Education for Students with Disabilities. Available at: http://www2.ed.gov/about/bdscomm/list/aim/publications.html.

[19] Association for Research Libraries. (2012). Report of the ARL Joint Task Force on Services to Patrons with Print Disabilities. Available at: http://www.arl.org/bm~doc/print-disabilities-tfreport02nov12.pdf.

[20] Nichols D. A matter of justice: Eisenhower and the beginning of the civil rights revolution. New York: Simon & Schuster; 2007.

[21] The California State University Office of the Chancellor. (2013). Coded Memorandum AA-2013-03: Accessible Technology Initiative. Available at: http://www.calstate.edu/AcadAff/codedmemos/AA-2013-2003.pdf.

[22] Keller, J. (December 12, 2010). Cal State's Strong Push for Accessible Technology Gets Results, *Chronicle of Higher Education*. Available at: http://chronicle.com/article/Cal-States-Strong-Push-for/125683/.

[23] Zou, J. (June 23, 2011). California State U. Report Warns of Accessibility Issues in Google Services, *Chronicle of Higher Education*. Available at: http://chronicle.com/blogs/wiredcampus/california-state-u-report-warns-of-accessibility-issues-in-google-services/31935.

[24] Burgstahler S, Corrigan B, McCarter J. Making distance learning courses accessible to students and instructors with disabilities: a case study. Internet Higher Educ 2004;7(3):233–46.

[25] Waller A, Hanson V, Sloan D. Including accessibility within and beyond undergraduate computing courses. In: Proceedings of the ACM conference on accessible computing (ASSETS); 2009. p. 155–62.

[26] Lazar J, Wentz B. Ensuring accessibility for people with disabilities. In: Buie E, Murray D, editors. Usability in government systems: user experience design for citizens and public servants. Waltham, MA: Morgan Kaufmann Publishers; 2012. p. 191–204.

[27] Yu D, Parmanto B. U.S. state government websites demonstrate better in terms of accessibility compared to federal government and commercial websites. Gov Inf Q 2011;28(4):484–90.

[28] Goodwin M, Susar D, Nietzio A, Snaprud M, Jensen C. Global web accessibility analysis of national government portals and ministry web sites. J Inf Technol Politics 2011;8(1):41–67.

[29] Hanson V, Richards J. Progress on website accessibility? ACM Trans Web 2013;7(1):1–30.

[30] Gulliksen J, Axelson H, Persson H, Goransson B. Accessibility and public policy in Sweden. Interactions 2010;17(3):26–9.

[31] Mirri S, Muratoir L, Salomoni P. Monitoring accessibility: large scale evaluations at a geo-political level. In: Proceedings of the ACM conference on accessible computing (ASSETS); 2011. p. 163–70.

[32] Lazar J, Olalere A. Investigation of processes for maintaining Section 508 compliance in U.S. Federal web sites. In: Proceedings of the 14th international conference on human-computer interaction (HCII); 2011. p. 498–506.

Culture change

11

INTRODUCTION

We rarely concern ourselves with that which is not there. Historically, persons with disabilities have been excluded from full participation in our society and thus overlooked as technology is designed. The exclusion of persons with disabilities has been the product of a cultural perception that they are less capable and thus correctly excluded.

A colleague of mine who uses a wheelchair describes the frequent response he receives from restaurateurs when he encounters restaurants with inaccessible entrances, "You know, we don't get many people in wheelchairs who want to eat here." When one of the authors of this book has advised a company of its inaccessible offerings, invariably, an early corporate response is, "We weren't thinking about the blind [or fill in disability of choice] when we developed/selected that product." The corporate speaker perceives this state of mind as an excusable oversight, an indication that the company did not act out of bigotry or invidious intent. This author stifles the temptation to scream at, say, the banker with the inaccessible ATMs, "You forgot that blind people use money and banks?" and thinks of the Steve Martin *Saturday Night Live* skit where he offers as an excuse to the judge that he forgot bank robbery was a crime. At the same time, this author reluctantly admits that he rarely thinks about the accessibility of a restaurant he enters unless he is with his wheelchair-using colleague. The corporation with the inaccessible software that explains its inaccessibility as the product of thoughtlessness is saying, in truth, persons with disabilities are beneath our notice.

As technology developers create, enhance, and license their offerings, the invisibility of people with disabilities in our educational, social, and business life supports their exclusion from the definition of who "we" are and who constitutes the market. Technology not designed to include persons with disabilities will rarely be fortuitously accessible. As the resulting inaccessible tech offerings become pervasive in higher education, fewer students with disabilities can participate on an equal basis and therefore are increasingly absent from the campus; the inaccessible workplace software excludes the disabled employee, and the inaccessible social media silences the voices of those without access. Thus, invisibility begets inaccessibility, which, in turn, begets further invisibility in a pattern that, unless interrupted, becomes a death spiral. As the virtual world becomes entangled in every cell of the "real" world, the right to live in the world, to compete and participate equally, becomes increasingly impossible and meaningless without access to technology.

The invisibility of persons with disabilities stems in part from exclusionary practices, both intended exclusion, such as institutionalization, sheltered workshops, and separate schools, and passive exclusion, such as architecture that excludes those with mobility impairments. It also stems from a set of widely held cultural beliefs about the meaning of disability and therefore those who have a disability—beliefs that see a disabled person as incapable in some fashion that restricts that person's ability to participate as a full member of society.

Changing the cultural meaning of disability is critical to making inclusion the default in technology. Only rarely are access problems beyond the state of the art, and with time, these few seemingly "unsolvable" access problems will be solved. For example, working with the National Federation of the Blind, Virginia Tech has developed a car that translates information that sighted people process visually, into tactile information that allows a blind person to drive a car. Converting digital images that convey information into tactile graphics is becoming increasingly easy. Instances where accessibility, if considered at the beginning of the design process, would add significant cost to development are nearly unknown. Thus, the problem is cultural, and it is not a new one, simply a familiar one in a new guise: the majority identifies a group as outside the definition of "we," and practices exclusion that, in the memorable words of Ralph Ellison, produce "The Invisible Man" [1].

To understand how to break the cycle of invisibility/inaccessibility/invisibility, we have to understand the seemingly well-meaning and benign mind-set that underlies the exclusion of persons with disabilities and how the myths and narratives that have been loaded on as perceived innate characteristics, as have happened with other historically excluded groups. We also have to understand the counter-narrative that is necessary to equal opportunity and that does not yet have broad currency—in the population at large and with those who have a disability.

Overturning deeply rooted cultural mindsets requires daily contrary evidence, but we are a long way away from seeing retail clerks at the mall who are Deaf, dwarves, or who use a wheelchair. Those with invisible disabilities in the workplace have strong disincentives to come out unless they need an accommodation. As a result, many who perceive themselves as nondisabled are not aware that some of their valued co-workers are, in fact, disabled. Rather, the daily examples of well-known fully functioning persons with disabilities are so rare that we are at what might be called the "Ralph Bunche" stage of disability rights, where public speakers invoke Stephen Hawking as a demonstration that people with disabilities can be full contributors to our society, just as speakers who urged racial justice in the 1950s pointed to the Nobel Peace Prize–winning American diplomat as the example of what African-Americans could achieve if afforded the opportunity.

This chapter has a modest aim. After exploring our cultural understanding of disability, its impact, and the development of a competing, liberating narrative, we will outline some policies, procedures, and best practices that can make an enabling narrative about disability a routine part of corporate action within institutions.

We will also outline steps that can create an economic market for accessibility, despite the small numbers associated with many individual disabilities. Should these steps be taken and have the expected impact, it should result in more persons with disabilities being visible in our educational institutions, our social life, and our workplace, increasingly less as oddities to be remarked upon and more as "one of us."

THE CULTURAL MEANING OF DISABILITY

What common physical or mental traits are shared among those who have dyslexia, quadriplegia, paranoid schizophrenia, cerebral palsy, and deafness? Seemingly, there are none of significance. By contrast, what traits are shared by those who are merely myopic and those who are blind, or by those who are moody and those who are bi-polar? Seemingly, many. Yet we define those who are moody or myopic as persons without disabilities and those who are blind or bi-polar as disabled. In short, we define those who are disabled as those who are sufficiently unlike "us," that is to say, those who have a trait or characteristic to a degree that it takes them outside the norm. Hence, a line is drawn between being shorter than average and being a dwarf.

One could attempt to dispute the arbitrariness of the classification by saying that a person with a disability is one who needs a reasonable accommodation or assistive technology, but accommodations are entirely majoritarian concepts: we do not define the stepstool for the short person seeking to reach the top kitchen shelf as assistive technology for the "disability" of being short. Rather, the stepstool is simply a practical way to deal with the person's lack of physical stature—one of a number of characteristics held by that person, but not seen as defining or determinative. By the same token, when a class of sighted students is taught by a blind teacher, we do not think of the lights being on in the classroom as a reasonable accommodation for the students, even though the teacher does not need it to teach and it is an expense only occasioned by the drawback that the students require light as a result of their physical characteristics.

Two persons wear sunglasses. The first wears them to reduce the possibility of developing cataracts from the continued effect of unmediated sunlight. The second wears them because of photophobia. We classify only the second person, based on this information alone, as one who has a disability.

The boundaries of disability are significantly fluid in two senses. First, in the individual sense, there is an open frontier between those who are disabled and those who are not—during a physical activity, such as bodysurfing, driving, or running, or while sedentary, asleep, or exchanging bodily fluids—one can cross the border from seemingly not disabled to disabled. This may make "them" (people with disabilities) even more frightening to "us" and therefore more important to exclude and put out of sight for one's sense of well being. At the same time, the social definition of what traits are considered disabilities changes with time. Historically, homosexuality was classified as a mental illness rather than a normal human variation, but finally in 1990, the World Health Organization became the last recognized standard maker to recognize that sexual orientation is not a mental illness. At the same time, persons suffering from certain chemical addictions, once viewed as simply having moral failings, are now viewed as having a disability.

At the end of the day, all that can be said of having a disability is that if you have one, the disability places you, to the extent it is perceivable, as belonging to "them" and not being part of "us." As a consequence of being "one of them," the importance of your disability becomes exaggerated. Someone who uses sight for a particular task assumes that sight is therefore required to do that task efficiently and considers the blind person "amazing" for accomplishing the same task as well or better using alternative techniques.

THE PREDOMINANT DISABILITY NARRATIVE OF "DISABILITY AS TRAGEDY"

Disability is limiting, a tragedy, something to be cured, a matter of pity. This view is so ingrained in our culture that to suggest an alternate view is heresy. The resulting dialogue goes like this: "Really, if you had a choice, wouldn't you have sight?" "Perhaps so. But if you had a choice, would you like to be more handsome, wittier, smarter, or younger?" "But that's different, I can live a full life even so." "So can I." [skeptical noise.]

This narrative of disability as a significant tragedy is reinforced by charities and organizations "for" people with disabilities, like "Jerry's Kids," and "Families Fighting Autism," whose funding depends on painting a heart-rending view of those with disabilities and those who, perhaps for good reason, view disability through a medical lens. Visual images that produce an "Aww" or "OMG" help promote this view of disability. It is pervasive and affects not only how those without disability view those who do have disabilities, but also affects the self-image of persons with disabilities and their own understanding of what their possibilities are.

The tragedy narrative results in a protective approach that is seen as benign, but in fact diminishes the humanity of the person with disability as someone to be taken care of. It is at odds with the notion that disability rights extend beyond the right to be well-cared for. As such, it is a limiting narrative that echoes the narratives that dogged those fighting in earlier days for racial justice ("We take care of our own and they are happy") and gender equality ("Now don't you worry your pretty little head, young lady") faced from people who mistakenly viewed themselves as having a benign view of African-Americans and women, but were steadfast in the belief that these groups possessed characteristics disentitling them from full participation on an equal basis.

And, as was true with the response to racial and gender bigotry, some persons with disabilities internalize and accept the majority stereotypes, and their actions in accordance with the stereotype, in turn, are taken as affirmation by the majority of the correctness of its view. This creates a dilemma, of course, for those who know better. If you are blind, you are offered the opportunity to pre-board on the assumption that you need more time, compared, say, to the sighted person who is laden with small children and all the necessary gear that comes with traveling under those circumstances. To accept pre-boarding reinforces popular limiting notions of blindness by those who observe it, yet it is nice to get to be first in line.

The tragedy narrative creates turmoil between those who are not disabled and accept that narrative and those who are disabled. Those who wish to take custody of the person with a disability, even if only long enough to grab that person's arm, unasked, and take them to their destination, are offended by resistance. They do not see their "kindness" as an offensive and unwarranted assertion of superiority and bigotry. Thus, as has always been true of minorities, those with disabilities must search for gentle ways to communicate their right not to be patronized.

Because of the traits that the tragedy narrative assigns to disabilities, it is still the case, 25 years after the passage of the Americans with Disabilities Act (ADA), that disability rights are not yet accepted as civil rights. When an educational or professional institution announces a diversity program or event, it generally covers race, ethnicity, gender, and, more often now, sexual orientation. Rarely is disability included as a diversity issue.

The failure to include disability rights in civil rights is a testament to the power of the tragedy narrative in modern culture: people with disabilities are perceived to be excluded because of the inherent nature of disability, not because of false cultural attributions to those with disabilities. But when segregation of "them" is reduced, cultural narratives are challenged about what it means to be one of "them." The inaccuracy of what some white Americans believed to be innate racial characteristics was more widely recognized when racial segregation in public places and employment was challenged. Women, as segregation in employment and higher education was challenged, faced a more complicated task in promoting comprehension among men and women as to what was innately female and what was a cultural overlay, but at the end of the day face far less exclusion than existed in 1968, when Title VII of the Civil Rights Act was enacted and for the first time protected against gender discrimination in employment. Cultural notions as to the inherent nature of disabilities—"It's just common sense that a Deaf person cannot … [fill in the blank]"—are proving by far to be more stubborn and, as we shall see, aided by the greater segregation of persons with disabilities than has been experienced by racial minorities or women. Thus, the "problem," consistent with the tragedy narrative, continues to be perceived as the disability, rather than the exclusion of the person with the disability.

This "less-than-us" view of persons with disabilities justifies exclusion and even sterilization as benign, so long as persons with disabilities in the view of those without are believed to be well-cared for. This view of disabilities was embraced in American progressive thought, leading to the embrace of eugenics by public figures ranging from Woodrow Wilson to Margaret Sanger, and gained the force of law in 1927 when Justice Oliver Wendell Holmes, writing for the Supreme Court, upheld involuntary sterilization of persons with developmental disabilities with the famous phrase "Three generations of imbeciles are enough" [2].

Internationally, some progressive European countries are proud of how well their governments take care of those with disabilities and are confused by disabled citizens who express a need to own their rights.

One impact of the tragedy narrative is that it overstates the limiting significance of disability and, as has been true of the fights for racial and gender equality, the overstatement gains credence not only with the majority, but with the excluded group. As Chief Justice Warren stated in *Brown v. Board of Education*, "[t]o separate [African-American children] from others of similar age and qualifications solely because of their race generates a feeling of inferiority as to their status in the community that may affect their hearts and minds in a way unlikely ever to be undone" [3].

Our misperception of our own experience reinforces that limiting narrative. One example is the erroneous syllogism "I have sight and I use it to cross the street safely; ergo, the safest way to cross the street safely is to use sight, and those who do not have it cannot cross as safely." Of course, in circumstances of limited visibility, such as fog or large snowbanks, our hearing may be the more important sense for the task, but we are not consciously aware that we are relying on different cues and, in any event, feel uneasy because we are more practiced at using our sight for that task. Thus, a blind person crossing the street may expect to hear a passerby whisper "that's amazing," about a task the blind person has accomplished for years safely. (Some people with disabilities define the moment when equal participation will have been accomplished as when they will only be described as amazing because they found the cure for cancer or wrote a beautiful symphony and not for cooking a delicious dinner without sight.)

As an example of this misperception in the area of technology, counsel for Target, the retailer, in addressing the court on the inaccessibility of target.com, offered as exculpation for the accessibility barriers on the web site that even he did not know before the inception of the lawsuit that blind people used computers. While this was hardly an effective legal argument, it was intended as a statement of broader import: if someone as educated and experienced in the world as "learned counsel" does not know that blind people use computers, it is undoubtedly a little known fact among those without disabilities. It is likely he was right, even though there is nothing inherently visual about computer information; though vision is not necessary for access to digital information, the great majority uses vision to access computers and therefore would assume that vision is required. Because the blind are so largely excluded from education, employment, and cultural events, it is likely that the lawyer, like many of his peers, has never seen a blind person use a computer. And so, when the technology has accessibility barriers, something that need not be, it limits the opportunity to participate in the world."

Moreover, many of our aesthetic memories may be associated with one of our senses, and thus we assume that in the absence of that sense, the opportunity for awe-inspiring aesthetic experiences are lost, rather than recognizing that the other senses may be just as adequate as a vehicle for experiencing the joys of beauty.

Another byproduct of this narrative of disability is fear for our own integrity. Unlike the false narratives of inferiority associated with race or gender, the "different from/less than" narrative of disability has the component that the individual may cross from "us" to "them." The category "person with disability" is highly permeable, independent of an act of will. Absent transgender surgery, the principal author of this chapter is unlikely to wake up tomorrow differently gendered than today, and barring a surprising DNA analysis, is likely to continue to be classified as Caucasian. Becoming a person with a disability is potential in all of us who do not have or are not aware of having a disability. Thus, a distancing mechanism is more urgently needed to provide an illusion of "safety from crossing the divide."

Another distancing mechanism is to see disability as an act of divine retribution from which the perceiver imagines himself immune. Thus, epilepsy was historically viewed by the Catholic Church as the result of demonic possession that in turn was the result of a sin within the family. Former Congressman Coelho, author of the ADA, was diagnosed with epilepsy when he sought to qualify for the priesthood. Not only was he rejected on grounds of epilepsy as a matter of canon law (and lost his driver's license to boot), but was rejected by his deeply devout family, from whom he was estranged for more than two decades [4]. As with Oedipus, blindness is seen as the penalty for some taboo act.

Also further distancing are the sacred attributes given persons with disabilities. Tiresias is but one of many blind figures of myth to be credited with second sight, while in many cultures those who might be diagnosed as having mental illness are given status as shamans, curanderos, and prophets. In yet another canard, many believe blind people to have superior sexual experiences by attributing to them a heightened sense of touch. Saul (St. Paul) is said while on the road to Damascus to have fallen to the ground for 3 days and lost his vision as a precursor to his conversion. Ironically, scholars speculate that this had been caused by the same epilepsy that the church otherwise attributed to demonic possession. While assigning sacred traits to disability may be perceived as benign, anything partaking of the "them" definition permits societal treatment that we do not condone for "us."

THE SEGREGATING EFFECT OF THE "TRAGEDY NARRATIVE" OF DISABILITY

Exclusion from at least some aspects of society is seen as warranted based on the proposed attributes of "them." Thus, African-American males were admitted to Harvard, while, for reasons now long discredited, women were not; women were admitted to many country clubs, while African-Americans were not. The impact of each of those exclusions affects one's ability to participate fully in the economic life of this country.

Those who practiced race- and gender-based exclusion often based those actions on false attributions of characteristics to those groups. When the women's movement began a renaissance in the late 1960s after the passage of Title VII of the Civil Rights Act, there were many—within the civil rights movement and without—who believed that feminists were seeking to overturn the very nature of gender, as opposed to cultural baggage.

The plausibility and endurance of the tragedy narrative has led to a widespread failure to recognize the disability rights movement as a civil rights movement. The exclusion of persons with disabilities is seen as the result of the disability rather than cultural exclusion.

At the beginning of the 20th century, exclusion of persons with disability was still the order of the day. Those with a mental illness or a developmental disability, along with, often, the merely eccentric, were institutionalized indefinitely, confined to institutional grounds, or, on occasion, to a single room or wing. It is not surprising that the name of one of those early institutions, Bedlam, has taken on the meaning it has in our common parlance.

Even as institutions began to be emptied in the last quarter of the 20th century, walls have remained. The new abodes of those who had been in institutions are only marginally with us—on the urban sidewalks where we walk and they live and in the group homes inhabited only by others like themselves.

Those who were Deaf, had cerebral palsy, or were blind were separated, either in institutions, sometimes particular to their disabilities or lumped in with mental or developmental disabilities or, if at liberty, consigned to residential schools for students with their disabilities, and then, later, sheltered workshops where they did dead-end jobs for less than subsistence pay. A Deaf person's other characteristics, such as intelligence or problem-solving, were irrelevant. Deafness alone consigned you to menial work. All of this was seen as the product of social reform by those with a benign paternal concern for the less fortunate.

In many significant respects law has and continues to support the exclusion of those with disabilities. In 1966, Jacobus tenBroek, a seminal disability rights scholar or, perhaps more properly, the father of the modern disability rights movement, summarized the state of tort law on such a basic question as whether a blind man had the same rights to be on the streets as other citizens:

> *The majority of courts say that it is not negligence per se for a blind man to walk the streets without a companion or attendant; others that he may do so only in certain circumstances. Some say that it is contributory negligence as a matter of law to travel without dog, cane, or companion; others, that the failure to use one or more of these travel aids presents a question for the jury as to whether due care was employed. No courts say that a blind man may not, when taking the proper precautions, enter unfamiliar territory; most courts, however, emphasize the plaintiff's knowledge of the surroundings and the frequency of his presence. Some say that the plaintiff's knowledge that the streets are or may be defective or dangerous creates a kind of assumption of risk; others, that in the circumstances, the disabled person may proceed but must do so with due care in the light of his knowledge. The latter rule is also applied by some courts to blind persons in railway depots, at railway street crossings, and like places of similar danger, while others say that it is gross negligence for blind persons to be in such places alone. Some courts say that the disabled may proceed upon the assumption that the streets and highways are kept in a reasonably safe condition, and that cities and abutting property owners must expect the disabled to be abroad in the land and accordingly must take precautions necessary to warn or otherwise protect them. Others say that those who create, maintain, or tamper with the streets and public passageways are only under a duty to safeguard the able-bodied pedestrian.*

No courts have held or even darkly hinted that a blind man may rise in the morning, help get the children off to school, bid his wife goodby, and proceed along the streets and bus lines to his daily work, without dog, cane, or guide, if such is his habit or preference, now and then brushing a tree or kicking a curb, but, notwithstanding, proceeding with firm step and sure air, knowing that he is part of the public for whom the streets are built and maintained in reasonable safety, by the help of his taxes, and that he shares with others this part of the world in which he, too, has a right to live. He would then be doing what any reasonable, or prudent, or reasonably prudent blind man would do, and also what social policy must positively foster and judges in their developing common law must be alert to sustain. [5]

Lest the reader feel a comfortable sense of anachronism, one author of this chapter had occasion, not long ago, to counsel a lawyer representing a grocery store that had been held liable by a jury to a woman who had tripped over the cane of a blind store clerk on the ground that the store was negligent not to have a sighted companion with the clerk in all public areas at all times. The appellate court reversed, albeit without published opinion. In other areas, such as the right of a divorced blind parent to custody and visitation, the incapacity narrative is alive and well, though with some judges canny enough not to be explicit as to the role disability plays in their decisions.

Still, today in most states, a person with a mental or developmental disability who requires support in decision making is left to the Hobson's Choice of surrendering all autonomy to a guardian or subsisting without the necessary assistance. Although Jenny Hatch's well-publicized and successful fight for autonomy and decisions by New York Surrogate Court Judge Kristen Booth Glen may generate some autonomy, it is still far from being the common reality [6,7]. For now, we continue to sanctify through mechanisms like state guardianship laws the unconditional surrender of liberty and dignity of persons "qualified" by disability to persons defined only by their lack of that disability.

Visibility promotes change. Until the passage of the Rehabilitation Act of 1973, persons in wheelchairs were not much in evidence, in part because there was nowhere they could go that was accessible. Perhaps one of the most significant steps toward making persons with disabilities visible has been the ubiquity of the wheelchair symbol in parking lots and public bathrooms. The symbol is a mixed message, the positive part of which is that persons in wheelchairs engage in the activities of the world at large, while the need for special treatment underlines the limiting aspects of mobility impairments. Perhaps if President Roosevelt were to run for office today, he might no longer feel the need to avoid being photographed in his wheelchair.

The persistence of the exclusionary view should not be underestimated. A few years ago, one of the authors of this chapter reviewed e-mails in which the head of a disability student services office at a major public university asked the chair of the mathematics department for the accommodation of a calculator at exams for returning veterans with processing disabilities from closed head injuries, only to be told that the math chair questioned whether such students should even be allowed to matriculate.

Exclusion has been stunningly effective in making those with apparent disabilities invisible and thus, as technology has been developed, not part of the market equation.

THE COUNTER-NARRATIVE: A DISABILITY IS A TRAIT TO BE DEALT WITH IN LEADING A NORMAL LIFE

The counter-narrative is that a disability is one of the many characteristics that make up an individual and, as such, is something that the individual must address in selecting how to accomplish various life tasks. From this point of view, a disability is simply something that requires, on occasion, the creation of alternative techniques for accomplishment. For a sensory disability, alternative techniques must be developed to accomplish tasks in the absence of that sense, just as a short person uses a stepladder to reach a kitchen shelf that would be within the grasp of a taller person.

Sometimes the possibility of alternative techniques is found in technology. For example, for someone with dyslexia, adjusting a digital page to reduce the number of lines on the page and words on the line may be her "stepstool."

At the heart of this narrative is that a disability is a characteristic, like hair color, height, intelligence, or athleticism, that will shape your opportunities, your interests, and your accomplishments, but that will not, except in trivial ways, prove an insuperable barrier to that which you wish to accomplish, so long as you can find alternative techniques that will address whatever limitations the disability would otherwise impose.

This view requires the elimination of separation, recognizing, as did the Supreme Court in *Brown v. Bd. of Education,* that segregation from the majority imports a sense of inferiority of the separated minority that may even convince the minority of the truth of that inferiority.

It is no surprise then that Jacobus tenBroek, a blind constitutional law scholar at the University of California, Berkeley, in "The Right to Live in the World: The Disabled in the Law of Torts," labeled this narrative as "integrationism" and its counterpart "custodialism." He contrasted the two narratives thusly:

> The actual physical limitations resulting from the disability more often than not play little role in determining whether the physically disabled are allowed to move about and be in public places. Rather, that judgment for the most part results from a variety of considerations related to public attitudes, attitudes which not infrequently are quite erroneous and misconceived. These include public imaginings about what the inherent physical limitations must be; public solicitude about the safety to be achieved by keeping the disabled out of harm's way; public feelings of protective care and custodial security; public doubts about why the disabled should want to be abroad anyway; and public aversion to the sight of them and the conspicuous reminder of their plight. For our purposes, there is no reason to judge these attitudes as to whether they do credit or discredit to the human head and heart. Our concern is with their existence and their consequences.

To what extent do the legal right, the public approval, and the physical capacity coincide? Does the law assure the physically disabled, to the degree that they are physically able to take advantage of it, the right to leave their institutions, asylums, and the houses of their relatives? Once they emerge, must they remain on the front porch, or do they have the right to be in public places, to go about in the streets, sidewalks, roads and highways, to ride upon trains, buses, airplanes, and taxi cabs, and to enter and to receive goods and services in hotels, restaurants, and other places of public accommodation? If so, under what conditions? What are the standards of care and conduct, of risk and liability, to which they are held and to which others are held with respect to them? Are the standards the same for them as for the able-bodied? Are there legal as well as physical adaptations; and to what extent and in what ways are these tied to concepts of custodialism or integrationism? [5]

Dr. tenBroek then comes down in favor of "a policy entitling the disabled to full participation in the life of the community and encouraging and enabling them to do so."

The clearest national normative statement of this narrative has been in the U.S. ADA. Among Congress's findings embodied in the legislation are the following:

(1) physical or mental disabilities in no way diminish a person's right to fully participate in all aspects of society, yet many people with physical or mental disabilities have been precluded from doing so because of discrimination …;

(2) historically, society has tended to isolate and segregate individuals with disabilities, and … such forms of discrimination against individuals with disabilities continue to be a serious and pervasive social problem;

(3) discrimination against individuals with disabilities persists in such critical areas as employment, housing, public accommodations, education, transportation, communication, recreation, institutionalization, health services, voting, and access to public services; …

(5) individuals with disabilities continually encounter various forms of discrimination, including outright intentional exclusion, the discriminatory effects of architectural, transportation, and communication barriers, overprotective rules and policies, failure to make modifications to existing facilities and practices, exclusionary qualification standards and criteria, segregation, and relegation to lesser services, programs, activities, benefits, jobs, or other opportunities;

(6) … studies have documented that people with disabilities, as a group, occupy an inferior status in our society, and are severely disadvantaged socially, vocationally, economically, and educationally;

(7) the Nation's proper goals regarding individuals with disabilities are to assure equality of opportunity, full participation, independent living, and economic self-sufficiency for such individuals; and

(8) the continuing existence of unfair and unnecessary discrimination and prejudice denies people with disabilities the opportunity to compete on an equal

*basis and to pursue those opportunities for which our free society is justifi-
ably famous. ... [8]*

These findings reflect Congress's intent to follow the counter-narrative and con-
struct the ADA to require equal opportunity and equal access in the most meaningful sense, so that a person with or without a disability truly has the same
opportunity.

EFFECTING CULTURE CHANGE—HOW TO MAKE THE COUNTER-NARRATIVE, EQUAL OPPORTUNITY, A REALITY IN THE CONTEXT OF TECHNOLOGY

The custodial view of disability will have its death when citizens regularly see the
contrary evidence, persons with disabilities participating fully and, on occasion, suc-
ceeding in all spheres of life. Of course, that will not occur until the battle for equality has been won. Ray Charles expressed a similar paradox brilliantly in the song
"Them That Got": "That old sayin', them that's got are them that gets is something
I can't see. If ya gotta have something before you can get something, how do ya get
your first is still a mystery to me."

Thus, we must focus on the foundation: what will remove enough barriers to allow persons with disabilities to shed their invisibility cloaks?

CLEAR ORGANIZATIONAL POLICIES

First, each institution must have an accessibility policy that states the normative
guidance and degree of importance the institution attaches to equal access for persons with disabilities. It must not be a double super-secret policy, but one that the
institution announces to the world, so that consumers, especially consumers with
disabilities know what to expect. Microsoft, for example, publishes an extensive
and detailed accessibility policy [9]. With a few notable exceptions, like SharePoint,
Microsoft has succeeded for some time in having products accessible at the time of
their introduction to the market. IBM, which has at various times promoted accessibility, has, if not a policy, an accessibility statement of some detail [10]. It becomes
believable that Pearson, which still offers much in the way of inaccessible content
and software, is committed to changing that, given its detailed policy statement that
commits it not only to accessibility, but to being open about the accessibility status
of its products [11]. Google, with many inaccessible products, but recent efforts to
address the accessibility of some, contents itself with a single precatory statement,
"Everyone should be able to access and enjoy the web. We're committed to making
that a reality" [12]. Apple congratulates itself as done with the job: "We've done everything possible to make anything possible" [13]. Apparently, Apple doesn't think
it is possible to let consumers know which apps for iOS are inaccessible or to require developers to follow Apple's API for accessibility. These may reflect economic

concerns at Apple, but in the absence of a public policy, it seems doubtful that the public or Apple employees can know where Apple strikes the balance between accessibility and economics, other than it falls short of its claim that it has done everything possible. But, at least, accessibility is there as a focal point. Facebook consciously falls short of promising equal access, stating only, "Facebook is committed to creating a great experience for all people. Learn about the built-in features and technologies that help people with disabilities get the most out of Facebook" [14]. Amazon, to the surprise of no one in the disability community, has no public accessibility policy. Fortuitously, the authors of this book discovered that the publisher of this book, Elsevier, has one of the more thoughtful and detailed public accessibility policies [15].

It is not that accessibility policies are self-executing that makes them significant; they are not. Rather, the policies legitimate actors within the institution who press for accessibility and can foster a sense of corporate responsibility. Moreover, the existence of a policy can help make the issue visible and part of the conversation.

A number of educational institutions, some after legal prodding and some not, have produced some thoughtful and thorough accessibility policy statements addressed to web accessibility, EIT accessibility, or both. They vary in focus, length, and detail, and cites to a number of different models appear below. However, the introduction to Ohio State University's web accessibility policy best captures that which is necessary to further the narrative of equal opportunity. That policy introduction states as follows:

> The creation and dissemination of knowledge is a defining characteristic of universities and is fundamental to The Ohio State University's mission. The use of state of the art digital and web based information delivery of information is increasingly central in carrying out our mission. Ohio State is committed to ensuring equal access to information for all its constituencies. This policy establishes minimum standards for the accessibility of web based information and services considered necessary to meet this goal and ensure compliance with applicable state and federal regulations. [16]

Others worthy of review include those of Penn State, George Mason University, Oregon State, University of Montana, and Temple University. A policy is just a first step [18–22].

Early agreements between the National Federation of the Blind and a number of e-commerce sites simply set an accessibility standard and a deadline. Given that changing the companies' culture was not addressed and given the dynamic nature of the web sites, the resulting accessibility was variable over time. The CEO might have been gung-ho for accessibility, but if the person responsible for the next release and its features on a timely basis reports to a middle manager who is not reviewed for accessibility, then accessibility may fall victim to the pressures of time and the CEO may be none the wiser.

To keep accessibility top of mind, companies must undertake to ensure that new releases onto a web site or of software are tested for and determined to be accessible before release. Thus, the recent consent decree entered into by H&R Block with the Department of Justice and NFB requires user testing of any "substantial proposed change" to the web site, mobile apps, or the online tax software prior to release and requires the Accessibility Coordinator to certify that all new releases have been made accessible prior to their release [22].

Pre-release testing addresses the problem of "later." When accessibility is an afterthought and persons with disabilities are told to wait for accessibility to follow, their ability to compete is significantly compromised. Their consequent inability to perform tasks between the time new software is introduced and the time it is made accessible also contributes to the stereotype of disability as incapacity.

Similarly, when accessibility bugs develop, their priority should not float, but should be incorporated into existing bug fix or service level agreements. Thus, the H&R Block agreement provided, "[t]he Modified Bug Fix Priority Policies shall ensure that any bugs that create nonconformance with WCAG 2.0 AA to www.hrblock.com, its mobile applications, or its Online Tax Preparation Product are remedied with the same level of priority, speed and resources used to remediate any other equivalent loss of function for individuals without disabilities" [22].

The H&R Block agreement contains a number of other procedures and requirements for training to keep accessibility in the "conversation" in the corporate environment, but two are critical: (1) performance reviews of the Web Accessibility Coordinator and "all employees who write or develop programs or code for, or who publish final content to, www.hrblock.com, its mobile applications, or the Online Tax Preparation Product ... of the degree and effectiveness with which each took accessibility considerations into account in the performance of their respective duties ..." and (2) reporting on accessibility issues to the Chief Information Officer. The first ensures that those who are evaluated will become accessibility evangelists within the company for the sake of their own job security and advancement. The second ensures that the status of accessibility is visible at a top executive level. Finally, the requirement of user testing for accessibility ensures that some persons with disabilities will be "visible" to at least some in the corporate world.

Having a locus of responsibility for accessibility is critical. Several companies, Microsoft and IBM among them, as well as some state agencies, such as Minnesota's MN. IT, have a position called Chief Accessibility Officer. The success associated with that position, of course, is tied directly to the authority and reporting associated with the position.

Involvement of persons with disabilities, particularly consumer organizations of persons with disabilities, such as the National Federation of the Blind, Autism Self-Advocacy Network, National Council on Independent Living, and the National Association of the Deaf, ensures a wealth of knowledge and an approach that is authentic, rather than merely plausible (as imagined by someone without a disability).

Different procedures are called for in noncorporate environments like universities. There the acquisition of technology is diffuse, with decisions being made by individual departments, the CIO, the CBO, admissions, HR, development, and a host of other bailiwicks. Thus, presidential leadership is required to get sign-on throughout academe. When that happens, some extraordinary procedures and policies can produce a set of best practices, which when enforced can change the landscape. Two of the most thoughtful and thorough such procedures in post-secondary education may be found at http://ada.osu.edu/resources/Links.htm and http://accessibility.temple.edu/.

Making accessibility the default for those more episodically linked to technology is also key. Thus, it is desirable to build in for, say, content creators at the universities reminders to put alt tags on images, followed, if ignored, by "Are you sure? Failure to label will make this image inaccessible to blind users." Templates that will reject uploading of image PDFs can also help.

CREATING MARKET DEMAND

The final key to culture change is dissemination and the creation of market demand. Institutions subject to the ADA or similar laws must create a market in which they create a demand for accessible instructional content and technology from those who are not directly subject to the ADA. Without that, persons with disabilities are faced with the kind of dilemma that existed when all of the technology for accessible voice-guided ATMs existed, but none was used. The banks, for their part, stated that they would be happy to use voice-guided ATMs, but none of the ATM manufacturers was offering them. The ATM manufacturers, on the other hand, said they would be delighted to make accessible ATMs, but no bank was asking for them.

To create the market demand requires an evidence-based procurement process, one that requires vendors to describe how their products are accessible in responding to requests for proposals and contracts that require representations and warranties of accessibility and indemnities for suits against the institutions for the inaccessibility of the product. Thus, Oracle advises those from whom it purchases as follows:

> *Accessibility is important to Oracle, for business, legal and ethical reasons. We are committed to providing accessible solutions to our employees, our customers, and our customers' customers, by developing and deploying products that conform to the U.S. Section 508 standards, and the Web Content Accessibility Guidelines version 2.0 at the AA level, including the Guidance on Applying WCAG 2.0 to Non-Web Information and Communications Technologies if applicable. We expect your product to also be developed to these same standards, and that you issue an accessibility conformance statement such as the Voluntary Product Accessibility Template that indicates the degree of conformance. [23]*

Ohio State recommends the following language for RFPs:

All content, interfaces, and navigation elements to be used by University faculty/ staff, program participants, or other University constituencies must be compliant with the Americans with Disabilities Act, as amended. Compliance means that a person with a disability can acquire the same information, engage in the same interactions, and enjoy the same services as a person without a disability, in an equally effective and integrated manner, with substantially equivalent ease of use.

There are multiple approaches to providing equally effective and substantially equivalent ease of use. A product will be considered to have met this standard based on a review by the University or when the vendor demonstrates that the work clearly meets the applicable current portions of the Ohio State University's Minimum Web Accessibility Standards through documented accessibility testing.

The Ohio State University Minimum Web Accessibility Standards are implementation guidelines for its Web Accessibility Policy, adopted in 2004. They are based on Section 508 §1194.22 of the Federal Rehabilitation Act, the standard of legal compliance for U.S. government institutions. The goal of MWAS is to ensure websites and web-based applications are functionally accessible to people with disabilities, as described in Section 508 §1194.31, Functional Performance Criteria. We understand that the 508 criteria are being revisited, and will likely come to harmonize with W3C WCAG 2.0 AA compliance. The criteria in the middle column of the table elaborate MWAS in an attempt to align it with current and emerging standards.

The accessibility testing process must be described in the proposal along with the completed chart (included below), and may include but is not limited to code reviews by internal or external experts, evaluations with accessibility checking software, vendor test bedding with assistive technologies, testing by users with disabilities, or testing by a third party organization.

Please answer the following questions:

Do you have clients who require accessibility (Federal govt., international, local company policies)? If so, in outline, how are they ensuring your product meets their requirement?

What standards are followed for coding of interfaces (if 508, what parts, if WCAG 2.0, which level)?

Do you do testing with users with disabilities? If so, can you explain the process and identify, roughly, the range of disabilities and access technologies used?

What experience do developers on your team have coding for accessibility?

What are your company's internal standards for developing with accessibility in mind? (Note: may have been answered by question 2.)

Does your company have a road map for accessibility going forward? If so, can you give us a general outline (goals, milestones)?

Have you tested and/or developed your mobile apps (especially iOS) with accessibility in mind?

If we find that there are changes that need to be made to web/mobile interfaces/apps, what guarantee can we have that these will be implemented to our satisfaction prior to go-live/going forward?

Would your company indemnify OSU against legal action related to accessibility?

Please complete the following chart to indicate your organization's ability to support Ohio State's ADA compliance guidelines.

[include the entire MWAS implementation guidelines from above, adding a column with "meets/partially meets/does not meet" and a column for vendor comments]. [24]

George Mason University, for its part, has contract language as follows:

All e-learning and information technology developed, purchased, upgraded or renewed by or for the use of George Mason University shall comply with all applicable University policies, Federal and State laws and regulations including but not limited to Section 508 of the Rehabilitation Act (29 U.S.C. 794d), the Information Technology Access Act, §§2.2-3500 through 2.2-3504 of the Code of Virginia, as amended, and all other regulations promulgated under Title II of The Americans with Disabilities Act which are applicable to all benefits, services, programs, and activities provided by or on behalf of the University. The Contractor shall also comply with the Web Content Accessibility Guidelines (WCAG) 2.0. [25]

George Mason's approach is also "trust, but verify." It requires Voluntary Product Accessibility Templates (VPATs) from vendors and does its own accessibility testing. Recognizing the complaint that academics who want the best and the brightest now will incorrectly elide "the vendor did not consider accessibility in creating technology that would advance my research" to "requiring accessibility will slow the advance of knowledge," Ohio State has wisely created an exception policy that conditions the use of inaccessible technology on both a plan with the vendor to address accessibility barriers within a fixed time frame and a written plan for accommodating those with disabilities in the interim. This is an important step to migrating the perception that the person with the disability is the problem to the perception that the problem rests with the tech vendor.

The federal government had the opportunity to help create an accessible tech market with the enactment of Section 508 of the Rehabilitation Act, which appeared to require, under some circumstances, that government entities "buy accessible." That statute has failed in its promise, and government purchasing agents treat the Section 508 requirements as simply a slalom pole around which they must navigate to complete the procurement. Few understand and fewer are trained in the requirements for accessibility. The General Services Administration, for its part, has been the cause of many accessibility barriers in recent years by listing as scheduled items (items that agencies can purchase with a purchase order and no competitive bidding) inaccessible phones, Google Docs and a host of other inaccessible products. It is too soon to say whether the actions of the Office of Federal Contract Compliance Programs of the US Department of Labor, requiring government contractors to hire persons with disabilities at a level reflecting the overall workforce, will have any impact. For now, it appears that we must rely on post-secondary institutions and private enterprise to create the market demand that will make accessible technology the default rather than the rare exception.

We are not yet at the point where the procurement procedures followed by Oracle and these universities are sufficiently common to create a tipping point in the market. But when they do, the competition is on among vendors to be the first on the block with accessibility. When this happens, the doors to those with disabilities whose participation has been frustrated by technology barriers will end, and the culture change will truly be underway.

BARRIERS AHEAD

Three areas of rapid technological change pose immediate questions for effecting culture change in time to integrate accessibility: educational technology, mobile computing, and cloud computing. Identifying a triggering event and the levers for culture change to produce accessible results in these areas are critical endeavors.

EDUCATIONAL TECHNOLOGY

Educational institutions, regardless of grade level, spend billions of dollars per annum purchasing new technologies for classroom use. The assumptions are that the more technologies can be put in to the hands of students from all ages, the more advanced their education is going to be.

Some schools pay no attention to accessibility in acquiring technology. Thus, a frequently recurring example of technology deployment set up to fail is when schools choose to deploy things like e-readers, such as the Kindle Paperwhite e-reader or the KoboGlo, which have no text-to-speech or Braille support for use in the classrooms. These may be less expensive than an iPad, and thus more appealing to school districts with more limited resources, but result in putting students with disabilities disproportionately at risk. The administrator may believe that the school has no blind students at the moment, not understanding that when one shows up, it will be too late to effectuate a fix. Typically, the students and the teachers who must use the technologies are the last to know that the schools will be deploying new technologies for use in the classrooms. By the time it becomes apparent to everyone that the chosen technology is inaccessible, it is often already widely deployed in the classrooms and expensive and difficult to alter.

Other schools may try to meet the diverse needs of their students, but the administrators who make the purchasing decisions for new technologies may have only partial information on what to do. For example, a school district may know that Apple iPads are accessible to persons with disabilities and select them as the means to deliver curricula to students in the classrooms, thinking that since the Apple iPad has accessibility support on-board by default, all of their accessibility problems will be solved. Regrettably, if the app that delivers the content is not itself accessible, then students will still not be able to access curriculum. If the administrator thinks to consult his IT staff, they may well be knowledgeable, but probably are not knowledgeable about accessibility. An accessible platform with inaccessible content is still inaccessible.

Thus, it is clear that school districts and educational institutions should make part of the decision making process talking to knowledgeable members of the user communities, and also make a demonstration of the full content delivery and its accessibility features a pre-requisite for the signing of a purchase agreement. If accessibility needs are not clearly defined and required in the procurement policy, the access for students and staff with disabilities will remain a costly afterthought. But action needs to be taken to make it easier for schools to get the information they need so that they can fulfill their obligations to all students. At the moment, accessibility is not a sufficient marketing plus to motivate the technology community to be the source of accurate and complete information.

Even when the right procurement decisions have been made, the problems are not at an end. Classroom instructors are often not trained to use the accessibility features of a new technology, and teachers and students end up learning how to use the technology together in the classroom. This type of classroom environment presents significant challenges to the students with disabilities who must use access technology in class in order to stay productive. Students with disabilities then must master a new technology, how it works with their access technology, and workarounds for the new tool's shortcomings—assuming it works with access technology at all.

More difficult still are those areas where there is no accessible choice, not because accessibility is beyond the state of the art, but merely because the developers have not chosen to address accessibility. Gaming, for example, is now a significant technology platform for classroom use, but at present there are no accessible gaming consoles in the market. Mainstream students may be more fully engaged by using gaming for education, but students with disabilities are simply left behind. For any student with a disability who wants to study science, technology, engineering, or math (STEM), having no access to lab equipment is also another problem they are likely to face. Yet, there are well-documented efforts, describing how students with disabilities can be given full access to technology and engineering curriculum, such as the AccessComputing and AccessEngineering alliances at the University of Washington [26].

As things stand, however, poor design and poor procurement policies often conspire to shut out students with disabilities from equal access to educational opportunities. These examples show both the urgency of the situation and, hopefully, the potential for a resolution. With some creative problem solving on the part of the software and hardware designers as well as the educational institutions, what is now a terrific hurdle can be turned into an opportunity to give *every* student a quality education.

MOBILE COMPUTING

As mentioned in previous chapters, out-of-the-box accessibility features on mainstream mobile devices have changed the world for consumers with disabilities. Though not gone altogether, the financial burden on people with disabilities of obtaining separate accessible products has certainly decreased over time. Expensive add-on software or specialized hardware is no longer a requirement for a person with disabilities. Though Apple has been leading in this arena, other operating systems' providers like Microsoft and Google have recently been more proactive about designing accessible mobile operating systems (OS) and mobile devices. The progress that we witnessed in the mobile computing area is a perfect opportunity for the information technology companies to demonstrate that they value all consumers, including people with disabilities.

To become a leading information technology company in the mobile computing space, Apple, Google, and Microsoft, and even Blackberry, realized that they need developers who can create innovative apps to help increase the adoption rate for their specific platforms. All of these companies put forth lots of effort to educate developers on how to proficiently create apps. To protect their brand, some companies even go so far as to require that app developers follow set criteria in order to post apps in an app store.

However, none of the companies listed above is willing to make accessibility criteria mandatory for app developers; none of them is even willing to create a rating system so that consumers or institutional purchasers can assess accessibility before they buy an app. This creates a manifest contrast between a policy that requires in-house developers to come up with accessible apps and makes an accessible API available to third party developers, but does not enforce that standard. As a consequence, in spite of the efforts of the company, users find themselves with more inaccessible than accessible apps. Our recommendation to all of the players in the mobile device market who want to gain a competitive advantage in the mobile arena is that they insist that accessibility design criteria are mandatory for all apps developers. Making accessibility a requirement, and making the requirement easy to fulfill, is not only going to help the consumers, but will gain app developers and OS providers a loyal customer base. It will also be a critical advantage in the education and federal government sphere, where accessibility is at least theoretically mandated.

Mobile computing is the ideal platform right now for making a real difference. The flexibility, the lower cost of entry, and the ease of app development make it a great launching pad for an open, all-user-friendly, consumer-need-oriented, responsive environment [27]. If the operating system providers are willing to talk openly about accessible design to create awareness for accessibility with the help of the user community, mobile computing can be accessible to everyone.

CLOUD COMPUTING

Cloud computing is at present the most challenging area for people with disabilities to access. It also has the broadest impact on the employment prospects of people with disabilities. Organizations in both public and private sectors are making the decision to migrate to the cloud, often because of economic reasons. The cloud offers many benefits in terms of flexibility, increased data storage, and outsourcing of technology management tasks.

Very few companies, if any, are evaluating cloud productivity tools to see whether they are accessible to employees with disabilities. Few businesses have a procurement policy that requires vendors to provide proof that their products are accessible beyond the VPAT. The stark result is that generally the employees with disabilities are terminated or forced into dead-end jobs, because they can no longer do their chosen job. At the time of this writing, none of the commonly used cloud productivity tools is accessible, in spite of the existing web accessibility standards. Training documentation on how to use these tools with access technology is virtually nonexistent.

The heart of the vast potential of the cloud is that it promises to be an environment where anyone can participate in the workforce from anywhere. For much of the disability community, that promise has so far proved to be an empty one when it comes to using cloud-based tools such as the Google suite. The ubiquity of such tools is plain: according to *U.S. News & World Report*, 66 of its 100 top-ranked schools use Google Apps [28], as does the federal government. The impact on those students and government employees with vision or manual dexterity impairments is devastating. No lack of skill is at fault here; only the entirely preventable and fixable creation of inaccessible cloud productivity tools is keeping employees with disabilities out of the workforce. Changing the culture to change the behavior is urgently called for here.

SUMMARY

So long as persons with disabilities are excluded from participation in society, specifically in participation in technology, they will continue to be invisible and will not be considered as new technology is developed. This chapter discussed some of the culture changes that must take place to ensure a future of equality in access to digital information. Promoting policies and procedures at institutions to make accessibility part of the internal conversation at these institutions will produce and create a market for accessible technology, which will enhance the participation of persons with disabilities, which should in turn create a new dynamic where greater visibility results in greater accessibility. Digital inclusion in the future needs to be planned for right now. The world that we live in today is a physical world inter-twined with the digital world, and without equal access to digital information and technologies, people with disabilities, to paraphrase Dr. tenBroek, will be excluded from living in the world.

REFERENCES

[1] Ellison R. The invisible man. New York: Vintage International; 1995.

[2] *Buck v. Bell*, 274 U.S. 200, 208; 1927.

[3] *Brown v. Board of Education*, 347 U.S. 483, 494; 1954.

[4] Carmen C. Tony Coelho urges more activism for rights of people with disabilities. [Web log comment]. Retrieved from http://epilepsyu.com/blog/tony-coelho-urges-more-activism-for-rights-of-people-with-disabilities/; 2013, July 11.

[5] tenBroek J. The Right to Live in the World: The Disabled in the Law of Torts, 54 Cal. L. Rev. 841, 866–68; 1966.

[6] Vargas T. Woman with Downs syndrome prevails over parents in guardianship case. *Washington Post*. Available at: http://www.washingtonpost.com/local/woman-with-down-syndrome-prevails-over-parents-in-guardianship-case/2013/08/02/4aec4692-fae3-11e2-9bde-7ddaa186b751_story.html; 2013, August 2.

[7] Savchuk K. The ruling that could change everything for disabled people with million-dollar trusts. [Web log comment]. Retrieved from http://newyorkcourtcorruption.blogspot.com/2013/09/former-surrogate-judge-kristen-booth.html; 2013, July 10.

[8] 42 U.S.C. § 12101.

[9] Microsoft. Microsoft commitment to accessibility. Retrieved from http://www.microsoft.com/enable/microsoft/mission.aspx; 2015.

[10] IBM. Accessibility at IBM. Retrieved from http://www.03.ibm.com/able/access_ibm/accessibility_statement.html; 2007, September 4.

[11] Pearson Higher Education. Accessibility statement. Retrieved from http://www.pearsonhighered.com/educator/accessibility/index.page; 2015.

[12] Google. (n.d.). Accessibility: everyone should be able to access and enjoy the web. We're committed to making that a reality. Retrieved from https://www.google.com/accessibility/.

[13] Apple Inc. (US). Accessibility: We've done everything possible to make anything possible. Retrieved from https://www.apple.com/accessibility/; 2015.

[14] Facebook. Facebook accessibility is on facebook. Retrieved from https://www.facebook.com/accessibility/info?ref=page_internal; 2015.

[15] Elsevier.com. Accessibility policy. Retrieved from http://www.elsevier.com/about/policies/accessibility-policy; 2015.

[16] The Ohio State University. Web accessibility policy. Retrieved from http://ada.osu.edu/resources/osu-web-accessibility-policy.pdf; 2003, July 1.

[17] PennState. Policy AD69 accessibility of PennState web pages. Retrieved from http://guru.psu.edu/policies/ad69.html; 2011, August 2.

[18] George Mason University. Non-discrimination and reasonable accommodation on the basis of disability, Univ. Policy No. 1203. Retrieved from http://universitypolicy.gmu.edu/policies/non-discrimination-and-reasonable-accommodation-on-the-basis-of-disability/; 2012; October 8.

[19] Oregon State University. OSU policy on information technology accessibility. Retrieved from http://oregonstate.edu/accessibility/ITpolicy; 2012, February 22.

[20] University of Montana. (n.d.). EITA policy and procedures. Retrieved from http://www.umt.edu/accessibility/policy/default.php.

[21] Temple University. Temple university accessibility statement. Retrieved from http://www.temple.edu/about/temple-university-accessibility-statement; 2015.

[22] US Department of Justice. Settlement agreement with national federation of the blind and H&R Block: inaccessible websites and mobile applications. Available at: http://www.ada.gov/hrb-cd.htm; 2014, March 25.

[23] Document Supplied to Author by Peter Wallack of Oracle Corp.

[24] The Ohio State University. Web accessibility standards—suggested purchasing procedures and contract language to help meet MWAS. 2015. Retrieved from http://www.osu.edu/resources/web/accessibility/#purchasing.

[25] George Mason University. Assistive technology initiative; procurement accessibility language. Retrieved from http://ati.gmu.edu/policy/procurement/; 2014.

[26] University of Washington. Access engineering. Program funded by National Science Foundation to broaden participation in engineering by increasing participation of people with disabilities. Retrieved from http://www.washington.edu/doit/programs/accessengineering/overview/about-accessengineering-project; 2015.

[27] O'Brien K. Mobile banking in the emerging world. *New York Times*. Available at: http://www.nytimes.com/2010/11/29/business/global/29iht-mobilebanks29.html?pagewanted=all&_r=0; 2015.

[28] Google. (n.d.). Apps for education. 66 of the Top 100 schools (according to US News & World Reports) are using Google Apps for Education. Retrieved from http://www.google.com/apps/intl/en/landing/top100schools/.

Index

Note: Page numbers followed by *b* indicate boxes and *t* indicate tables.

Printed in the United States
By Bookmasters